FATHERS, FAMILIES, AND THE STATE
IN FRANCE, 1914–1945

Fathers, Families, and the State in France 1914–1945

Kristen Stromberg Childers

Cornell University Press   ITHACA AND LONDON

First published 2003 by Cornell University Press

Printed in the United States of America

Library of Congress Cataloging-in-Publication Data

Childers, Kristen Stromberg.
    Fathers, families, and the state in France, 1914–1945 / Kristen Stromberg Childers.
        p.   cm.
Includes bibliographical references and index.
    ISBN 0-8014-4122-6 (cloth : alk. paper)
    1. Fathers—France—History—20th century.   2. Family—France—History—20th century.   3. Family policy—France—History—20th century.   I. Title.
    HQ756.C467 2003
    306.874′2′09440904—dc21

                                                                    2003009151

Cornell University Press strives to use environmentally responsible suppliers and materials to the fullest extent possible in the publishing of its books. Such materials include vegetable-based, low-VOC inks, and acid-free papers that are recycled, totally chlorine-free, or partly composed of nonwood fibers. For further information, visit our website at www.cornellpress.cornell.edu.

Cloth printing   10 9 8 7 6 5 4 3 2 1

for Tom

Contents

Illustrations

Acknowledgments

I am indebted to many people for their assistance and guidance in completing this book. The University of Pennsylvania and the Mellon Foundation have provided generous support for writing and research over the past several years. I am also grateful to the Fulbright Commission, which provided me with the opportunity to carry out the necessary research in Paris. At the Archives nationales, Mlle. Bula of the Section contemporaine and Mme. Barbiche of the Section moderne were helpful in locating sources and in obtaining *dérogations* for many of the documents requested. M. Nicolas Buat was extremely accommodating of my requests to see documents at the Centre des archives contemporaines in Fontainebleau.

In Paris, Michel Chauvière and colleagues at his seminar on family associations provided valuable perspectives on my own work and on French family policy in general. I appreciated André Burguière's help and advice, as well as that of Bernard Comte, Francine Muel-Dreyfus, and François Weil. Laird Boswell and Dave Smith both served as obliging guides to the archives and to French academic life, for which I am most grateful. My thanks also go to Michelle Bolduc, Elisa Camiscioli, Jennifer Milligan, and Daniella Sarnoff for their friendship and support. And I wish to thank Susan Watkins, Sarah Fishman, Leslie Page Moch, Françoise Thébaud, and Susan Whitney, who read parts of the work in earlier incarnations and offered useful comments.

At the University of Pennsylvania, I have benefited from the friendship and good suggestions of many advisors, colleagues, and friends. Kathy Brown and Kathy Peiss both took time to offer constructive criticism and helped me see the larger implications of the project. Bruce Kuklick and Jonathan Steinberg were supportive both personally and professionally, as was the fine staff of the History Department at Penn, including Deborah Broadnax, Joan Plonski, and Valerie Riley. Lynn Lees nurtured this project from the start and offered constructive comments and encouragement in just the right amounts. Lynn Hunt, whose own work provided inspiration and whose advice in the first seminar of my graduate career helped shape this project, has been a wonderful teacher and guide from the very beginning.

At Cornell University Press, I wish to thank Catherine Rice for her enthusiasm and encouragement, as well as Melissa Oravec, Teresa Jesionowski, and Evan Young. My mother, Jean Stromberg, has been helpful beyond measure in the completion of this book, from the first big decisions to the last finishing touches. Finally, I want to thank my husband, Tom Childers, who has been a wonderful source of support at every step along the way. Tom's sense of history, language, and humanity has been a marvelous inspiration for this book and for my life.

KRISTEN STROMBERG CHILDERS

Philadelphia

FATHERS, FAMILIES, AND THE STATE
IN FRANCE, 1914–1945

Introduction

In 1947, a bold new operetta premiered at the Opéra Comique in Paris. The performance, titled *Les Mamelles de Tirésias* (The Breasts of Tiresias), was based on a play by Guillaume Apollinaire, "poet of the Avant Garde." A young Francis Poulenc had attended the first staging of *Mamelles* in 1917—in the midst of what may have been the bloodiest year of World War I for the French—alongside luminaries from the artistic world such as Matisse, Picasso, Braque, Derain, Modigliani, Dufy, Léger, Cocteau, Aragon, Breton, and Satie. In 1944, during the dark years of the German occupation, Poulenc set the surrealist play to music, and it premiered amid much fanfare in June 1947.

In the prologue to *Les Mamelles de Tirésias,* the theater manager tells the audience that the opera is basically a morality play without any consistent plot. He exhorts the listeners to "learn the lessons of war and make more children, you who made hardly any." *Mamelles* tells the story of Thérèse, a bored housewife who tires of her chauvinist husband and decides to become a man herself. She opens her blouse to release two balloons, symbolizing her breasts, which she pops. She announces that her new name will be Tiresias, alluding to the blind prophet who lived as both man and woman. Her husband is disgusted with her transformation and declares that since women are no longer willing to be mothers, men will make children on their own. In Act II, the husband is blessed with fatherhood; to his utter delight, he produces 40,049 children in one day. The opera proceeds through a series of sketches related to the activities of these many children, before finally ending with marital reconciliation between a once-again feminine Thérèse and her husband. The characters assemble on stage at the finale to reiterate to the audience: "Hear, oh French people, the lessons of war, and make children."[1]

On the opening night, an elderly gentleman in the audience cried out

1

"Decadent!" while another lady exclaimed from her seat, "But it's *horrible!*" One reviewer noted with glee that during the intermission fans and critics of Poulenc squared off on the stairways; although they did not come to blows that evening, they gave every indication of doing so at future performances.[2] Despite these outbursts, the international press was generally well disposed toward Poulenc's *oeuvre* and it was deemed a great success.

Critics have been divided on the meaning of *Mamelles;* while some saw it as an earnest plea for repopulation, others considered it a farce ridiculing the government's pro-natalist efforts as well as the feminist movement. Perhaps much of the confusion comes from Apollinaire's own contradictions— as the critic Ned Rorem writes, "Apollinaire in his life seemed at once patriotic and anti-military, condescending to women and socially egalitarian. . . . Did he coin the term Surrealism . . . to justify his ambiguous comedy which promised to be feminist, pacifist and liberal, but winds up hawkish, nationalist and reactionary?"[3] Whatever the interpretation, it is clear that concerns of gender are at the heart of Apollinaire's words, performed first during the Great War and set to music by Poulenc in the midst of another war and the cataclysm the French were to find themselves a part of in 1944.

In the first half of the twentieth century, France was fixated on the possibility of war with Germany, the integrity of the State, and changing gender roles. It is impossible to understand modern France without reference to these concerns, and gender occupies a central position in this history.[4] Scholars have consistently demonstrated the decisive role of gender in defining public discourse and policy on fundamental concerns of social reform and national identity. This approach has been particularly salient in historiography of the Third Republic and the Vichy regime, where links between gender identities and the public good were at the forefront of French debates on national decline, war, population growth, and social citizenship.[5] Much of the literature on gender in modern France has, quite appropriately, focused on representations of women and their relationship to the nation as mothers and producers of future generations.[6]

But what does *Les Mamelles de Tirésias* tell us about gender in modern France? Although Thérèse is a dynamic heroine, the true hero of the story is the unnamed "Husband," who responds to his wife's changing gender identity by electing to become a father on his own. Arguing that children are a man's greatest wealth, he gives birth to more than 40,000, and revels in their exploits, while a concerned gendarme—a representative of the state—asks him how these children can all be fed. It is fatherhood that takes center stage in *Mamelles.* Can men be good fathers without good mothers? Do children really enhance a man's reputation and his standing in society? What do men have to do with the crisis of the state in modern France?

This book examines the interactions between fathers, families, and the state in France from 1914 to 1945, exploring the modeling of family roles for men and the integration of paternity in formulations of citizenship and social policy.[7] Debates on fatherhood were central to political and social discourse and went to the heart of major issues facing French citizens of the late Third Republic and the Vichy regime. In controversies over voting rights, public assistance, labor policy, and social class, the father appeared as a key figure in visions for France's social and political future and as a critical concern for architects of the expanding welfare state. As they addressed the role of the father and fatherhood, participants in both the public and the private sphere found themselves drawn into a discussion about nothing less than the nature of government, the shape of the modern family, and the future of the nation. When fathers, rather than just mothers, are integrated into the history of the two world wars and the interwar years, a far more complex—and politically revealing—relationship between gender and the state comes to light.

Women were not the only "gendered" beings in the eyes of the French state. In fact, French legislators made every effort to cast men in certain gender-specific roles that would enhance the protection of the family and, ultimately, the nation. Few men, however, could live up to such expectations about their masculinity and their fatherhood, expectations that were in any case often inconsistent and imprecise. Nevertheless, diverse elements in French society throughout the early twentieth century attempted to make men's gender and family roles key to the apportionment of resources and privileges in the French nation. Their failure to succeed in this project tells us two important things. First, the French state did not view male citizens as gender-neutral beings against whom they contrasted women, "the sex." In fact, the Third Republic and especially the Vichy regime took a keen interest in male citizens' family lives and the potential benefit that inhered in them; yet the regime(s) found men intractable, and in the end unhelpful, in their attempts to build a stronger France. Perhaps, then, it was not the fact that women were "*the* sex" that led to their second-class citizenship in France, but rather that they were perceived as being of the *wrong* sex in the early twentieth century.

This leads us to a second crucial point, which concerns the place of Vichy in the course of French history. The history of the Republic in France has been inextricably connected to that of fatherhood; the founding act of the Republic, in fact, was the decapitation of the father-king, and each successive regime from Napoleon to father-Pétain has advanced the debate about good fathers, bad fathers, powerful fathers, or inadequate fathers. The Vichy regime marked the apotheosis of reactionary measures to reinstate fatherhood as the litmus test of good citizenship. In its spectacular failure, Vichy demonstrates that while convincing arguments can be made for the continuity of Vichy's policies with both the Third and the Fourth Republics, in fact 1945 did mark a definitive break in the history of the French state. After the Liberation, gender was no longer the basis for exclusion from the franchise nor was it the driving principle behind the establishment of the new social security system. The Vichy regime's failure pushed this particular means-test to the rear, to be replaced, perhaps, by standards of sexuality in the late twentieth century.[8]

In the early twentieth century, however, social activists and legislators of different political persuasions may have had opposing views on the role of the father in civil society, but all were forced to deal with him as a competing source of power over French families. This competition was played out from the local gatherings of family associations to the benches of the Chamber of Deputies. Under the Vichy regime, the state struggled to reconcile paternal power and governmental authority, but its efforts were ultimately frustrated by certain fundamental contradictions between the reality of men as fathers and the social welfare schemes of public authorities. In the shaping of French political culture and the emergence of the welfare state in twentieth-century France, these conflicts over the nature of paternity, fathers, and fatherhood occupied a surprisingly central role. The history of these conflicts and their meaning in the evolution of modern France make up our subject here.

The intertwining histories of paternity and citizenship in France are distinctively rich and deserving of scholarly examination. From the paternal imagery surrounding Louis XVI during the Revolution to Marshal Pétain's claims to national fatherhood during the occupation, paternity has been an essential means of defining relationships between citizens and the state.[9] While monarchical and authoritarian regimes made wide use of paternal metaphors, conservatives, republicans, socialists, and communists also struggled with the ever-changing notion of fatherhood and strove to reconcile the often conflicting interests of fathers, families, and the nation. Linguistically, fathers in France were accorded a special status as *pères de famille,* or "fathers of a family," an expression that symbolized the father's unique collective and relational identity and finds no direct translation in the English language. Nowhere in Europe were the problems of the family a more pressing national priority than in France, and nowhere was the *père de famille* more closely linked to concrete political agendas and social policies.[10]

Not surprisingly, therefore, historians of France have dealt with the history of fatherhood in a variety of ways.[11] The historical interest in the subject has only increased with contemporary debates about fatherless families, paternity tests, and the relationships between fathers and their children.[12] Yet, curiously, historians have shown little inclination to examine paternity as a politically relevant concept. A number of new studies on masculinity have been more successful in integrating constructions of men as gendered beings within the larger social and political currents of early twentieth-century Europe.[13] The Great War not only traumatized men at the front, it also unleashed a plethora of fears about male homosexuality, which was thought to flourish in the trenches.[14] The war also generated new models of masculine identity evident in the robust specimens promoted by fascist movements in Europe. The martial bearing of the young men of Hitler's SS or the idealized male archetypes of fascist art provide ample evidence of a close connection between fascism and a cult of male virility in the interwar years.[15] Fascism itself was synonymous with the term "virility," and masculine virility was held up in opposition to femininity, homosexuality, and Bolshevik internationalism.[16] The study of masculinity, war, and fascism, therefore, has yielded rich and important conclusions about the interaction between male gender and politics in the early twentieth century.

The importance of paternity to fascist rhetoric in France has begun to be explored recently by French historians.[17] It is perhaps not surprising that fascist groups would have espoused a hierarchical, authoritarian, and male-dominated vision of society that foreshadowed the Vichy regime; what is more astounding is the way in which the rights and responsibilities of the father infused the political and social discourse of many *non*-fascist groups in the interwar years. The relationship between paternity and masculinity was a complicated and often contradictory one, not least in fascist ethics. On the one hand fatherhood was promoted as the eminent expression of virility, and on the other hand references to a man's family life were thought to weaken his image of strength and independence.[18] In France, unmarried men had for centuries been denigrated in particularly vicious terms, a phenomenon that only became more acute in the intensely pro-natalist interwar years. Yet the harmony of a man's paternal characteristics with his other duties in the public world of masculine pursuits was often highly problematic.

In occupied France, the rhetoric of virility and masculinity coalesced around a veneration of manhood developed in the leadership school of the Chateau d'Uriage and the Chantiers de la jeunesse.[19] Although not strictly fascist, these movements participated fully in the ethics of physical and mental fitness, obedience to authority, and disdain for weakness common to fascist rhetoric elsewhere.[20] The new men of Uriage, however, were seldom the long-suffering *pères de famille* promoted by family activists, and in fact the real-life burdens of paternity often detracted from their image as independent and manly beings.[21]

Notwithstanding these recent studies of masculinity and fascism in France, the relationship of fatherhood to political participation, social welfare, and the family has not been woven into the analysis of gender roles for men in the same way as motherhood has been for women. A man's paternity shaped his relationship to the political world and defined the nature of his private virtue. It was in his role as representative of the family that a father negotiated the interchange between public and private worlds and that his masculinity intersected with the interests of the state. For all of the literature on gender in modern France, this crucial intersection has often been over-looked. Men's family life was an integral part of their male identity and a field of social and political contention in the national community.

While studies of maternalism and the emergence of the welfare state have underscored the interdependence of gender and citizenship in the early twentieth century, little attention has been focused on the critical conjunction of paternity, politics, and nationhood in the same period. Maternity has occupied a more obvious place in the political and social discourse of many European nations through public celebrations, philanthropic discourse, and mass infant health campaigns. What happened to fatherhood as gender prescriptions for women came to rely increasingly on maternal identity? Was paternity transformed to meet the new political and social exigencies of the early twentieth century?

The French obsession with the *père de famille* was not simply an imported version of fascism, a variation *à la française* of reactionary social policies that had no resonance in a republican nation committed to equality and frater-nity. Rather, preoccupation with fatherhood was a long-standing French tra-dition. It appeared in the programs of workers, employers, women's groups, and Catholic associations, and it cut across class and political affiliation as a question of national importance.[22] Discourse on paternity was more than a matter of conservative social ethics, one more attempt to subordinate women and return them to the home with restrictive gender prescriptions. *Les Mamelles de Tirésias* gives us one indication of how such themes were pre-sent even among the avant garde in Paris. Debates on the *père de famille* were complex, contradictory, and motivated by political objectives that were at once vague and well defined.

While roles for women within the family were often promoted as ideo-logically clear-cut, this was not the case for the role of men. Whereas a woman's role as mother was frequently explicit and undisputed for conven-tional bourgeois society, a man's role as father could be plagued with doubt and interrupted by the distractions and demands of the greater world—workplace, military service, political life—predicaments that could essen-tially rob him of his paternity itself. While social reformers portrayed women as biologically, morally, and socially destined for motherhood, the demands of paternity were not as deeply inscribed in a man's body or character. After all, the behavior code of a proper father, consisting mainly of working and providing for one's family, was not inextricably linked with biological pater-nity. Men could work and earn money whether or not they were fathers, and many contemporaries decried the fact that men could eschew their duty to raise children with their earnings. While paternity was an obligation or a burden to be accepted and could thus seem less consequential in the complex life of a man, motherhood was an unmistakable corporal transformation thought by many to fulfill the woman's entire "destiny."

Paternity could therefore be exposed to doubt and cynicism as well as acclaim. In the Third Republic and under Vichy, pro-natalists and familists attempted to make fatherhood synonymous with good citizenship but immediately encountered a number of intractable dilemmas. First and foremost, they were forced to confront the definition of paternity itself, to endorse its symbolic virtues while confronting the deleterious effects of the countless real-life bad fathers threatening France's families. Social reformers who vaunted the father figure as the key to national regeneration managed to place fathers at the center of social and political debates, but who exactly was this father in the midst of the controversy? What were the specifics of his gendered role within the domestic circle, and how was his status in the public worlds of work and government determined by his family life? French policymakers held strong views about gender roles within the family, but as they repeatedly discovered when they tried to make policy conform to philosophy, such roles were not only less obvious than they had assumed but also quite problematic.[23] Gender roles for men were deeply contested because fatherhood did not coalesce easily with state efforts to assist women and children. Fathers represented both a competing authority for state power and a rival of women for public resources, even as they were seen as essential to the project of reforming French families. The ways in which policymakers, public authorities, and concerned individuals attempted to reconcile these contradictory qualities constitute a major theme of this study.

The development of family policy in France has too often been portrayed exclusively as the province of a few highly motivated and influential men. A wide variety of other familist organizations flourished in early twentieth-century France, many of which are described elsewhere in this volume. These organizations cared intensely about gender and family structure, and particularly about the role of the *père de famille* in the political constitution of the nation. Although republican pro-natalists such as Fernand Boverat of the Alliance nationale contre la dépopulation did play a key part in the administrative structures and policymaking circles of the late Third Republic and the Vichy regime, other groups of concerned citizens, especially members of social-Catholic organizations, also exerted considerable influence on the shape of French family policy.

Paternity cannot be overlooked as a mobilizing agent and organizational structure for family associations and their relations with public authorities.[24] Many organizations in early twentieth-century France were based on groups of *pères de famille* who named themselves in proud recognition of the number of children their members had fathered. The *père de famille*, in fact, became the symbol *par excellence* of many family associations because he represented a return to order, optimism about the future, and a means of redistributing state resources through his patriotic parenthood. The father therefore provides an expedient entry point into the discussion of public activism, social citizenship, and the development of welfare policies in twentieth-century France.

Analyzing the role of fathers in the proposals and practices of family associations refutes the notion that men were victims of a conspiratorial coalition between state reformers and wives in the development of welfare policies. According to Jacques Donzelot, in the late nineteenth and early twentieth centuries the workingman was stripped of his autonomy and rights by an increasingly interventionist state whose administrative tentacles reached far into the private family sphere. Aided and abetted by wives who enforced ever stricter norms of hygiene and decency, men were unwittingly besieged by an acquisitive welfare state intent on supplanting the father's authority.[25] Fathers, however, were active participants in the process of state intervention into family lives, often adamantly soliciting assistance and at the same time betraying considerable anxiety about doing so. Many held up their paternity as a national duty eminently worthy of recognition, even as they feared the appearance of supplicating the state for aid. Fathers were therefore key players in the development of social assistance schemes, both as rallying symbols and as interested parties in the negotiation of public policy. Ignoring the *père de famille* obscures the vibrancy of debates about family structure, paternal rights, and social responsibility that continued in and around pro-natalist circles.

The participation of concerned groups of citizens in the crafting of family policy reached its apotheosis under the Vichy regime, when family associations were granted a legal status and official consultative rights within the government. Many scholars have pointed to the remarkable continuity in personnel and policies between the Third Republic and the Vichy regime in the administration of family assistance.[26] Although Vichy officials carried out many of the provisions of their predecessors, particularly as defined in the 1939 *Code de la famille*, the Vichy years constituted an exceptional period in French history that deserves special analysis in and of itself. Letters and visitors poured into Marshal Pétain's office suggesting policy modifications and demanding that the family be granted a position of honor in the new state. Here as well, the status of the *père de famille* was debated as never before. With the ideological support of Pétain himself, it appeared as if the Vichy regime would finally be able to realize the long-cherished goal of many conservative family supporters and to reinstate traditional family values and gender norms in France.

Miranda Pollard and Francine Muel-Dreyfus have outlined how the Vichy regime actualized these traditional gender norms, drawing on supposedly "eternal" truths about the nature of women and men and putting them to use in service of the reactionary National Revolution.[27] Muel-Dreyfus and Pollard offer convincing analyses of women under the Vichy regime, but again the main focus is on the complexities of female rather than male gender. Although Pollard discusses some of the implications of Vichy's masculinist policies, her study describes the importance of women in the great national "cleaning up" of the National Revolution, while men are rendered "metaphorically invisible," useless in the feminine work of renovating France.[28] This approach obscures the importance of fathers, however, as Vichy propaganda did insistently push them forward and brought them to the center of debates about domestic policies and national renewal.[29] In works that explore the complex ideology and administration surrounding women, men appear more simplistically as active perpetrators of the "familial imperialism" of the Vichy regime. As "superior" beings, they benefited from the ideological support of a government that wanted only to restore power and privilege to fathers at the expense of women. Yet the motivations behind and the impact of Vichy's family policies were not so clear-cut. If propagandists borrowed from a long tradition of beliefs about women and mothers, they also drew on a culture of convictions about fathers that was far from uniformly good. Fathers under the Vichy regime were subject to the same distrust, humiliation, and usurpation that had plagued fathers of the Third Republic. Men were also subject to intense state censure and were derided by state propaganda in ways that went beyond accusations of "feminization."[30] In a regime in which they were to be accorded all advantages, rights, and status, fathers were nevertheless the object of punitive laws and, despite the rhetorical acclaim they received, found their authority undermined by the very regime that officially acclaimed them. To ignore this dimension of Vichy policy is to fundamentally misunderstand Vichy itself.

The great irony of family policy under the Vichy regime is that given the opportunity to create a state based on paternal authority and true to the ideological prescriptions of the regime, policymakers were unable and even unwilling to carry it out. Vichy authorities may have advocated a return to traditional family structure and strong fathers, but in the end even zealous partisans of patriarchy recognized the contradictions inherent in a policy granting fathers powers that interfered with those of an expanding welfare state.[31] Advocates of the *père de famille* faced an inescapable conflict between paternal authority and the authority of a state that would inevitably supplant it. This study examines the contest between fathers and the state in France and explains the limitations of an ideology that promoted fathers even as it found them problematic for the regeneration of the nation.

Our analysis begins with an examination of the legal foundations of father-state relations in France. Legal texts, government debates, court cases, and the discourse of social reformers reveal the impact of the Napoleonic

Civil Code in defining family life and paternal prerogatives during the late nineteenth and early twentieth centuries. Chapter 1 examines major acts of legislation, from the *Code civil* to the *Code de la famille,* that affected fathers in their relations to families and the state. Here, the growth of fears about inadequate and abusive fathers and the ideological conflicts inherent in the expansion of state administration become clear.

Building on the legal foundations, chapter 2 analyzes the role of paternity in public discourse and popular imagery during the First World War and on into the interwar years. Why was the father key to national regeneration and defense, and how did fathers become useful in the various political and social conflicts facing the Third Republic? In a thematic analysis, images of what the proper family man was supposed to look and act like are brought to light through advertisements, family magazines, social welfare exhibitions, workers' tracts, pro-natalist propaganda, and Catholic treatises on the family. These popular representations illustrate the central role of the *père de famille* in contests over power and authority within the Third Republic and the ways in which various social and political groups portrayed fathers.

The origins and goals of the National Revolution must be understood within the context of France's capitulation in the war, an approach that demonstrates how the "strange defeat" revitalized long-standing conservative goals for family reform. In official discourse, the family was promoted as a link between the past and the future, essential to legitimating the new Vichy regime and to quelling the divisiveness of the Third Republic. Examining government texts and propaganda, as well as school lesson plans, public lectures, and administrative directives, chapter 3 moves to Pétain's conscious use of paternal metaphors as a model for relationships between citizens and the state and investigates the images and social groups summoned to prop up the authority of the regime.

In chapter 4, images of the "new men" sought by the Vichy regime come to the fore. Most powerful in expressing these ideals were the propaganda campaigns aimed at turning defeated soldiers into virile workers and apostles of the National Revolution. Looking at images from pamphlets and internal memoranda concerning the Service du travail obligatoire and the Chantiers de la Jeunesse, as well as representations of paternity from expositions, the family press, and Vichy's own bureau of propaganda, this study examines the portrayal of fathers in Vichy ideology and how these portrayals differed from the representations of the Third Republic.

In chapter 5, the concrete administrative ramifications of Vichy's discourse on the family are examined through the policies enacted during the occupation that pertained to fathers. Office notes, records from the administrative bodies established to deal with family issues, and the profusion of letters received by Pétain's cabinet chronicle the accomplishments of the family movement and the role of family associations in promoting the *père de famille.* Finally, this study examines the *Code de la famille* in practice and explains the ultimate incompatibility of Vichy's ideological convictions about the father with its perception of the needs of French families.

Throughout this book, my emphasis is on public rather than private manifestations of fatherhood in civic society. Another interesting topic, certainly, would be the examples of real-life fathers and their lived experience during the Third Republic and the Vichy regime. However, this more personal and individual approach would not get at the ultimate meaning in the government debates, the popular representations, and the legal controversies surrounding the very essence of paternity in early twentieth-century France. To be sure, individual men and women and their concerns do appear in cases brought before the courts, in personal letters to Marshal Pétain, and in cautionary tales told by concerned activists. Yet here I use diverse sources in advertising, legal documents, social and religious tracts, and government propaganda to demonstrate that at the highest levels, there was in fact a vibrant and critical discussion of paternity in the French state among participants from all across the political spectrum.

Throughout this animated conversation, few could agree on the most appropriate criteria for defining proper fatherhood or find consensus on the state's interest in men's family lives. Far from being a paean to fatherhood or a lament on its decline, this book aims to show that in the constant reevaluation of fatherhood and its merits, men's gender identities have been more tenuous, and less constant, than much previous scholarship on gender has seemed to imply. The French state did not view women alone in gendered terms; rather, it was dedicated to putting gender norms for *both* men and women to work in the business of renovating France. What this study reveals is that, ultimately, this approach was doomed to failure. In the latter half of the twentieth century, the French Republic was forced to rethink the conceptual basis of citizens' rights and responsibilities; the rights of the family unit and social solidarity for all workers became the new criteria upon which the postwar state would be built.

1

Paternity, Law, and Politics in the Third Republic

In 1801, as the turmoil of the Revolution gave way to a new Napoleonic paternalism, the Institut national de France sponsored an essay contest in which the respondents were asked to take up the question: "What should be, in a well-constituted Republic, the scope and the limits of the power of a Father of a family?" The Institut had already proposed the same question twice before, but none of the treatises previously submitted corresponded adequately to its views and it was sponsoring the contest for a third time. Following the upheavals of the Revolutionary years, resolving questions of paternity and politics seemed an essential part of the reconstruction of a new and more stable order. The scholars of the Institut held out hope that the forthcoming civil code would lend weight to the principles developed in the prize-winning treatise and reaffirm the powers of fathers in domestic and public society.[1]

The Civil Code of 1804 did, in fact, support the principles of the selected essay, far more than it realized the outlines of projects for a code elaborated under the Convention a few years earlier. In a series of three proposals brought forward by Jean-Jacques Cambacérès, the Convention had refined and articulated projects for a system of family law that condemned the tyrannical and arbitrary power of fathers and aimed to establish a new family order based on natural affection and reason rather than coercion and law.[2] Yet by 1799, shortly after Napoleon Bonaparte's *coup d'état,* the presentation of a fourth legal project demonstrated that the climate surrounding the legislation of family relations had changed dramatically, and provisions for paternal authority over children and wives was again firmly grounded in legal stipulations more closely resembling those of the *ancien régime.* With the promulgation of the Civil Code in 1804, French fathers again had the right to punish and incarcerate their children for their offensive behavior, a proviso that granted them more power than fathers in any other European country except for Sardinia.[3]

The Revolution unleashed a torrent of critical debate on the interaction between family, politics, and the state that certainly did not cease with the rigorous and reactionary provisions of the Napoleonic Code. Throughout the nineteenth century and well into the twentieth, dissension over the respective rights and obligations of families, fathers, and the state continued to erupt into political battles whose participants defied clear-cut divisions of class or political affiliation. Indeed, in the early twentieth century, the linkage of paternity and political authority continued to define power relations between citizens and the state and prescribed relations among individuals in the domestic sphere.

To understand these complex relations, one must begin by following the fortunes of the *père de famille* in the late Third Republic, tracing the articulation of power relations through laws that targeted the less-than-ideal father who had either abused his charges and neglected his duties, or was unable to survive in a system that seemed to penalize him for accepting the burdens of paternity. Understanding the legacy of the Revolution and the Civil Code on paternal legislation provides a crucial foundation for understanding the profusion of legislation surrounding the family in the late nineteenth and early twentieth centuries. The relationship between fathers and the state was enacted in legislation against a background of both consensus and strife among political parties and social classes in the late Third Republic. At a time when maternity was exalted as the one truly suitable and noble vocation for women, paternity was surrounded with contradictory currents of opinion that held up the *père de famille* as crucial to national regeneration while at the same time defining his position and authority as increasingly problematic for the operation of the Republic. While discourse on the virtues of fathers will be addressed later on, here the focus is on analyzing the ways in which, from the *Code civil* to the *Code de la famille* of 1939, the privileges of fatherhood were defined, modified, and dismantled by administrative powers in the early decades of the twentieth century.

Despite the reversal of paternal fortunes brought about by the Civil Code, the uncertainty and apprehensions over paternal power conspicuous in the Revolution left a taint on fatherhood in general that could not be completely erased by attempts to bolster paternal prestige in the nineteenth century. The efforts of social critics and legislators to counteract the inadequacies of less-than-ideal fathers propagated an idea of "tyrannical," "deficient," and "absent" fathers that came to cast doubt on all fathers in the twentieth century.[4] How did jurists, politicians, and philanthropists of the twentieth century replay the strains of doubt and misgiving over fathers elaborated 150 years before? What did citizens of the Third Republic believe was wrong with

French fathers, and what did they anticipate doing about it? This chapter looks at the expressions of distrust and criticism of early twentieth-century fathers manifest in social commentary admonishing bad fathers and in concrete legislative acts that curtailed their power. As the state attempted to assume greater responsibility for what went on inside the family sphere, it came into increasing conflict with traditional nineteenth-century notions of paternal independence and authority. With a vigor that spanned social classes and political affiliations, concerned French men and women petitioned the government and appropriate associations to reform relations between fathers, families, and the state, and urged legislators to generate a new family code that would correct the errors of the last century and a half.

The winning essayist in the 1801 contest sponsored by the Institut national de France recognized the duties of fathers to prepare future citizens for the nation. After great political upheavals, the principles of government could be established only through firm and just laws that protected property, liberty, and security. The present hour, however, required fashioning *new men,* and this was a task that could only be accomplished slowly, within each family, and that would send forth a new and improved generation of citizens as tribute to the state.[5] To obtain these happy results, the essayist believed, paternal power should be extensive and should include rights to punishment, prohibition of marriage, and the ability to pass on inheritance as a father saw fit. Broad paternal prerogatives, however, were always to serve the higher interests of the state:

> Well-organized paternal power is the most powerful support not only of public morality, but also of the government itself. Yes, the happiness of a state, its morals, and even its most precious institutions depend on paternal power. Perfect morality is the primary source of a people's prosperity; and where does one find such morality if not in the heart of families?[6]

In the earlier years of the Revolution, jurists appeared more concerned with preventing abuse of power by tyrannical fathers; by the turn of the century, public authorities and social critics seemed to fear far more the anarchy erupting from weak fathers. Even if a father misused his power, the Institut believed, "one must always determine whether it is more dangerous to leave children without limits, or to submit them to an authority that is no doubt occasionally arbitrary, but most often salutary."[7] The "excesses" of the Revolution had come to an end—just in time, legislators believed, to prevent chaos and utter lawlessness in society at large.

If notions of the state and fatherhood were interdependent and mutually reflective, how would the complex relationship of power be negotiated? To what extent did the Civil Code of 1804 actually reflect the aspirations of the

Revolution with respect to family law? The Code did embody a fundamental revolutionary desire for a formal system of laws regulating family life, and although many paternal powers were reinstated and extended, the Napoleonic order did *not* return families to the *ancien régime*. Nevertheless, fathers were acknowledged in the Code as the civil magistrates and cornerstones of society, law, and morality that Consulate legislators thought them to be.

Under provisions of the Civil Code, *la puissance paternelle* regained its title and much of its content; its scope was extended once again past the age of a child's majority for consent in marriage. Legislators hesitated to restore to fathers the right to incarcerate children for unlimited periods, but fathers could "correct" children under fifteen by having them detained for renewable periods of one month, in consultation with civil judges. In order to preserve the love for property and fatherland that legislators saw as emanating from a father's right to dispose of his heritage, the Code did grant greater paternal leeway in apportioning worldly possessions, stopping short of permitting a father to totally disinherit a child. Article 340 of the Code, prohibiting investigation into paternity for illegitimate children, was also a significant stipulation of the law that would be debated for decades to come. The explicit repudiation of unwanted accusations of paternity protected men and the institution of marriage from the perceived excessive egalitarianism of the Revolution, and its reactionary vehemence provided a backdrop against which legislators of the Third Republic would struggle.[8] The Code thus perpetuated the idea that paternity was primarily an act of volition on the part of the father and sustained the aura of inviolability surrounding paternity by shielding it from the degradation of mere procreators.

Despite the enthusiastic zeal of the Revolutionaries to purge fatherhood of its corrupt and arbitrary attributes, the authors of the Civil Code preferred to count on the support of undiminished fathers rather than risk the anarchy engendered by a society of morally orphaned citizens. The Code was a symbol of cooperation and collaboration between the state and the family, in which fathers were consecrated as the first essential link in the long chain that constrained the individual in the name of liberty.[9] The representation of the family as a bounded unit over which a father had dominion, however, was slowly transfigured over the course of the nineteenth century. After decades of relative calm in the realm of legislation, the family, and the role of fathers in particular, once again became a subject of wrenching debate for legislators of the Third Republic.[10] The suppositions of the Civil Code about the nature of paternal authority and the social status of its possessors became increasingly difficult to reconcile with the new social, political, and economic realities of the late nineteenth century wrought by industrialization and urbanization. In the wake of such radical societal transformations, public authorities could no longer sanction a father's unquestioned rights over his family with the confidence manifest in the Napoleonic Code.

The Civil Code remained virtually untouched until a new generation of republican legislators were brought to power in the last decades of the nineteenth century. Laws on the family remained relatively untroubled during the nineteenth century, through social upheaval, revolution, and reaction, whether under the July Monarchy, the Second Empire, or the early Third Republic. On the one hand, liberal politicians were averse to proffering suffrage rights or greater autonomy within marriage to women, and the outlines of the Civil Code coincided happily enough with their own views on the family.[11] On the other hand, conservative politicians, such as Théodore Benoit-Champy from the Côte-d'Or, wished to expand the rights of *puissance paternelle,* but his generally well-received proposal became a casualty of the *coup d'état* of December 2, 1851. Benoit-Champy submitted his recommendations to the Deputies in August, but the National Assembly was dissolved before any further discussion of the project was possible.[12] Only certain utopian socialists and feminist groups directly attacked the family as configured by Napoleon's Civil Code; for the most part, the Code provided a basis for family life to which most French men from across the political spectrum could agree with only minor reservations.[13]

If modifications to the actual Code were limited throughout the nineteenth century, the family itself nonetheless became the focus of increasingly intense debate and scrutiny as the century wore on. Heightened concern about the family in public discourse belied the stability of Napoleonic law, for whereas "family" as a juridical term appeared only briefly in the Civil Code in references to guardianship and in the term *conseil de famille,* the family as a discrete entity was proclaimed loudly as the natural and primordial unit of society by jurists and social reformers alike.[14] The family was a useful symbol that served in the rhetoric and political manifestos of Catholic thinkers and social conservatives, but workers and utopian socialists picked up the strains of this chorus as well.[15] Both Right and Left claimed to defend the family and its social mission, while conservatives and republicans alike worried about its demise.[16]

Indeed, the family was both a symptom-bearer of the ills of modern French society and a key element in its rejuvenation. Against a backdrop of "depopulation" that only intensified after defeat in the Franco-Prussian War of 1870, politicians on all sides agreed that the family was a "problem" the state could not afford to ignore. French birth rates began to decrease as early as the late eighteenth century, and by the end of the nineteenth century the French population was reproducing itself at the lowest rates in the world.[17] While conservatives blamed this depopulation on the decline of traditional morality and religious values, republicans looked to other causes. Radical republicans, for example, linked the declining birth rate not only to moral disintegration, but also to the profound economic transformations of the age. Among the bourgeoisie, they believed, couples may have limited their families to one or two children because they wished to maintain a certain social and economic status. Among the working classes, on the other hand, oppressive poverty and the risks associated with childbirth made family life unattractive for many.[18] Whatever politicians indicated as the root cause of the problems of family life, condemnations of the shortcomings and recommendations for the rebirth of the French family were abundant in public debate in the nineteenth century.

Statesmen and political partisans were not the only public figures concerned with family life and its ramifications for the nation. The nineteenth century witnessed the appearance of several major philosophers and theoreticians who focused on the family in their writing and teaching. In his *Origins of the Family, Property and the State,* Friedrich Engels set forth the idea that the degrading effects of capitalism prevented the working classes from having a healthy home life and that marriage itself was simply another phase in the appropriation of property and the transmission of goods.[19] Scholars influential in establishing the new discipline of sociology also took up the cause of the family. Most notable among these were Frédéric Le Play and Émile Durkheim in France.

Le Play was one of the most ardent critics of the Civil Code. He fiercely resented the abolition of primogeniture and the limitations on a father's testamentary rights, changes he saw as contributing directly to the fracturing of paternal authority and the disintegration of society. In works such as his *Méthode sociale* (1879), Le Play amassed an impressive number of "scientific" family monographs to study domestic life in societies around the world. He classified families into three main groups: the "patriarchal family," in which all grown sons stayed within their father's household; the "unstable family," in which children left home as soon as they could survive on their own; and the "stem family," in which one child stayed in the father's household and inherited his property. Le Play saw the stem family as being the only form of domestic organization that could prevent social anarchy and as a happy medium between the suffocating strictures of the patriarchal family and the excessive individualism of the unstable family. He asserted that the civil and political liberty necessary to modern society could only develop within the context of a strict hierarchy within families, one that granted the patriarch important powers. His scientific observations, moreover, were linked to a concrete political agenda; in 1865, Le Play pressed for reform of the laws on inheritance overturned by the Revolution and the Civil Code.[20]

In his courses and writing on the sociology of the family, Émile Durkheim also attempted to reconcile the tension between individualism and social solidarity inherent in modern societies. Durkheim found fault with the impassioned partisanship of Le Play's discussion of the family and with his inability to keep personal feelings out of his scientific observations. Durkheim also, however, devised a system of classification for the evolution of family structures over time and space. Unlike Le Play, he did not assign "moral" value to his observations, but his idea that the modern family was changing—from a structure of unlimited paternal authority and solidarity to a unit in which individual desires, as well as the state and society, exerted ever greater control—alarmed many social reformers. The important role Durkheim granted the state in modern family life was almost as outrageous to late nineteenth-century moralists as were Engels's views on marriage. In his course titled "Introduction à la sociologie de la famille," given at the University of Bordeaux in 1888, Durkheim described the modern or "conjugal" family as characterized by the "ever-increasing intervention of the State into the interior life of the family." The state was not merely a new influence in domestic life, he believed, but was necessary to its very existence: "the conjugal family would not have come into being without the intervention of this new factor, the State."[21] Although Durkheim's assertions were heretical to many who decried the decline of the French family, his role in the establishment of the new field of family sociology was significant.

Philosophers such as Durkheim and Le Play helped to focus concern about the modern family and gave credence to the idea that families were shaped, for better or worse, by the laws and institutions that governed them. If deficient laws or economic want had transformed the family, perhaps further purposeful alterations could restore it to its former glory or even fashion a new family system better adapted to human nature and to modern democratic society. Alongside the identification of the family as a social phenomenon worthy of scientific study, therefore, came a host of scientific experts and institutions claiming authority in this new field of research and reform. Families became a target of intervention and a means of social control during the nineteenth century, as the development of family science necessarily implied classifying families into categories of "normal" and "deviant." The traditional bourgeois family was held up as the norm, whereas any family that did not conform to that set of values and practices (usually urban, working-class families) quickly became an object of overly solicitous and intrusive concern.[22] The Civil Code postulated a law-abiding and just father of means in its formulation of family law; in the later decades of the nineteenth century, however, this supposition became increasingly difficult to uphold.

The discrepancy between such legal standards of paternal behavior and the reality of late nineteenth-century fatherhood crystallized around a new law on the divestiture of paternal authority. The law of July 24, 1889, protected "morally abandoned" and mistreated children from the abusive behavior of their parents and stipulated that parents might lose all legal authority over their children if they had been convicted of crimes or if they had incarcerated their children under provisions of *correction paternelle*.[23] Sylvia Schafer has explored the complicated motives behind the passage of this law and its tremendous implications for relations between families and the state. The law elicited profound ambivalence among legislators, who saw it as either an incontrovertible assault on the sanctity of paternal power as prescribed by nature and the Civil Code, or the logical progression of the state's efforts to protect children against abuse and danger, whatever its source. Support or opposition for the law did not break down neatly according to political ideology: both Right and Left echoed and commingled these two very different positions.[24] The law symbolized a compromise between conservatives who wanted to protect innocent women and children from debauched, drunken, working-class fathers but hesitated to endanger paternal rights in general, and republicans who wished to protect future citizens from dangerous and immoral environments but were loath to compromise a husband's authority over his wife. The authority of husbands was particularly at issue as the Naquet Law reinstating divorce had been passed only five years earlier. In the end, the only principle that all sides could agree on readily was the protection of young children against mistreatment by all-powerful and corrupt fathers.[25] For purposes of this study, the most important impact of the law on *décheance de la puissance paternelle* was in its presumption that paternal behavior was no longer outside the purview of state control. Instead of bolstering a father's authority and power within the family, legislators of the Third Republic were more attuned to the notion of the best interests of the child, and they promoted the welfare of children over and against unlimited paternal prerogatives. Ultimately the law of 1889 marked a decisive change in the boundaries between public and private life established by Napoleonic law and signaled a new progression in the fortunes of paternity in France.

What had happened in the eighty-five years since the promulgation of the Civil Code that enabled the passage of a law so radical in its impact on the rights of fathers? How did the economic, social, and political changes wrought by the nineteenth century change the formulation of family policy and the guiding principles of relationships between fathers and the state?[26] One useful way to examine such changes is to follow the evolution of *correction paternelle*, that singularly harsh paternal right French fathers enjoyed over children of theirs who had seriously aggrieved them in some way. Statistically speaking, *correction paternelle* did not affect a large percentage of French children, and it was finally expunged from the law books in 1935. The fact that between 1851 and 1896 an average of more than 1,000 adolescents a year were incarcerated or threatened with incarceration by their fathers is nonetheless significant.[27]

In the early nineteenth century, *correction paternelle* was a natural extension of a father's role as domestic magistrate; he was the first line of discipline and constraint within a hierarchy that extended from individuals to the state. Authors of the Civil Code imagined fathers who would avail themselves of this right to be just and enlightened rulers, and certainly men of substantial wealth, since children were detained at the instigator's expense. A series of laws waiving the obligation to pay for the upkeep of one's incarcerated children changed all that, however: in 1841 and again in 1855, the state eliminated the cost of feeding and housing a child for poor families who could not afford it. Paternal correction had thus become the prerogative of fathers of humble means, not just an aristocrat's method of disciplining an intemperate youngster.[28] Such laws on indigence generated a momentous change in both the purpose and the clientele of *la correction paternelle.*[29]

Georges Bonjean, who was responsible for investigating cases of paternal correction in the Seine department, published a book in 1895 that went a long way toward breaking down any lingering illusions about the social status of solicitors for *correction paternelle.*[30] In his *Enfants révoltés, parents coupables,* Bonjean indicated that in his Département, the great majority of requests came from the working classes, 78 percent of them from the manual professions alone. Very few of them were liable for any associated expense because of their status as indigents. Furthermore, paternal correction was a phenomenon associated almost exclusively with great urban areas, and its popularity seemed to evolve in tandem with forces of modernization and industrialization. The fact that demands for paternal correction skyrocketed during the depression of the 1890s suggests that the incarceration of children was linked to destitution, originating with parents who could not afford to keep them, rather than a desperate last resort for frustrated disciplinarians.[31] The expansive rights granted fathers under the Civil Code, therefore, had been appropriated by a new kind of father. The late nineteenth-century petitioner for *correction paternelle* was poor, working-class, and living in an industrial center; he was himself not a powerful and impartial dispenser of justice within his family, but a laborer caught in a hierarchy of oppression and destitution.

Most social observers were not particularly sympathetic to the difficult circumstances of working-class fathers, however. Karl Marx acknowledged paternal abuse within working-class families but emphasized the fact that men could not help but mistreat their children and exploit their authority because they themselves were exploited by the capitalist system. Bonjean, on the other hand, accentuated the moral failings and degeneracy of such men and argued that they were unworthy of the title of *père de famille.*[32] In his emotionally charged account, Bonjean described the demands for paternal correction as emanating from unworthy, drunken, and debauched men who often punished their children for refusing to hand over earnings to satisfy their own dissolute desires. Many demands, he asserted, also came from bro-

ken homes, where fathers living in concubinage simply wished to rid themselves of bothersome children from a former, legitimate union.[33] The
scourge of despotic fathers was now emanating from a new source; in the
minds of Revolutionaries a century earlier, inordinately empowered fathers,
often aristocrats, had threatened the Republic with their unlimited auto-
cratic rights. In the late nineteenth century, however, the very impotence
and inadequacy of fathers was cause for alarm, and reformers sought to curb
the tyranny that sprang from the moral weakness of fathers and endangered
the well-being of the nation.[34]

Such a mistrustful and critical view of poor fathers certainly galvanized
legislators' will to strip unworthy individuals of the privileges associated with
fatherhood. But while the statistics on *correction paternelle* suggest that economic and social constraints motivated many demands, legislators, like Bonjean, targeted the moral and psychological characteristics of the father
himself. The 1889 law on *déchéance paternelle*, for example, not only acted to
protect innocent children, but also extended the state's powers in passing
moral judgments on their abusive fathers. In the legal realm, after all,
déchéance can be defined simply as the loss or divestiture of rights due to a
failure to accomplish an obligation. It holds other important connotations,
however, not simply of divestiture but of a fall from grace, or the passage to
an inferior moral or spiritual state.[35] Furthermore, *déchéance* also implied a
kind of irretrievable loss or downfall rather than a legal process that could
potentially be reversed. In targeting working-class fathers, therefore, social
reformers and legislators focused on the inherent qualities of the man
rather than the circumstances that may have made family life difficult.

According to the historian Françoise Hurstel, a new concept of incompe-
tence and inadequacy, *carence*, came to characterize fathers in the late nineteenth and early twentieth centuries. This ideological construction of
fatherhood was the deformed reflection of the father's real decrease in
power within the family, but whereas this decreasing power, manifest in
changing law, was the result of unsteady economic, social, and legal structures, social reformers put fathers themselves on trial for their shortcomings.[36] Hurstel's analysis is reminiscent of Jacques Donzelot's understanding
of the workings of state encroachment on family life in the late nineteenth
century, in which government authorities wielded an inordinate amount of
power over working-class families, and over fathers in particular. In her
analysis, the late nineteenth century witnessed a pitched battled over the inadequacy of fathers between two antagonistic social classes: dispossessed fathers on the one hand, and bourgeois representatives of the state on the
other. By the twentieth century, however, the notion of *carence* had spread to
encompass fathers in general; whether rich or poor, all fathers were placed
on trial by the new experts on family life and child welfare.[37]

While this analysis is compelling in many important respects, social and political lines cannot be so easily drawn between prosecutors and defense in this turn-of-the-century trial of paternity. Social reformers and state representatives did in fact dispossess fathers of rights, often transferring them to the state and public authorities. But they often did so with profound ambivalence and even regret about the implications of their actions, rather than with the ominous determination that might be inferred from Hurstel's account.[38] Just as reformers in the Revolution had no intention of destroying the family altogether, Third Republic legislators did not set out to diminish the rights of the upstanding and worthy father they hoped was the norm. It was not simply the designs of public authorities that served to generalize such mistrust of fathers and cast a pall over fatherhood in the early twentieth century, for welfare reformers were not prosecuting alone. Legislation limiting the power of fathers drew on a widespread cultural sense of distrust and antagonism toward fathers and their powers, a dissatisfaction that spanned social classes and political affiliations in the years leading up to the Great War and on into the 1920s and 1930s. Public authorities were spurred on by a critical analysis of fatherhood that emerged in the first half of the twentieth century from many different sources; it is to this cultural critique and the legislative responses to it in the twentieth century that we now turn.

The Civil Code's formulation of family law rested on certain assumptions about paternity that anticipated that fathers would be revered and respected rather than brought under scrutiny by legislators and social reformers. Napoleonic law, after all, went so far as to outlaw—in article 340—any undue investigation of natural paternity. Legitimate paternity was based on a man's legal union with a mother of a child, rather than on any legally or biologically defined relationship between a man and a child. Article 312 of the Civil Code stated that a child conceived during marriage has as father the husband of its mother.[39] This rather circuitous logic was derived from the Roman legal heritage and the notion of *pater is est,* which established paternity exclusively through marriage and a man's own will to recognize a child.[40]

If illegitimate paternity was outlawed by the Code, however, married men still retained the right to "research the paternal origins" of a child if they had significant reasons to doubt that the child was their own. "Notorious misconduct" of the wife could lead to such a disavowal, as well as a physical accident or absence that made the likelihood of a husband's paternity very small.[41] A man who wished to disavow his wife's child, however, was faced with an arduous task, for the rule *pater is est* proved remarkably tenacious. To disavow a child, a husband had not only to prove his non-paternity through sufficiently damning evidence of his wife's adultery, but additionally to prove the paternity of another man, something that was virtually impossible to do.[42] The authors of the Code had, after all, operated on the logic that "nature has covered the transmission of our existence with an impenetrable veil" in prohibiting research into illegitimate paternity.[43]

The Code, therefore, raised the specter of doubts on legitimate paternity yet offered little solid recourse if a man wished to disavow his fatherhood. The establishment of paternity for early twentieth-century legislators was based on legal and social definitions rather than biological determinations, and even medically certified impotence was unlikely to convince a court that a husband was not also a father.[44] The obfuscation of biological paternity was also manifest in the presumption that men under eighteen years of age were incapable of procreating, since the legal age for contracting marriage was eighteen, and therefore a boy under that age could conceive no legitimate child.

In the hands of legislators, paternity was more a product of social convention than a biological given.[45] Not only was paternity less obvious than maternity; many jurists believed it was "materially impossible" to establish paternity, for although humankind had been successful in unveiling many secrets of nature and testing her limits, the secret of paternity had defied all efforts of investigation. Henry Lavollée noted that "even Aristotle and Alexander did not attempt to seek out, in the mysterious laws of the reproduction of souls, a means of discerning the children they had brought to life."[46] Creators of the Civil Code had anticipated that the cloud of secrecy and majesty surrounding paternity could be upheld by laws limiting unwanted paternity suits and that paternal rights could be kept safely above the mêlée of social and political changes.

By the end of the nineteenth century and the beginning of the twentieth, however, the ambiguities proceeding from the *pater is est* rule were difficult to ignore and led legislators to reexamine the legal foundations of fatherhood and initiate a revision of the Civil Code itself. In 1893, Radical-Socialist deputy Claude Goujat from the Nièvre suggested that a commission be named to overhaul the Code, because "laws age just as men do, and a century is a ripe old age for a piece of legislation." The 1804 Code, he believed, was the work of a "despotic government and an Assembly of slaves handpicked by their master." The new assembly, elected by universal male suffrage, was now obliged to replace such outdated relics of a former age with provisions "more befitting modern ideas and social and intellectual progress."[47] The Code's conception of paternity figured prominently among those provisions crying out for reform.

Perhaps, in fact, the Code's elevation of paternity invited precisely the kind of attacks that came forth in the Third Republic. In particular, the contradictions inherent in the idea that legitimate (but not illegitimate) paternity might be investigated biologically prompted legislators to question whether nature might reveal her secrets in the birth of "natural" children as well.[48] In 1895, another Deputy in the sixth legislature, Arthur Groussier, a member of the Parti ouvrier socialiste revolutionnaire, proposed a law that would lift the ban on paternity suits and attempt to remedy the social ills that sprang from such a mistaken conception. It was understandable, he said, that the legislator would want to prevent illicit parentage from coming to light, but it "is inadmissible that one allows suits which defend the rights of the husband but never those of the child." What was the purpose of society if not to protect and sustain the weak, whether that weakness sprang from nature, from human institutions, or from "the will or cowardice of other men?"[49]

The same year, another champion of legalizing *la recherche de la paternité*, Gustave Rivet, put forward his third proposal to overturn article 340 and permit paternity suits for illegitimate children (it would not be his last). A deputy from Grenoble, Rivet placed himself among the radical Left and eventually became vice president of the Gauche démocratique. Rivet argued that the numbers of abortions, infanticides, and abandonments of children were growing every year and that considering the dire demographic situation of France, no one could afford to ignore the terrible plight of unwed mothers.[50] He praised governmental advances in the protection of mothers and infants but claimed that such measures only palliated the effects of the real disease that needed to be eradicated. The unwed mother, after all, bore all the shame and guilt for a state that was "more than a little the work of another." Despite Rivet's censure of such debauched seducers, he nonetheless thought that women and children would be better served if the obligations of paternity were forcibly imposed on these men:

> In the interest of the innocent child, and in the name of the rights of woman, one must assure the child and the girl who has been seduced the protection of the father, a protection more efficient and just than that of the commune or of the State. One must admit investigation into paternity.[51]

The irony apparent in Rivet's proposal that the very man who had abandoned a woman could also best provide for her salvation mirrored a widespread tension many legislators experienced between the desire to preserve the family and a zeal to punish the father who had failed in his duty as its natural protector.[52]

Rivet's proposal to authorize investigation of paternity was finally enacted as law on November 16, 1912. He and Radical Deputy Julien Goujon insisted that the purpose of the law was not to establish an inquisition into paternal origins but rather to enable the judicial recognition of a paternity that was "recognized and accepted, at least in germ, by the author of the birth of a natural child."[53] Again, Rivet recognized that he walked a fine line between deferring to paternal authority and will on the one hand, and protecting the weak and disadvantaged on the other. A social reformer such as Rivet hoped to make men more responsible for their actions and to reform society as a whole; one cannot easily classify him as simply a prosecutor in the trial of working-class fathers.[54] In any event, despite the fact that republicans of the Left such as Rivet harked back to Revolutionary traditions in pressing for the right to investigate paternity, legislators had actually surpassed the license of their forebears. In the refashioning of family relations, Revolutionaries wished to emphasize the natural affection and will in paternal bonds; they had not imagined that paternity could be impressed on a man against his will.[55]

In his preface to the *Code manuel de la recherche de la paternité*, Émile de Saint-Auban wrote:

> Article 340 is dead; its death is an assuagement to the conscience. It decreed injustice and savagery. It smiled on the worst selfishness. It encouraged unmentionable instincts. It released the male into the world like a wild beast in the jungle. For men, it condoned rutting like animals. It atrophied any sense of responsibility. . . .[56]

Whereas Article 340 was supposed to have protected the family, legislators of the early twentieth century believed that too many men had abused the law for their own selfish protection and freedom from responsibility. Saint-Auban's denunciation did not fall on any particular social class or political group; instead it signaled a sense of contempt and unease with the characters of men in general. Likening would-be fathers to rutting animals certainly was a marked contrast to the presumptions of Roman law and the Napoleonic Code. The law of 1912 had transformed the definition of paternity, making it at once more transparent and more shrouded in mystery than ever. The "social convention" of paternity was being dismantled in law, and with a virulence that suggested that no new invention of the father could amend the errors of so many unworthy men who had fallen from grace.

While legislators debated the suppression of Article 340 and suggested that the "secrets" of paternity might be unraveled, other social commentators questioned whether there was much to be discerned about paternity after all. Certain feminists were quite adamant in their condemnation of fathers and the "amateurs of bourgeois morality" that deliberated on the subject of paternity as if it were a serious natural phenomenon. Madeleine Vernet, a liberal bourgeois feminist, wrote in 1905: "For me, paternity doesn't exist," indicating that she doubted the existence of anything like "paternal sentiment."[57] In her social study on paternity, Vernet contrasted paternal feelings to maternal ones and found men lacking at every level of biology, morality, and social responsibility.

Men, for example, only possessed sexual organs, rather than "paternal organs," whereas women's sexual organs were essentially maternal, making her a mother nine months before she actually gave birth. Women, according to Vernet, were the only true authors of the masterpiece of human life, because a man quickly abandoned his sexual companion most of the time anyway. "The rest of the time, when he is married, if he acts like a father according to the law, it isn't nature that dictates this feeling of paternal obligation, it is only established convention."[58] For Vernet, a family was made up of a woman and children, and therefore the proposal to create new laws that tried to secure so vague a concept as paternity were misguided:

> This so-called "paternal sentiment," so vaunted on the stage and in novels, is so unreal, so unnatural, that it can develop perfectly well in a man who thinks he is the father of a child, but who in reality he did not create. . . . This is the most effective negation of paternity. It attests to the fact that paternal love is not a primordial natural feeling, and has no physiological basis.[59]

Vernet's proposals were for a basic restructuring of domestic organization and a negation of men's role in the family altogether. Her views were obviously quite radical and would have found little support in mainstream public opinion, yet she was not alone in questioning the nature of paternity itself. In the public discourse surrounding paternity in the early twentieth century, doubts about defining fatherhood continued to arise: was paternity based on sentiment? on biology? on the discharge of certain responsibilities?

Echoing the idea of man's moral decline, the Union de pensée féminine wrote a letter to the Ministers of War and of Public Education proposing a program of education about paternity in barracks and in state schools. Lydie Martial of the Union reported that men needed to be educated about their reproductive organs because they were unable to regulate their own sexual impulses.[60] Their disorderly reproductive instincts wreaked havoc on women, children, and society as a whole. Men may be proud of being able to make love at any hour, she reported, but this indiscriminate power led to man's fall into "a state of inferiority in which he can make no progress towards a normal, active and fertile state of fulfillment or morality."[61] Whereas motherhood was promoted by many as making a woman more beautiful, moral, and socially useful, the transformations wrought on men as fathers were far more ambiguous. If paternity had to be "taught" in order to save men from moral and physical degradation, how could fathers be held up as exemplars of virtue and social progress? In the first decades of the twentieth century, the accusations of *déchéance* and *carence* that had plagued certain classes of unworthy fathers at the end of the nineteenth century were multiplying to encompass fathers of every kind.

The notion of deficient fatherhood could also be read in population statistics of the early twentieth century that seemed to indicate that men, and therefore fathers, were increasingly rare and wanting. The discourse on deficiency was inscribed in demographic reality, for France suffered an enormous "hemorrhage of men" in three wars between 1870 and 1945.[62] The French casualty rate during World War I was proportionally the highest in Europe: 16.5 percent of those mobilized were killed, as opposed to 14.7 percent of German soldiers. Between August 1914 and November 1918, an average of 930 Frenchmen were killed every day: these dead French soldiers, laid out head to foot, would have formed an uninterrupted line from Paris to Berlin three times over.[63] Of those men conscripted to fight in the war, the generation born from 1891 to 1897, who would have been in their mid-thirties in 1930, were the hardest hit. This cohort constituted more than one-third of all men drafted, and these contingents lost an average of one man out of every four.[64]

Alongside the devastation of an estimated 1.5 million dead, the war had produced three million wounded and had permanently disabled another 1.1 million men.[65] Not only were millions of able-bodied soldiers destroyed by the war; population experts warned that the death of so many men had left 1.4 million babies unborn—the very citizens who were essential to the renewal of France after this annihilation.[66] Fewer men also meant fewer opportunities for women to fulfill their preordained roles as wives and mothers: male casualties had created an unprecedented "surplus" of single women whose chances of finding a marriage partner were slim.[67] Contemporaries may have disagreed on the exact number of "excess" single women, but the fact that many young, fertile women were unlikely to find husbands caused much consternation and public controversy.[68] It also gave statistical representation to the persistent charges of *carence* and insufficiency haunting men in the early twentieth century. Fathers had been targeted in law for the deficient way in which they had fulfilled certain paternal obligations; now it seemed that the very existence of France was at risk because of their numerical insufficiency.

In the face of such staggering casualty rates, social commentators obviously did not hold men themselves accountable for their deaths or attribute their actual loss to personal or moral failure. Women, in fact, seemed to bear a disproportionate amount of blame for the demographic situation in postwar France, and they were often criticized sharply for seeming to enjoy themselves with makeup and other frivolities on the home front while men were being slaughtered in the trenches. Postwar literature often detailed the anxiety and alienation of the *poilu* who returned home to find his wife changed into a more independent, sexually liberated, and "masculine" being.[69] In 1919, for example, a group of *poilus* from Montigny-en-Gohelle brought a case to the court of appeals of Douai against their wives, whom they accused of absconding with household funds. The women apparently had taken their husbands' money, declaring that robbery did not exist between spouses, and the returning soldiers had no legal recourse. The men addressed their request to the Minister of Justice, pleading, "we hope very soon to see a law in the newspapers that would apply to all these thieves, because, really, when one has spent 4½ years at war, every *poilu* should at least be granted some peace of mind."[70] The war in fact could be seen as deepening misunderstanding and mistrust between men and women in France and setting back such initiatives for greater women's equality as the vote.[71]

While the nationalistic and conservative Bloc National that dominated the parliament after the war did continue to uphold men's rights over women's rights, as in a law of July 1920 that outlawed all forms of female (but not male) contraception, legislators also set about to make life in the absence of men easier for women and children. The desperate demographic situation of France certainly did solicit concern on the part of legislators, but they were determined to find a way to make up for the loss of so many *pères de famille* if real flesh-and-blood fathers were lacking. During the War, for example, the government passed a series of laws on marriage and the legitimation of children by proxy, which further dissociated paternal functions from the man himself. In 1915, the Chamber adopted a proposal to allow women certain civil rights when their husbands were away at war: to draw up contracts, to exercise *la puissance paternelle,* and to authorize the marriage of their children.[72] A year later, the Senate passed a new law that made it possible to legitimate children whose parents had been unable to marry because of the mobilization or death of the father. Children whose fathers had died in service since August 1914 could be legitimated by a court procedure, as long as correspondence or other documents manifested "a will on the part of both parents to marry and legitimate the child."[73]

In addition to procedures that made the physical presence of the father less relevant in determining the status of children, the French state set about providing for the thousands of orphans who would be left without paternal guidance after the war. The parliament instituted a new system of protection for children who had lost their fathers, known as Pupilles de la nation. From 1919, the Office national des pupilles de la nation dispensed pensions for the estimated 750,000 orphans who became wards of the state until the age of eighteen.[74] The legislature thought that the best way to honor the valiant sacrifice of French fathers on the battlefield was to replace them: now the state would "adopt" such children and offer them the material and moral protection of a proper father. A deputy proclaimed, in proposing a law to lower the age of majority for orphans:

Public solicitude will watch over [these children], of course. They will become, in this great fraternal country, "pupilles de la nation." But we should have a higher goal, which is to enable war orphans to form a new family, to enable them to have a new father or mother who will replace those absent and will maintain the memory of those lost in the heart of the child. . . .[75]

The *Revue philanthropique* addressed the problem of war orphans in 1920, describing the plight of legions of "mutilated families" in which the father had fallen during the war. In a study directed by several medical authorities, the *Revue* suggested that the war widow should become the central figure around whom French families be reconstituted. Even "psychologically or physically mutilated" veterans could be grouped into new families with a solicitous adoptive mother.[76] The rejuvenation of France, therefore, would necessitate rehabilitating its families, but men were not necessarily essential to the process. In its zeal to make up for the loss of so many men, the French state risked making them redundant.

The assumption that the state might be able to step in for lost fathers after World War I was in sharp contrast to public authorities' proclamations on mothers and the proper performance of their sacred duties. If there was doubt about the biological nature of fatherhood, hygienists and philanthropists focused on the physiology of motherhood, encouraging, for example, breastfeeding over other forms of childcare that created no link of physical dependency between mothers and infants.[77] In the interwar years, childcare experts campaigned to make maternity safer and successfully lowered infant mortality rates by encouraging practices that were more hygienic and healthy for babies.

In addition to the Roussel law of 1874, which regulated wet-nurses, legislators passed laws granting women maternity leave, in hopes of increasing the number of healthy babies born. The Engerand Act of 1909 ensured that women who took up to eight weeks off to give birth could reclaim their jobs, and the Strauss act of 1913 awarded maternity allowances for some women and required many more employers to grant maternity leave.[78] While feminist critics pointed out the weakness of maternal legislation and recognized the law's refusal to grant women real citizenship rights, many saw such laws as an essential first step toward the recognition of the social function of motherhood that could eventually justify greater rights for women.[79] In the same spirit of pro-natalist concern, the Millerand government established a national "Fête des mères" in 1920, celebrating motherhood and awarding medals to mothers of five children or more.[80] The state-sponsored commemoration of mother's day was a potent symbol of the rhetorical importance accorded maternity, made even more striking by the lack of any similar day honoring fathers. Fathers could not, in fact, be venerated in such glowing terms, for without medical directives for new hygienic practices or the formation of intimate bonds with infants, a father's relationship to his small children seemed rather tenuous. For propaganda purposes, fatherhood was less organic, less compelling, and less tractable than motherhood, and there was no Father's Day to parallel Mother's Day in the Third Republic.

A father's tie to his offspring was repeatedly contrasted to a mother's noble affection and sense of responsibility for her children. The lawyer Maria Vérone, in a debate on natalism that included Deputy Roulleaux-Dugage (a conservative Progressiste), described a young woman who came to her office, distressed by the fact that she could not press a paternity suit and that therefore her child had no name.[81] After asking the young woman if she herself had recognized the child, Vérone proceeded:

> So [your child] bears the name of a brave girl who has courageously accepted her maternity. So you can't investigate paternity, what does it matter? You would be giving your child the name of a man who has abandoned her; it is more just and moral for the child to bear your name, which is that of an honest woman and a decent mother of a family.[82]

The audience responded warmly to Vérone's anecdote, and she went on to discuss the problems of alcoholic fathers who misused their voting rights and abused their children. The exaltation of motherhood in the interwar years often came at the expense of fatherhood or simply ignored fathers altogether. While emphasizing motherhood as the *only* proper role for women hardly granted women the civil and political freedom many yearned for, the valorization of maternity afforded mothers a certain recognition that was not forthcoming for fathers.

Some social critics and reformers contended that fathers had long been the focus of family activism and that the focus of family assistance should now shift to mothers and involve them more. E. Lancelot, for example, wrote:

> We have for too long limited family activism to the humiliating gestures of the *père de famille* which elicit public pity. . . . The family movement has proceeded without mothers, who participate only exceptionally. . . . No place has been made for mothers in the family movement, and this is regrettable and disturbing. . . .[83]

Fathers were compared in unflattering terms to mothers, for a mother's absence within the family was exceptionally unfortunate, whereas a father's absence was unexceptional. In a report issuing from the League of Nations on children in "moral danger," rapporteur Mlle Chaptal emphasized that it was the mother who was the center of the family and who made a home sound for children. Her work outside the home, therefore, was terribly destructive for family life:

> The juvenile judge also adds the voice of his experience to those of all others who deplore the deficiency of family life [*la carence familiale*] and the absence of the mother from the home, for whatever reason. As the pivot of the house-

hold, her role there is essential; she makes up for the absence of the father and often fulfills a role as mediator and an element of conciliation between paternal severity and the indiscipline of children.[84]

In this report the mother was heralded as the mainstay of family life, while the father was portrayed as an absent and shadowy figure: he spent little time at home, but was a severe and arbitrary disciplinarian of his children when he was with them. Thus fathers were reproached for their deficiencies and absence even as family specialists, doctors, and mothers' rights activists were unsure of the specific benefits of their presence.[85]

Other commentators derided the pathetic actions of fathers who tried to solicit public support for their paternal rights, yet who had resigned their important obligations as fathers. At the annual Catholic encounter Semaines sociales de France held at Versailles in 1913, for example, M. J. Terrel stressed that a father's responsibilities were social as well as individual; if fathers did not accept these burdens, Terrel argued, society would be forced to compel them to do so or to replace them altogether. Speaking of the paternal duties of education, Terrel wrote: "yes, one must have the courage to say that in France fathers of families have for too long discharged themselves of their responsibilities . . . some onto the public authorities, others onto religious authorities."[86] After the war, the newspaper *La Famille française* published an article on "The Decadence of Paternal Authority" in its monthly edition.[87] Jean Guirand wrote:

> More than once, I have seen fathers crying in front of me while detailing the terrible sufferings inflicted on their paternal hearts by their own children. . . . They are partly responsible, for if their authority is disdained, it is because, all too often, they themselves have abdicated it.[88]

Even if some critics wished to reaffirm the rights and privileges of fatherhood, they often cast doubts on fathers themselves and accentuated their moral shortcomings rather than placing blame on others or on the transgressions of the state. How could fathers expect to be revered and supported if they were unworthy of such status?

Paternity came under fire from analysts of family life from across the political spectrum. In addition to the social-Catholic views of participants in the Semaines sociales, newspapers such as *L'Humanité* abounded with stories of abusive fathers, each more depraved and drunken than the last. In November 1936, for example, *L'Humanité* ran a story about an incestuous and alcoholic father who had abused his daughter Suzanne. Auguste-Emile Tisserand, having lost all sense of morality through drink, had taken advantage of his daughter until after years of mistreatment Suzanne finally found the strength to denounce her *père dénaturé* to the police.[89] The newspaper condemned another inveterate alcoholic father from Saint-Quentin in 1937 for similar abuses against his daughter. Emilien Bocquet had kept his adult daughter prisoner in a completely dark, enclosed room for more than ten years.[90] In the socialist newspaper *Le Populaire de Paris,* the same lurid accounts of paternal inadequacy appeared throughout the interwar years. In 1939, for example, *Le Populaire* reported on a father who had been sentenced to two years in prison for mistreatment of his three young children. His children, found filthy and covered with vermin, were now being entrusted (the paper reported) to the Assistance publique.[91] These are merely a few of the many reports of violent fathers that filled the pages of these newspapers in the 1930s.

In addition, fatherhood came under intense scrutiny from socially concerned women of various stripes. Bourgeois feminists gathered at conferences such as those sponsored by the Ligue française d'éducation morale to discuss the problems of domestic life and the role of fathers. D. Parodi's examination of a father's power, for example, was hardly confidence-inspiring:

> To tell the truth, the prestige of the father is greater because he remains the most distant . . . he is represented first and foremost as all-powerful and infallible. . . . But, children grow up. The child discovers the fallibility of his father, the very narrow limits of his powers, his knowledge, perhaps even of his virtue. . . .[92]

Another speaker at the same conference proclaimed that fathers were no longer pontiffs, magistrates, judges, or foremen; in the modern family, a man was now merely a father and a spouse. Furthermore, he no longer held the same extensive rights he had before, and important family functions had been taken over by state and society.[93] While fathers could be replaced, and their functions taken over by others, however, there was little suggestion that any other association or authority could step in for mothers. Alongside the aggrandizement of motherhood in the late Third Republic, therefore, attitudes toward fatherhood also were transforming; but these changes seemed to subtract from a father's uniqueness and power rather than add to it.

Negative judgments of fatherhood seemed to flourish in the climate of the interwar years as family reformers and social critics scrutinized the problems of the French family and set out to amend laws regulating domestic life. In the political and legal narrative of the period, entrenched supporters of paternal rights were repeatedly disappointed in their efforts to enhance or simply protect the authority of fathers, and they failed to achieve their cherished goal of instituting a system of family suffrage.[94] The rights of fathers were further eroded in the interwar years by new laws punishing men who abandoned their families and abolishing *correction paternelle* altogether. Yet if fathers continued to lose their prerogatives in the 1920s and 1930s, the family itself moved increasingly to the center of public debate and animated discussions amidst gatherings of concerned citizens and legislators in parliament.

New administrative and institutional agencies were set up within the highest levels of government to address problems of fertility decline and family order. Most notable among these was the Conseil supérieur de la natalité, established by the Bloc national government in 1920, a commission with consultative powers in which Fernand Boverat of the Alliance nationale contre la dépopulation played a key role. Boverat's prominence in the history of the family movement in the interwar years attests to the fact that the pronatalist lobby was a powerful and remarkably unified association of different groups whose propaganda and policy efforts met with considerable success.[95] Between 1920 and 1932, the "family movement" counted approximately 600,000 members in its ranks; its influence on social policy, however, and its success in bringing the problems of the *famille nombreuse* to the fore were even more substantial.[96]

In the Chamber of Deputies, legislators organized a Groupe de la protection des familles nombreuses that counted 348 out of 532 deputies as members in 1918. This was to be expected in the conservative bias of the postwar years, and most members of the group were right-wing Catholics. Although the proportion of sympathetic deputies dropped after the elections of 1924 and the victory of the Cartel des gauches, it was clear that the family cause was no longer merely the province of the conservative Right.[97] By 1928, the renamed Groupe de défense de la natalité et de la famille, under the direction of the Radical Socialist Adolphe Landry, boasted 359 members out of 612 deputies, or a three-fifths majority in the Chamber.[98] Out of these deputies who supported the family cause, the members of the Action démocratique et sociale and the Gauche unioniste et sociale were best represented, with 79 percent and 89 percent, respectively, of their members belonging to this group.

The most spectacular addition to this group came in 1936, when all seventy-two of the Communist deputies joined the pro-natalist group; in 1932 none of them had belonged at all. Fernand Boverat was amazed to note that the Communists offered the only substantial pro-natalist program in 1936. This was due to a change of policy in Moscow, where Stalin had abruptly outlawed abortion and declared that people were the most precious capital of all.[99] French Communists, hurrying to effect a dramatic about-face in light of new directives from Moscow, joined the Groupe de défense de la natalité et de la famille en masse. Socialists and Communists vacillated on population issues throughout the interwar years, and obviously there were many diverse reasons for supporting the family cause in the political sphere. Although these statistics varied, the numerical strength of the pro-natalist lobby was substantial from the Armistice of 1918 to the fall of France in 1940. What the Communist contingent demonstrates is that in French political culture, family concerns were far from the exclusive preserve of the far Right.

In addition to establishing and expanding state instruments for family policy within the administration, concerned French citizens banded together in leagues and associations aimed at addressing the problems of France's declining population and deteriorating families. Chambers of commerce convened to discuss matters such as the birth rate and the rejuvenation of the family, and in 1920 the textile manufacturer Eugène Mathon established the Comité central des allocations familiales. Also in 1920, Eugène Duthoit, a Catholic professor at the University of Lille, convened a major meeting of natalist and family associations that drew up a "Declaration of the Rights of the Family."[100] Many of these leagues and associations gathered together fathers of large families who wished simultaneously to protect paternal rights from the administrative encroachment of the state and to solicit support and resources from government coffers. How, then, did the rights of fathers fare in the political climate of the interwar years? Did the powerful pro-natalist lobby succeed in giving power and privilege to fathers as primary bulwarks in the defense of the French family?[101]

Despite the strength and cohesion of the natalist movement, few of the Catholic and socially conservative groups who wished to bolster the traditional French family through the *père de famille* succeeded in implementing their reforms. Although most pro-natalists were hesitant to challenge the authority of husbands and fathers by providing mothers with privileges that implied full citizenship rights, they were less concerned than their Catholic counterparts with the personal status of the *père de famille* when it was not directly instrumental in producing more babies. Pro-natalists such as Fernand Boverat were concerned with birth rates, not men's rights, and they believed that a worthy *chef de famille* would support such policies as paying benefits for large families directly to mothers rather than fathers.[102]

Once again, drawing strict political lines around supporters of fathers' rights is an impossible task. It is certain that most politicians who proclaimed the glories of the *paterfamilias* and argued for greater paternal power originated from the center and Right. Many critics from the Left, such as Deputy Marcel Cachin, found the idea of a father representing his son's interests at the electoral urn repugnant.[103] While most advocates of greater paternal authority emanated from Catholic and conservative milieus, however, the issues surrounding paternal power in the interwar years were so significant as to involve commentators from across the political spectrum in debating the merits and shortcomings of fathers. Maurice Thorez, leader of the Communist Party, for example, espoused traditional views of the French family with the father as leader and creator of many children.[104] Yet despite such endorsements, preoccupation with the family in the interwar years did not result in legislation favoring specifically paternal rights and rewards that many activists pressed for and that many pro-natalists of all stripes embraced in their rhetoric. In fact, the legislative record of the interwar years demonstrates that fathers continued to come under fire for the moral and material failings that exercised legislators of the *fin-de-siècle*. Throughout the 1920s and 1930s, their privileges were progressively dismantled by policymakers intent on promoting the best interests of children and families rather than the interests of fathers. Of course, to our modern sensibilities, there is no reason the interests of the father should have been upheld over the interests of children and families. What *is* significant is that in an era in which men were supposed to have all the advantages, there were *not* in fact groups arguing for the preservation of their personal rights. These debates demonstrate, in fact, the surprisingly double-edged nature of men's privileged legal status.

One of the ways in which legislators attempted to protect the interests of French families was through the criminalization of *abandon de famille*. A law passed on February 17, 1924, penalized individuals who abandoned their spouses and children without material resources, especially those who failed to pay the food allowance decreed in a divorce settlement. Although the law technically applied to both men and women guilty of abandonment, fathers were clearly the intended targets of the legislation, and the Union fraternelle des femmes drafted the actual bill presented to the Chamber. Louis Marin, a conservative member from Nancy and the sponsor of the bill, indicated that it was impossible to correct the myriad ways in which families could be abandoned morally or socially; the purpose of the bill was simply to pursue those who failed in the pecuniary obligations to their families that had been established by law.[105] Vice president of the Chamber of Deputies in 1924 and leader of the right-wing Union républicaine démocratique, Marin envisaged the law punishing men who willfully, or at least consciously, inflicted material injury on their children or their dependent parents, a circumstance that had become all too common in the postwar years.[106]

Yet if its focus was on material responsibility, the law on *abandon de famille* also held powerful moral connotations, similar to laws on *déchéance de la puissance paternelle*. For *abandon* implied not only pecuniary abnegation, but also an ethical failure to carry out duties flowing from one's authority and status. According to one legal dictionary, *abandon pécuniaire* was a crime outlawed by the Civil Code, but the primary definition of the term was of a moral nature. It defined *abandon* as "an act, by the father or mother, seriously compromising the health, security and morality of one or several children, by mistreatment, pernicious examples of habitual drunkenness or notorious misconduct, lack of care or of necessary direction."[107] Legislators were aware of the more vague definition of *abandon moral* and regretted the fact that the law gave them limited power in prosecuting offenders guilty of crimes against the family.[108]

Again, court records and correspondence with the Ministry of Justice demonstrate that despite the inclusion of women in the text of the law, most cases brought to justice were directed at fathers who failed to provide for their children or pregnant wives. Throughout the late 1920s and 1930s, many groups, including the Alliance nationale contre la dépopulation and the Union féminine civique et sociale (UFCS), took up the cause of *abandon de famille* and frequently interceded with government authorities in the prosecution of particular cases that had been brought to their attention. The UFCS, for example, wrote to Prime Minister Edouard Daladier in June 1939, demanding greater deterrents and penalties for men who abandoned their families. The UFCS reported that "numerous are the fathers who abandon their families at news of the arrival of a third child; most often this is not because of poverty, but because they prefer a woman of lax virtue to their own family."[109]

Similarly, Fernand Boverat of the Alliance nationale took up the case of Madame Verdy, a midwife from St. Cloud whose husband had abandoned her and their three children when he was mobilized for war. Boverat informed the Minister of Justice that this case was "typical" and decried the injustice of a legal system that granted scoundrels such as Monsieur Verdy immunity from prosecution by civil courts by virtue of military status. The Ministry of Justice saw as an outrage that soldiers who were granted family allowances or who were even exempt from military service because of their family obligations should continue to receive any benefits when they had in fact abandoned their families. The Ministry of War and National Defense was hesitant to transfer to civil courts authority over soldiers, and it tried to maintain jurisdiction over such cases, but in 1939 and 1940 there were more pressing matters for the military to deal with. With the avid support of the Alliance nationale and voices within the government itself, the court of Versailles finally sentenced Auguste Verdy to three months in prison. The court learned that he had earned more than ten thousand francs between June and August 1939, including more than 900 francs in family allowances, and had paid his wife only 700 francs. Population and family experts argued that mobilization often meant financial stability, sometimes even gain, for men, rather than personal disruption and danger, and were ardent in their support of the women and children forgotten at home.[110]

Champions of the idea that a man's salary had a familial character, which supported women and children at home, had met with success in 1932 when a new law was passed making family allowances universal and mandatory. Demands for a "family wage" had been part of French labor discussions from the nineteenth century on. Laura Frader notes that at the turn of the century many male workers in trades such as leatherworking and metalworking argued for the family wage citing their positions as fathers and upright family men.[111] Support for the family wage waned somewhat prior to the First

World War with the increasing acceptance of women in the labor movement, but it picked up again after World War I as concerns about depopulation and inflation grew.[112] In the 1920s, many large employers and industrial leaders had voluntarily established *caisses de compensation* that awarded workers a family bonus (*sursalaire familial*) for children instead of instituting across-the-board salary raises.[113] The family bonus was payable to either a mother or a father, which provoked the ire of both CGT (Confédération générale du travail) activists and Communist unions, who invoked the exclusive rights of the worker as a father and family man.[114]

The French government itself set up a *caisse* for state employees, and by 1932 the idea that the family allowance system should be rendered uniform and mandatory had achieved a considerable degree of consensus among pro-natalists, family activists, and political parties. The law of March 11, 1932, stipulated that all employers in business and industry were required to pay out family allowances for their workers' children—a set amount for the first two children, and a higher sum for children after that. In addition employers had to affiliate with a *caisse de compensation* approved by the Ministry of Labor.[115] In debates leading up to the passage of the law there was disagreement among familists on whether or not family allowances should be legally required by the state. Some feared that such legislation would destroy the liberal, voluntary system crafted by industrialists, simply opening the way for greater meddling from the state and making workers' salaries another contentious issue in the war between classes. Most groups, however, like the Alliance nationale, argued that both inequities in the current system and the primordial need to encourage population growth through support to large families mandated regulation of family allowances and intervention by the state.[116] In the end, supporters of state intervention far outnumbered those who balked at the idea, and the law on family allowances, one of the most important acts of social policy of the interwar years, came into effect in 1932.

The family allowance act was touted as a grand success for pro-natalists and family activists, and its material support of families, which continued to expand in the late 1930s, certainly did raise the standard of living of impoverished families with children. Yet in analyzing the preconceptions about fathers and attitudes toward family life emanating from the debates on family allowances, it is clear that such a measure was not an unalloyed triumph for the embattled *père de famille*. Family allowances *did* pay fathers an additional percentage of salary for their charges at home, but many social reformers believed that paying fathers extra money was misguided since they were all too likely to spend it on drink or other immoral pursuits. Even the government's own Social Insurance Commission argued that payments should be made directly to the mother, since she was the one who took care of the children, and certain large *caisses* continued to direct all their payments to the mother, even after 1932.[117] Because of the large number of women in the French workforce, payments were never, in fact, paid exclusively to fathers, and thus family allowances cannot be seen as primarily fortifying paternal power and status.[118]

More importantly, allowances aimed at assisting fathers with the burdens of family life exacerbated charges of paternal inadequacy and failure. Family activists were extremely sensitive to this issue; they argued constantly that allowances were not any kind of charity or handout, but rather were simply a reimbursement for the material burdens accepted by working fathers who were fulfilling civic duties. Yet the tenacious accusations of material inadequacy evident in discussions of family allowances were hard to shake. Even if such allowances represented a measure of social and redistributive justice, in dispensing such aid the state also risked turning fathers into the pitiful supplicants so abhorrent to many social reformers. Not long after the new law on *allocations familiales,* Fernand Boverat set out to prove that allowances for dependents were totally insufficient to maintain a large family at the same standard of living as a *célibataire.*[119] Although his report in 1934 to the Conseil supérieur de la natalité (CSN) met with favor, and the CSN issued a declaration castigating bachelors and their privileges, such comparisons only accentuated the inferiority of the *père de famille,* emphasizing yet again that his ability to provide for his children through his own work and value alone constantly came up short. Despite the fact that they were intended to enhance the position of fathers through augmenting their resources, these family allowances in fact severed the direct association between a man's work and his ability to provide, and shifted some of the financial burden of children onto employers, other workers, and the state. Although there was considerable consensus in France around the idea that children were a national resource whose expense should be distributed more evenly among families, family allowances did not ultimately serve to promote paternal interests, and in fact threatened to erode further the autonomy of fathers, even among those who claimed to be their greatest supporters.[120]

In the years leading up to World War II, the interests of the family, and most importantly those of children, consistently triumphed over considerations of the status and authority of fathers. The family allowance system did not signal a radical shift in attitudes toward paternity, nor did it protect fathers from the criticism of reformers, who continued to target weak and abusive fathers. In 1935, legislators finally outlawed *correction paternelle* altogether, substituting a system of "supervised re-education" for wayward youngsters. Although instances of paternal punishment declined dramatically in the interwar years, an average of 160 requests for the incarceration of children were still brought forward each year from 1922 to 1928.[121] The law of October 30, 1935, granted the judge greater leeway in determining the length and form of punishment for a child, confirming the fears of many nineteenth-century liberals who warned of the perils of an increasingly interventionist state.

The gradual assumption by the state of certain paternal prerogatives was mirrored in another new law protecting children of abusive parents who had been divested of *puissance paternelle.* In 1937, a proposal to modify the 1889 law on *déchéance* was accepted by the Chamber of Deputies; the proposal stipulated not only that parents who had "shown no interest" in their children placed with public authorities or a third party were to be stripped of paternal authority, but also that this power and the rights associated therewith could be reinvested in a guardian or institution.[122] Once again, although this legal reform technically applied to both mothers and fathers, it was clearly fathers whose bad behavior had drawn the ire of public authorities and legislators.

The Comité de vigilance et d'action pour la protection de l'enfance malheureuse, for example, deluged the administration with requests that unworthy fathers be punished to the fullest extent possible. In a brochure sent to legislators, the committee warned that children should not suffer for their fathers' misdeeds and advised the state to establish material and moral protection for all children of drunken or delinquent fathers, similar to the assistance extended to orphaned *pupilles de la nation* after World War I. The Committee further decried the fact that civil courts, particularly in the Seine department, were so slow to divest unworthy fathers of their *puissance paternelle* and pressed for greater rights for mothers, claiming that a true *chef de famille* was anyone who really took care of children. In the ninth point of their manifesto, titled "A Bad Father Cannot Be a Good Citizen," the committee claimed that a father who had abandoned his family, an act "prejudicial to the public good," must be punished with "exemplary rigor." Furthermore, the penalties determined by these courts should strip individuals of all their civil and political rights and should lead to instant dismissal for civil servants. In contrast to the censure heaped upon drunken and dangerous fathers, the committee advocated on behalf of mothers, asking that legislators consider a mother's rights over her children absolute, unless she has personally been divested of her authority by a court of law.[123] Alongside efforts ostensibly to render fathers more financially capable and socially secure through a system of family allowances, therefore, legislators and social reformers continued to dismantle the unquestioned authority of fathers in their own homes. In public debates, the specter of the besotted and debauched father haunted more positive representations of the beleaguered but worthy family man.

In the final years of the Third Republic, advocates who had for years pressed for greater governmental vigilance and defense of the French family finally saw their efforts achieve some success. Under the government of the Radical politician Edouard Daladier, who had no children himself, the protection of families and promotion of higher birth rates attained un-precedented levels of support within the administration. With the help of his Minister of Finance, Paul Reynaud, Daladier took the crafting of family policy out of the hands of parliamentarians and established a new complex of family laws through a series of presidential decrees. In February 1938, for example, Daladier rendered inheritance laws more flexible and discretionary, a goal cherished by family activists since the time of Le Play. In the decrees of November 12 and 13, Daladier expanded and modified family allowances, linking them more explicitly to salaries and to a standard mean salary for the department. In addition, the new laws provided for an *allocation de la mère au foyer,* set at 10 percent of the mean departmental wage.[124]

Not content with the still disparate and irregular provisions for the protection of families, Daladier pushed for the further reorganization of family policy and created the Haut comité de la population on February 23, 1939. The Haut comité, composed of representatives from the Ministries of Labor, Finance, Agriculture, and Public Health, as well as five additional experts, oversaw the development of a new assemblage of laws known as the *Code de la famille,* promulgated on July 29, 1939 and set to take effect on January 1, 1940. In June 1939, at the executive committee meeting of the Radical party, Daladier had declared his intention to guarantee the glory of France through the protection of its large families. "A deserted country cannot be a free country," he proclaimed.[125] The main innovations of the Code consisted of a single bonus of two times the mean departmental salary for a first child born to a couple within two years of their marriage. The allowance for the *mère au foyer,* which was granted until the last child was fourteen years old, was made mandatory in all major urban centers. Finally, the *Code de la famille* enforced stricter penalties for abortion and for public immorality and pornography, and made demography a required subject in schools.[126]

The *Code de la famille* took effect in fits and starts, and plans for its progressive implementation were greatly hindered by the events of 1940. The Code was not all that the Alliance nationale or other pro-natalist groups had hoped for, but in addition to its moral and economic reforms it provided a psychological boost for those who had long cried out for attention to the problems of the French family at the heart of the Republic. The stipulations of the Code continued to be hotly contested during the war and under Vichy, a subject dealt with in detail elsewhere in this volume. In July 1939, however, France once again had an expansive code of family laws that replaced the outdated Napoleonic Civil Code and systematized family life according to impulses the Revolutionaries of 1789 would have recognized as their own. The word *famille* was scarcely mentioned in legal texts of the early nineteenth century, but by the middle of the twentieth century it held a place of honor in the decrees of the last administration of the Third Republic, and it would be raised to a national motto under Vichy.

If the last years of the Third Republic were marked by the triumph of the family, could the same be said for the fortunes of fathers? Considering the evolution of laws on paternity and the progressive dismantling of paternal prerogatives throughout the late nineteenth and early twentieth centuries, the answer to that question must surely be "no." At the beginning of the nineteenth century, legislators were moved to ground paternal authority in specific statutes and laws that upheld the supremacy of fathers and ensured the stability of the nation. By 1939, however, laws on paternity served to limit and restrict the rights of fathers in the interests of the Republic rather than to maintain them. A subject of intense juridical debate in the Revolution and in the Napoleonic period, juridical fatherhood itself appears to have moved offstage in the *Code de la famille,* subsumed by discussions of the family and children. If the cherished ideals of partisans of the *père de famille* included expanded social, civil, and political rights for fathers, the increasingly interventionist politics of the Third Republic consistently repudiated such goals, and politicians acceded to or actively negotiated for the transfer of paternal prerogatives to the state and public authorities. In direct contrast to the principles informing the prizewinning essay at the Institut national de France, legislators in the late 1930s believed that a powerful *père de famille* might do more harm than good to future citizens of the Republic.

Aside from laws that directly targeted the rights of fathers, paternity was cloaked with an aura of doubt and attacked with insinuations of inadequacy and *carence.* As mentioned previously, the Civil Code was formulated for an ideal father of means, legislators banking on his virtues rather than hinting at his failings. By the mid-twentieth century, however, such presumptions appear to have been completely reversed. If the Institut national de France supported the view that perfect morality could only be found within families headed by a strong father, consider this quote from Jacques Lacan, writing in 1938 on the root of neuroses: "our experience leads us to locate the principal source [of neuroses] in the personality of the father, always deficient in one manner or another."[127] The laws of the early nineteenth century were a symbol of cooperation and collaboration between fathers and the state, an alliance of control that served to regulate and structure family life. In the France of the 1930s, however, the compact had been fundamentally transformed: fathers could no longer claim unquestioned authority over the nation's children, and they risked being made redundant by the new family policy designs of the state.

2

Icons of the *Père de Famille*

The Symbolic Power of Paternity in the Interwar Years

In 1913, on the eve of the war that would shatter the illusions of the Belle Epoque and cost France 1,400,000 lives, Fernand Boverat of the Alliance nationale contre la dépopulation turned his mind to the subject that he considered of critical importance to the nation: patriotism and paternity. Boverat asserted that the crisis facing his fellow citizens was in large part caused by the failure of men to live up to their obligations as fathers. He suggested that the commitment to fatherhood be considered as imperative as military service:

> The duty of paternity no longer exists! This duty has been, nevertheless, since the beginning of time, the fundamental condition for the life of all societies: those nations who disregarded it have all, without a single exception, disappeared rapidly; those who would disregard it today or tomorrow will inevitably suffer the same fate.[1]

More than a decade later, Georges Pernot, a conservative senator and a leader in the family rights movement, elaborated on this theme. Pernot emphasized that the nation was not simply an amalgamation of individuals, but rather "the homogeneous and organic body made up of all the paternities that it encompasses and which support it."[2] Throughout the early twentieth century, voices such as these were raised in defense, opprobrium, and exhortation of the duties and rights associated with paternity. Not only pro-natalists and promoters of family rights used the theme of paternity as a means of defining battle lines for social reform and appealing for political change in the Third Republic; commentators from other, seemingly unrelated fields did so as well.[3] In controversies over voting reform, labor policy, and citizenship rights, the father appeared as a crucial figure in the articulation of visions for France's future and as a critical concern for architects of the expanding welfare state. The motif of the *père de famille* was used to petition for and against a forty-hour work week, to extol the virtues of workers' gardens, and to argue for a reform of universal male suffrage. As they addressed the role of fathers and fatherhood, participants in both the public and the private sphere found themselves drawn into a discussion about nothing less than the nature of government, the shape of the modern family, and the future of the nation. How could the father's role be critical to the discourse of so many groups with different political aims? Why was the *père de famille* key to national regeneration in France and to the very order of the Republic?

To address these questions, one must turn to the theme of the *père de famille* as it came to the fore in public debates and shaped legislation and social policy in early twentieth-century France. By examining the various political and social issues in which the emblem of fatherhood was raised, one can discern what players in these conflicts hoped to gain through references to the proper role of the father. These political contests help to explain the father's perceived importance to the vitality of the nation, but who exactly was this protean father behind the popular perceptions? The proper family man could be easily distinguished from his antithesis, the "voluntarily sterile" bachelor, by the number of his progeny, but after conception his connection to these children, and to the family in general, was far from clear.

Drawing on images of fathers from family magazines, literature, conferences, expositions, and even architectural plans allows us to suggest some of the principles and criteria used to define the *père de famille* and illustrates the rhetorical power of his polar opposite, the *célibataire*. Prescriptions for a man's character and behavior as a *father* are less easy to find than those for a proper mother, due to the pervasive belief that while fatherhood was only one component, usually subsidiary, of a man's identity, a woman fulfilled her one true destiny in motherhood. Nevertheless, these sources indicate in both direct and indirect ways how fathers were supposed to educate their children, to behave in the privacy of their homes, to differ from and complement mothers, and to comport themselves in the public society of other men. In the interwar years, the emblem of the *père de famille* made manifest a struggle over the distribution of power and privilege in the reconstruction of the French nation, within the hexagon and across the seas.[4] Ideologically opposed groups of conservatives, Catholics, workers, and employers justified their demands for reform with paternal images and examples as they debated the allocation of resources within the expanding welfare state. Conservatives held up fathers, for example, as symbols of order and integrity in the political sphere, while unions argued that better domestic harmony would result from improving the working conditions of the family man. Leaders of the fascist leagues, such as Antoine Rédier of the Légion, extolled the virtues of patriarchs and of anti-Republican virility in general.[5] Men's family relations were far from irrelevant to the public concerns of work, government, and nation. Rather, paternal rights and responsibilities figured largely in debates from social-Catholic meetings to the halls of the Chamber of Deputies.

As described in chapter 1, the legal chronicle illustrates that despite the rhetoric of regeneration, paternity could be a highly problematic condition, occasionally requiring the state to intervene in order to correct some of the worst inadequacies of real flesh-and-blood fathers. Between the extremes of individual failure and national adulation, however, the father figure was useful in political and social conflicts: evoking paternity went to the heart of issues of citizenship and nationhood in early twentieth-century France. The father could be fashioned according to diverse models, much in the same way that women and mothers could be used to represent both the worst and the best of society. Unlike the preoccupation with mothers, though, the national obsession with paternity involved male political actors who were themselves potential objects of debate and whose positions of power could significantly change not only their own private lives but the requirements for citizenship in the nation. The French obsession with the *père de famille* made manifest a contest over opposing models of authority and a competition for the distribution of assets within the nascent welfare state.

What follows in this chapter is not a one-size-fits-all template for proper paternal behavior, but an assortment of the many diverse representations of fathers in the popular press and the social, religious, and political commentary of the late Third Republic. Representations may, of course, diverge considerably from real-life experience, yet my interest here is not so much in the actual day-to-day lives of fathers in the early twentieth century as in the way such fathers were portrayed, and became emblematic, in the major social conflicts of the day. What did actors in the competition for citizenship rights and welfare benefits have to say about fathers? What were the opposing models of paternity that animated such discussions? Rather than focusing on plotting variations over time, this chapter looks at cultural representations of fatherhood in the late Third Republic as a whole. What this approach demonstrates is that references to the proper role of the father appear in debates on topics as varied as working hours and workers' gardens, voting rights and leisure reading. In all of these concerns, activists portrayed the *père de famille* as a worthy figure who merited greater resources, rights, and responsibilities within the French nation.

Although the concern surrounding the *père de famille* cannot be explained away as merely another manifestation of natalist concern, fears for France's dwindling population did set the tone for debate and justified much critical self-examination within the nation.[6] Many associations and leagues were created throughout the late nineteenth and early twentieth centuries to address the issue of depopulation, the most notable perhaps being the Alliance nationale pour l'accroissement de la population française, founded in 1896 and later renamed the Alliance nationale contre la dépopulation.[7] In the late 1920s, the Alliance nationale alone boasted more than 40,000 members. During the decade following World War I, pro-natalist and family associations became a significant force in French politics, gathering together more than 500 different groups and representing more than 95,000 families. By 1930, more than 300,000 French families were represented in family associations throughout the country.[8] Many of these groups were made up of fathers of families, who in the tradition of Le Play argued that *chefs de famille* should be considered a separate estate with distinct social and political rights.

Natalist groups often saw the population problem as intimately connected to the welfare of mothers and babies, and they focused their efforts on improving public hygiene and health care for young women while teaching them *puériculture,* the science of infant care. Recent scholarship has contributed valuable research on the influential role women played in developing the "maternalist" policies of early twentieth-century welfare states, and also demonstrates that because motherhood was central to women's identities, women and their behavior drew a disproportionate share of the blame for France's population decline.[9]

Pronouncements on the fertility problem emanating from male social critics and policymakers offer important examples of attitudes toward women and their relationship to the nation, but such declarations did not preclude censure of men, who were also called to account for the sterility of France. Not only did natalists condemn men with the same charges of decadence and selfishness they leveled against women, but certain critics maintained that in fact men were *more* responsible for the depopulation of France, and that the demise of French families was attributable to men's egotistical shirking of familial burdens rather than with women's refusal to bear children. Men were particularly taken to task in the late 1930s as tensions with Germany continued to mount. In its leaflets and pamphlets, the Alliance nationale, for example, often depicted France's calamitous demographic situation through male figures, contrasting the robust, manly appearance of growing populations such as Germany's to the diminutive characterization of declining populations such as that of France (fig. 2.1). In February 1939, weeks before the Nazis invaded Czechoslovakia and shattered the Munich Agreement, it was surely not without significance that the German population was depicted in the hypermasculine bearing of a Nazi Party member, while the figure representing Great Britain appeared decidedly foppish, and, like France, less capable of projecting manly strength. Amid the growing realization that France might be unprepared for another war, natalist propaganda questioned the virility and potency of French men as they lagged behind their German and Japanese counterparts in siring children.

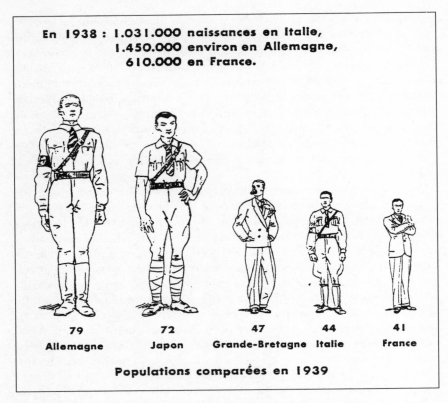

En 1938 : 1.031.000 naissances en Italie,
1.450.000 environ en Allemagne,
610.000 en France.

79	72	47	44	41
Allemagne	**Japon**	**Grande-Bretagne**	**Italie**	**France**

Populations comparées en 1939

Figure 2.1. "For Great Ills, Great Remedies Are Required." Alliance nationale contre la dépopulation, *Natalité* 23 (February 1939): 1.

In these representations from the Alliance nationale, one can only imagine that the productive father of *Les Mamelles de Tirésias*, with his 40,000-odd children, would have been a national hero.

In his monumental 1921 work on the disorder of sexual mores in France after the Great War, the outspoken professor Paul Bureau expressed his fervent belief that the deregulated sexuality of young men had caused France's difficult circumstances and that the selfishness of single men threatened to bring the courage of former heroes on the battlefields at Verdun and the Marne to naught.[10] *L'Indiscipline des moeurs* was, according to its author, an objective sociological study, based on the most rigorous social-scientific methods; its aim was neither to judge nor to condemn, but rather to analyze social phenomena and carefully describe their repercussions on French society.[11] Bureau asserted that France was the most "sexually developed" modern country in the world and that throughout the land, in ministerial cabinets and in peasants' fields, whenever men had the chance they would turn to the one subject that truly interested them: sex. When this titillating subject is broached, he reported, "faces become animated, eyes sparkle, and the intonation of the voice changes." Why, he proceeded to ask, do men of all ranks and walks of life, be they manual workers, businessmen, or intellectuals, demonstrate such fervent enthusiasm for and interest in the sexual act and all that precedes and recalls it? Bureau concluded that in modern society the sexual act had been completely disconnected from the consequences willed by nature, and that therefore young men mistakenly claimed *rights* to sexual pleasure, rather than accepting *responsibilities* of paternity.[12]

Furthermore, while young men and bachelors contributed most to the disorder of sexual mores, married men were liable for "conjugal frauds" and their nefarious consequences. In a discussion of how the practices and methods of voluntary sterility infiltrated the marriage bed from the wedding night on, Bureau explained the husband's error:

> Moralists dispute the question of whether the primary responsibility for conjugal frauds lies more with the husband, or rather whether it is wives who refuse to have children.
>
> I am most inclined to think that the fault is attributable to husbands. In the actual state of our morals, there are still a considerable number of wives disposed to follow the preferences of their husbands, as these preferences manifest themselves in selfishness or generosity. Even if a wife were to want only a limited family, it would be very rare that she maintain her resolution faced with the patient and persistent efforts of a husband capable of behaving like an honest man.[13]

Bureau considered "conjugal fraud" a trait of the calculating bourgeois, whose stubborn vigilance and fear of a noisy and disorderly household filled with many children held him back from loving his wife "honestly." Louis Blachère, a natalist and promoter of large families, saw the husband's calculations and reactions as key to the population problem and echoed this view. He believed that the natalist cause would be won only "on the day when a women informs her husband that she will become a mother and the sound of a champagne cork popping replaces that of a fist slammed on the table or a muttered curse."[14] Social commentators may have accused women of straying from their proper roles as mothers, but other conservative critics believed that men egotistically prevented women from fulfilling their duty in the interest of saving money and pursuing other passions. This was particularly true, some believed, of the bourgeoisie, whose *arriviste* ways led them to lavish all their money on one socially ascendant child.[15]

While criticizing bourgeois habits in general, Bureau was careful to point out that France's leading elite had failed to set proper standards of behavior and that they displayed in their own private lives no real concern for the nation's declining population. How could one be surprised at the indifference of the state to the interests of the French family, he mused, when "among the notable politicians of the Third Republic, almost none of them had a large family, and the immense majority had no children at all?" He reported that neither Thiers, Ferry, Gambetta, nor Waldeck-Rousseau, to name but four among many, had accepted the burdens of paternity. Furthermore, many of these men were not even married, or had contracted marriages that could scarcely be held up as examples for young people.[16] The immense majority of Frenchmen were indifferent to the family circumstances of their governors and seemed to find this irrelevant to their ability to lead. The premise that a wall of privacy should surround a person's intimate life was entirely wrongheaded, Bureau asserted, for while "we pretend to think that the views each of us hold with respect to reproductive discipline and practices has nothing to do with our actions and behavior in public," he saw such practices as central to the character of a governor.[17]

For Bureau, fatherhood not only endowed a man with children, but provided an education and apprenticeship in the exacting science of governance. Accepting the obligations of paternity certainly meant that a man was carrying out his patriotic duty to provide future French citizens, but it also meant that he was better qualified, and certainly more legitimately entitled, to play a role in the leadership and direction of the nation. The idea that fathers, and especially fathers of large families, were better leaders because they had willingly taken on familial burdens was central to the philosophy of many conservative politicians, family rights supporters, and beleaguered fathers who begrudged rights to all who did not share in the costs of child-rearing. The intelligence and experience gained through paternity was indispensable to the art of governance. The lawyer André Toulemon, for example, affirmed that no matter how conscientious, correct, and filled with good intentions and patriotism a parliamentarian might be, as long as he remained a bachelor he remained essentially incompetent. The delicate science of the family, he wrote,

> is not learned in books, nor in reports from commissions, but only by experience and through practice: a father of a family learns this science bit by bit, in proportion to his growing burdens, anxieties, and the constant and various demands that haunt and worry his laborious life.[18]

The superior attributes of a father were not limited to years of accumulated experience and concrete sacrifice; at times the father, or *chef de famille*, was described by social critics as possessing an indefinable aura of quality and good sense that eluded his bachelor counterparts. Evoking the *père de famille* suggested not merely a man who had conceived and raised children, but a superior being whose qualities and actions were essential in the fight against national decline. André Toulemon went so far as to describe fathers as an elite, comparing them to the nobility of times past, who were particularly qualified to lead:

> Democracy cannot endure the elites of yesteryear, for historical experience has shown that one may be very noble of blood and still not nourish a profound attachment to one's country. . . .
>
> But there is an elite in the nation . . . which more than any other group has concern for public interest and the future of the nation engraved deeply into their hearts and souls: this group is made up of fathers of families.[19]

The existence of this elite was perfectly compatible with a democratic system, Toulemon asserted, as it was an elite based on merit rather than on unfair advantage. The *chef de famille* was a figure that connoted sacrifice, courage, political expertise, and a bulwark against national degeneration and shortsightedness.[20] All these presumed qualities made him a perfect effigy for politicians and social critics who could argue in his place for causes whose advancement required either more model citizens like him, or greater power and privilege to those of his kind.

Nowhere was the superiority of the *chef de famille* more closely linked to a contest for political power than in the fight for a reform of voting rights, the *suffrage familial*. The principle behind family suffrage was that fathers of families should be given extra votes in elections, as they represented all the members of their household rather than just themselves. Debates on the family came up repeatedly in the Chamber of Deputies from the late nineteenth century into the interwar years and were a fundamental concept in the abortive Vichy constitution. At the birth of the Third Republic, the Baron de Jouvenel, a deputy from Corrèze, and the Comte de Douhet, deputy from the Puy-de-Dôme, put forward family suffrage proposals in the first legislature of 1871.[21] Adolphe Carnot, a member of the Institute and president of the executive commission of the Democratic Republican Party, argued in a similar vein in 1914 for an extension of the electoral rights of the *chef de famille*.[22] Henry Roulleaux-Dugage, a deputy from the Orne who registered himself as a conservative Progressiste, became the champion of family suffrage in the interwar years. Forty-six deputies specifically mentioned that they supported the family vote in their *barodet*, or statement of intent, for the 1924 parliamentary elections.[23] The family vote was also frequently a component of the political agendas of the fascist leagues, such as the Légion.[24]

The *vote familial* drew the attention of lawyers, parliamentarians, and social critics who believed the family vote would solve some of the problems inherent in the democratic system and set France on the right path once again. As late as May 1939, partisans of the family vote thought that reforming the electoral system would thwart Germany's aggression. The president of the Mediterranean Association of Large Families wrote to Edouard Daladier explaining that family suffrage "would not occasion financial burden for the state, and would constitute a solemn warning to foreign countries, as effective in maintaining peace as conscription in England." The measure had already received full support in the Chamber of Deputies, he wrote, and if passed "what would those across the Rhine and the Alps say when France gave families the right to express themselves? Would they really have the will to rise up?"[25] While proposals for family suffrage varied as to the number of extra votes granted or the rights of married women, the basic idea behind family suffrage was that *fathers* of families should be rewarded for their contributions to the nation with greater political rights, and furthermore that their voice should be more powerful than that of single men, who possessed neither the moral qualities nor the spirit of sacrifice that France needed.

Universal male suffrage was a travesty of democracy, advocates of the family vote claimed, as it gave bachelors, who represented only their own interests, the same power as fathers, who represented the interests of all those in their households. In a widely read book about family life from the 1930s, for example, champions of family suffrage wrote:

> From the beginning of time, well-advised statesmen, as well as philosophers, moralists, and historians have deemed that the voice of a father of a family should be a voice that is especially listened to; that one who is responsible for souls and property is more qualified than one who for all intents and purposes wants only to live and let live.[26]

The problem, according to proponents of the family vote, was that granting the vote to individuals allowed them to behave selfishly and to ignore the needs of French families. The unbridled individualism unleashed by the Revolution of 1789 had displaced the locus of authority within the Republic; now individuals, rather than families, controlled France, with obviously disastrous results. Supporters of the family vote referred back to Alphonse de Lamartine, who headed the provisional government after Louis-Philippe's abdication in 1848 and whose name was inextricably linked to the struggle for universal male suffrage. Lamartine would have been disheartened by politics in the 1930s, they believed, as he had anticipated a day when "the father of a family will have as many votes as he has women, old people, and children in his household, for in a well-constituted society, it is not the individual but the family that is the permanent unit."[27] The theme of the family as the fundamental unit of society was a constant of arguments in favor of family suffrage and was transformed and elevated to a national rallying cry under Vichy. Corollary to this theme, however, was the inference that the father alone was the natural and exclusive bearer of familial rights. Although a mother might inherit limited privileges upon the death of her husband, this was only a makeshift situation that attempted to compensate for the loss of a family's true leader.

Proposals for family suffrage appear reactionary and pointedly antidemocratic today, but contemporaries consistently shaped their arguments in terms of greater representation and maintained that endowing fathers with multiple votes was inspired by true republican doctrine and provided a solution to the injustice they suffered in a democracy gone awry. Not surprisingly, however, proposals for the family vote tended to emanate and gain support from the Right and the center rather than the Left. Fernand Boverat found Antoine Rédier of the Légion to be a supporter of his proposals for family suffrage, for example.[28] Enhancing a father's power vis-à-vis his children certainly coalesced better with conservative family traditions than with individual rights within the modern family. Nevertheless, *Familles de France*, a newspaper published by the Fédération nationale des associations de familles nombreuses, claimed that it was just and natural to give a father the right to represent his children in the political arena when he was responsible for representing them in every other way.[29] The Civil Code was based on the premise that children's rights were protected by entrusting them to their father or mother, so why wasn't it logical, they argued, to let the *père de famille* represent their interests at the electoral urn?[30] They argued that the fact that the number of deputies representing an area was based on the size of the population, rather than the number of voters, supported the claim that women and children too had rights to representation.

Partisans of the family vote regularly quoted population figures that manifested the injustice of representation in the most concrete way. Henri Roulleaux-Dugage, a moderate who had sponsored the last important proposal for family suffrage in 1923, continued to remind audiences of the figures: in 1925, out of 11 million voters, 7 million were bachelors or married men who had at most two children. These 7 million voters represented 16 million people, if one counted the few dependents in their households. On the other hand, he argued, the remaining 4 million men—fathers who had more than two children—represented 26 million inhabitants with far fewer votes. This meant that young bachelors, without experience or family burdens, triumphed over fathers of large families on election day (fig. 2.2). According to Roulleaux-Dugage, a minority of negligent citizens were deciding policy for unheard millions.[31] Roulleaux-Dugage's bill was only one of several family suffrage proposals considered in the Chamber of Deputies, and one of the most straightforward, as it granted a father one extra vote for every one of his children. Other measures, such as that of Georges Pernot, granted fathers one extra vote if they had more than three children, while that of Marcel Boucher granted fathers an extra vote for every group of three children a family had.[32]

In the many different proposals for family suffrage, the premise that the

La famille, qui fait vivre le pays,
doit peser plus lourd que le célibataire,
qui le laisse mourir

Figure 2.2. "The Injustice of 'Universal' Suffrage." *La Dénatalité mortelle* (Paris: Alliance nationale contre la dépopulation, 1939), 75.

distinct political rights of women and children could be represented effectively by husbands and fathers was presented as a given, even as the process by which this could happen was not spelled out. Justice for women and children was *not* a primary consideration in the promotion of family suffrage, but this fact did not prevent its advocates from expressing their indignation at the current "universal" system that completely ignored their rights. Emmanuel Harraca, an ardent supporter of family suffrage, wrote a history of the movement in which he quoted the Baron de Jouvenel, a sponsor of one of the first family suffrage proposals, in 1871:

> It is unacceptable to disregard the incontestable interest that women, minors and even outlaws have in the proper administration of public goods. . . . We must proclaim it loudly: everyone has the right to be represented in the political arena. . . . Logic and justice suggest that he (the head of the family) represent all the beings that he is responsible for, and that civil law places under his protection and responsibility.[33]

To Harraca, France faced the same imperative in the 1930s that it had in the 1870s: justice dictated that millions of unheard denizens of French households be offered representation through the head of their family. Whereas family suffrage supporters argued for the rights of their disenfranchised compatriots, critics such as Harraca were careful not to call them citizens, for the word "citizen" implied direct voting rights and civil autonomy that they would never grant to children and were certainly disinclined to grant to women.

Partisans of family suffrage advanced the rights of women and children (and even outlaws!) in their rhetoric, but parliamentary debates and political pamphlets reveal that in their view it was differences in prestige and obligation among *men* that were contentious. Fathers of large families, and those who supported them, believed that bachelors wielded an inordinate amount of political influence and that the nation would suffer at the hands of these social misfits, who were unconcerned with the plight of families in the present and with the survival of France in the future. It seemed to the family suffragists that the question of women's suffrage was almost irrelevant to the whole debate, even though feminists often framed their arguments for female suffrage in terms of benefits for the family unit as a whole. Whether one supported women's right to vote or not, parliamentarians were still faced with the pressing issue of balancing rights of citizenship among men. Certain provisions allowed a mother to take over her husband's voting rights after his death or incapacitation, but these rights were awarded not on the basis of citizenship for women but as a means of preserving the family as the primordial political entity. In his exposé of the problem in 1925, Deputy Roulleaux-Dugage explained that he obviously had nothing against granting women the right to vote, as he had proposed it himself, but such a measure was ineffectual in addressing the real problem of democracy in France.

If all you do is enfranchise women, you will have augmented the number of voters without eliminating the disadvantages of current legislation which lets the bachelor or the married man without children prevail over the voter who is a father of a family. You will have consolidated the current state of affairs; you will have augmented the majority of individuals and not that of representatives of the family.[34]

Of course not all members of parliament were as unconcerned about women's suffrage as Roulleaux-Dugage's dismissal would imply.[35] Association of family suffrage with proposals for the enfranchisement of women served, in fact, to fragment support for such propositions and helped to defeat the 1923 bill in the Senate. The fact that the Chamber of Deputies approved granting women at least partial voting rights in 1919, 1925, and 1932, and that each time the measure was rejected by the Senate, demonstrates the existence of an active women's rights movement following World War I that gained considerable parliamentary support.

Furthermore, the agitation generated around the issue of women's enfranchisement is instructive in discerning certain male fears and anxiety about women with political power. Newspaper articles and political cartoons, for example, often contained misogynous jokes about how women were likely to vote solely on the basis of a candidate's good looks, or how they would presumably stop cooking once they had marched to the electoral urn.[36] The housewife Thérèse and her comical behavior in *Les Mamelles de Tirésias* gives us one such representation. In France, the struggle for women's suffrage was long and difficult, involving complex political debates and shifting ideological currents that cannot be dealt with adequately here. The way in which Roulleaux-Dugage referred to women's suffrage, however, demonstrates that alongside the question of offering women full citizenship, the Assembly faced another distinct political problem in the interwar years: which men were the best citizens, and what rights were they due?

In 1936, the newspaper *Familles de France* published an article on family suffrage proposals submitted to the Chamber and Senate, outlining how each proposal sought to avenge the family man's impotence with respect to bachelors. Family suffrage, they hoped, would be the principle around which "all men, and men from every class" could rally.[37] The basic idea behind proposals for family suffrage, however, was that some men were better than others, and that fathers of families were both inherently more fit to govern than bachelors and had manifested their dedication by raising children for *la patrie*. Georges Pernolet expressed this assessment in one of the earliest discussions of family suffrage in the Chamber of Deputies, where he affirmed that only fathers with more than two living children should be allowed full electoral prerogatives. These fathers, he believed, were "complete citizens" because they guarded the nation from numerical extinction; they were also complete morally because no one could be trained in a better school of work, patience, and devotion. On the other hand, he said, "it is also irrefutable that a married man, even without children, is in all respects less incomplete than a bachelor, who might be a genius or a great man, but will never be more than a simple fraction of the true political unit: the family."[38] Pernolet made these comments in 1873, but the effort to calculate degrees of quality and privilege among men of different family status only took on more vigor in the interwar years. It was clear to all partisans of family suffrage that the bachelor had failed to perform his national duty; it was less apparent, however, precisely to whom the moral and governing qualities of fatherhood had been bestowed. Certainly *Familles de France* questioned whether a man, living out of wedlock with his mistress while having recognized his children, should be able to claim the same rights as an honest *père de famille*.[39]

The abundance of proposals for different modes of suffrage reform accentuated the contradictions inherent in the family rights movement and belied the notion of a simple rallying cry uniting men of all classes. Despite the confusion over which reform was more effective, the notion that family suffrage represented a measure of justice for the most deserving citizens was compelling enough to gain the endorsement of the Chamber of Deputies in 1923, and even to appear in the recommendations of the Population Committee established under the provisional government in June 1945.[40] Within the family suffrage movement, in the fervent polemics around natalism or even through the exaltation of the father's qualities, the *père de famille* was presented as a fundamentally important figure in the political and social discourse of the interwar years. Social reformers and philosophers who placed the *père de famille* at the center of their designs evoked not only a figure of authority who could sustain France through the exigencies of the postwar years, but also a figure who represented certain rudimentary struggles over democracy and the state that had plagued the Third Republic from its inception.

In the interwar years, this patriarchal view of society was most closely associated with conservative groups of the political Right who took issue with the way democracy was unfolding in early twentieth-century France. Catholics in particular often espoused the idea that children were an extension of the father's person, as laid out by Pope Leo XIII in the *Rerum Novarum* of 1891. Within the fascist leagues, such as the Croix de feu, rhetoric on the importance of patriarchy abounded, as leaders such as Colonel de la Rocque played the role of *paterfamilias* to their political followers.[41] Fatherhood was also a prominent theme for Antoine Rédier of the Légion, who frequently took up the problems of the *chef de famille* in the group's newspaper, *Le Rassemblement*. Rédier believed, for example, that only strong fathers and "real" men could take up the political challenges of the interwar years.[42] It is not surprising that such socially conservative groups would have supported a traditional patriarchal notion of society that took shape in advocacy for the family vote.

Also unexceptional is the fact that groups on the Left would have raised serious objections to the notion of family suffrage. Women gathered at the Socialist Congress of 1935 in Mulhouse were so opposed to the idea that they suggested that the legal emancipation of women be delayed if winning the vote was in any way tied to proposals for family suffrage.[43] While deputies such as Roulleaux-Dugage, a baron descended from an old family of parliamentarians, could wax eloquent about the justice of the family vote, Socialists considered that a crime against democracy had been averted when in 1939 Radicals thwarted the family vote.[44]

Yet the idea that a man with a family represented more than himself was not just a conservative conviction; it was a central principle in the development of progressive forms of social assistance, such as in the evolution of family allowances in France.[45] The Communist deputy Paul Vaillant-Couturier from the Seine argued that in a well-organized society women should be able to work or stay home according to their own inclinations: "The base salary of the man should be sufficient," he wrote.[46] Various Communist electoral posters in 1936 admonished people to vote Communist for the welfare of the family, and displayed prominent pictures of fathers holding their children. Conservative forces certainly fought to maintain the authority of fathers within an expanding bureaucratic state apparatus, such as in the fight for religious education, or in the struggle for family suffrage. Part of the critical discourse on paternity, however, was not simply based on a nostalgic wish to return to a pre-Revolutionary political past, but a blueprint for redistributive justice in a context of expanding state resources that engaged workers, employers, scientists, labor union members, social-Catholic reformers, feminists, and politicians from across the ideological spectrum.

Politicians, family-rights advocates, and social critics adopted the father figure as a useful symbol in setting forth ideas for change, but who exactly was the *père de famille* who animated their debates? While these groups all made allusions to paternity, they were unlikely to share the same conception of the proper role of a family man. The debates on family suffrage alone demonstrate the near impossibility champions of the father faced in achieving consensus about what constituted an ideal *père de famille*. Was he to be defined primarily by the number of his children, or were there other, less tangible qualities that would grant him status? A father's role was often portrayed as an important yet public and exterior role, in contrast to the mother's role of domestic child-rearing, and the duties of paternity were presumably addressed in discussions of work, government, or civil society. In this sense, fatherhood could be taken somewhat for granted, for a father's obligation to his family entailed providing material goods for his dependents while motherhood required prescriptions for care and interaction with family that were at once expanded and systematized in the interwar years.[47] Without similar comprehensive prescriptions for fatherhood, it is easy to overlook men as gendered beings who participated in private family life, especially in the context of a growing French glorification of motherhood and infant care. Furthermore, the comparative lack of pronouncements and directives on paternal behavior only seem to reify the timeworn gendered dichotomy between public and private worlds.

For contemporaries, however, men were not dissociated from family life in an artificial distinction between public and private worlds. In fact, men's familial qualifications functioned as a critical lens through which social reformers in early twentieth-century France understood fundamental problems of the Third Republic. Fatherhood, far from being taken for granted, lay on the fault-line of divisions that ran throughout the Third Republic and would break apart under the Vichy regime. For men, family life was inexorably linked to public roles and responsibilities, and contemporaries con-

structed definitions of fatherhood around the poles of good or bad, courageous or selfish, legitimate or illegitimate; all were extremes measured
against the standard of civic good. Because a man's family situation was important to his status in civil society, recommendations for and evaluations of
his role are revealed in imagery pertaining to the family and its activities.
Gathering evidence from literature, legal prescriptions, women's groups,
workers' organizations, and diverse associations with a variety of aims, it is
possible to discern a widely shared image of the "proper" family man and to
determine how he was distinguished from his counterpart, the "voluntarily
sterile" bachelor.

Henry Bordeaux was a popular and prolific writer in the interwar years,
and he often addressed the problems of the French family in his novels and
social criticism. Bordeaux was highly respected as a veteran of World War I,
a member of the Légion d'honneur, a recipient of the Croix de guerre, and
a member of the prestigious Académie française. In *Le Foyer,* published in
1937, he offers an eloquent and expressive description of a father, recalling
the memories of his friend Michel Rambert.

> No one could ever mistake the footsteps of my father. Rapid, even, and sono-
> rous, they could not be confused with anyone else's. As soon as we heard his
> resounding steps, everything changed, as if by enchantment. . . . Was there a
> question to resolve, a difficulty to bear, a danger to fear? When he was an-
> nounced, all this vanished: all worry dissipated, everyone sighed as if suddenly
> victorious. Aunt Dine in particular had a way of announcing, "He is here!"
> which would have chased away the most resolute enemy. It meant: Wait and
> see. . . . In one minute, justice will be served! Alerted to his presence, we felt
> an invisible might. It was a sensation of security, of protection, and of armed
> peace. It was also a perception of mastery.[48]

This description of a father's commanding presence signals the way authors
interested in the restoration of the French family depicted fathers as emblems of authority and justice. In literature and critical studies dealing with
paternity in the interwar years, the father's role as arbiter and commander
is a common theme, and many writers described the scope and nature of his
authority within the family.

For Catholic authors, the father's leadership could be likened to the supremacy of God the Father, and he was to be feared, respected, and obeyed,
often from afar. Pierre Méline, a Catholic theologian, believed that whereas
a mother had specific duties with respect to children, especially at a young
age, it was incumbent upon the father to govern the family, to punish its
members if need be, and to shape the mores of the family as a whole. The
father was the keystone of all authority in the household, the one who would

direct intellectual formation and orient the children's professional careers while "calming the useless effervescence of imagination." A father's authority, according to Méline, "is willed by God as a foundation of domestic society. . . . This authority is always mindful of its divine origins."[49] The comparison of paternity to divinity also came through in descriptions of a father's regulating and guiding role, which he exercised in a comprehensive yet distant manner, providing for a family's needs without becoming submerged in domestic matters. Another Catholic author, Madeleine Danielou, made this comparison explicit in quoting the New Testament, when Jesus asked his followers "who among you, if your son asked for bread, would offer a stone. . . . How much more will your Father in heaven provide for those who ask in his name?" God the father provided for his children on earth, and fathers of families were to provide sustenance for their individual families through work and sacrifice.[50]

Just as God surveyed from afar, fathers were removed from the business of everyday life at home. Their interests were in the exterior world, rather than in quotidian domestic cares, and their presence could be almost mystical, as in Henry Bordeaux's description of a father whose advent seemed almost as imposing as his physical presence. "The presence that a father owes his children," the family theorist Maurice Carité wrote, "is not measured by the number of hours he spends in their midst, and is not even necessarily linked to his physical presence. It is a disposition of the will, an openness of the soul."[51] The question of how much time a father should spend with his children or ensconced in the domestic circle was complicated by the fact that a man's occupation would naturally take him away from home. A man's family duties were essentially different from a woman's, and some observers asserted that interchanging these gendered roles would be ill advised. Mme Couvreur, who wrote the popular *Comment aimer pour être heureux,* thought it admirable that a man be interested in home life and that he perform certain services at home, but the partnership of the spouses should take into account the aptitudes and skills of the parents. Couvreur wrote:

> Helping his wife in the daily duties of housework, or in caring for children, is not in and of itself beneath the dignity of a man, because he is collaborating in the common enterprise of the home; this contribution, however, would be mostly of an exceptional character, and is not always desirable. . . .[52]

One of the characteristics of a father, in fact, seemed to entail a certain detachment from the everyday activities of home and family, a detachment that both afforded a man distinction and elevated his presence to the exceptional. Madeleine Danielou believed that a father's relative distance from his children originated in the fact that paternal feelings were initially less profound than maternal ones. A father looked to the future, to his lineage and what he could pass on to his children, rather than intimately experiencing the mysteries of birth and infancy. While a father's care was certainly different from that of a mother, it was no less important:

> A father is not as sensitive to the charm of very small children; he lives less closely with them and doesn't follow their adventures in the nursery or celebrate their little daily triumphs. But he carries an immense feeling of responsibility toward those he has put on this earth, for whom he must provide sustenance and an orientation in life. This responsibility does not weigh on him, but he carries it gladly, for having so many little children on his shoulders encourages him in his work.[53]

The sense of responsibility that fathers were to feel for their wives and offspring might not always have been a charge they would take up so gladly, but even without this ideal sentiment, familial burdens were an important societal institution that could combat men's natural selfishness and teach them the social virtues of community that were indispensable in civil society. Danielou wrote that one of the most important ways the domestic sphere served the nation was by firmly anchoring a man and "giving him duties and responsibilities which incite him to work and form him into a true citizen. What man would work without respite if it wasn't for his children?"[54] Whether writers believed paternal sentiments were less powerful than maternal ones, or thought that the hours spent at home were crucial, the spiritual and distant relationship fathers were thought to enjoy with their families was grounded in the reality of providing materially for everyone in their care.

Illustrations of paternal obligations to work emerged in many different areas; but whether in advertising, workers' demands, or family manuals, all linked a father's work to the sustenance of his family. Providing food for a child could be considered grounds for establishing paternity for an illegitimate son or daughter when a plaintiff sought to determine the father of an out-of-wedlock child. In 1912, authors of the law on *recherche de la paternité* posited that feeding a child was a de facto acknowledgment of paternity. Henry Lavollée, a jurist commenting on the legislation, wrote, "the most natural and the most imperative obligation of paternity is to furnish food for the child." The government obviously agreed, and the French legal system validated this rudimentary definition of a father, not only in determining biological fatherhood in paternity suits but also in defining the crime of family abandonment. In February 1924, a law was passed making *abandon de famille* a criminal offense; courts were entitled to pursue men who had been sentenced to provide a food allowance to their children and had not done so for the preceding three months.[55] The obligation to provide food for chil-

dren was ratified by article 203 of the Civil Code and was based on laws of
descendance rather than marriage, for the *obligation alimentaire* was considered an unavoidable duty even after a man was granted a divorce.[56]

Courts could decide that a father's work, and the product of his work,
were not his own personal property to dispose of as he wished, but had a familial character that required him to use them to maintain his children. In
order to perform this sacred duty, men clearly had to rely on their professions and the salaries they earned, and therefore workers' groups campaigning for better salaries used familial arguments to justify their demands.
Male workers in many parts of Europe and North America raised demands
for a family wage throughout the nineteenth century based on the notion
that the right to provide sustenance to a family was an exclusively male right.
Laura Frader points out that a "chorus of different voices" argued for the
family wage in France, and these discussions demonstrate that men's work
identities were profoundly marked by ideals of gender and family.[57]

Many workers, as well as government officials and even business interests,
saw family allowances as a fundamental measure of justice that redistributed
income more equitably between families who had to support many children
and families or bachelors who had none.[58] During the Semaine sociale of
1923, a yearly social-Catholic meeting that gathered religious, political, and
legal experts to discuss pressing social problems of the day, the Reverend
Père Desbuquois offered a seminar on the economic reforms needed for a
restoration of the family. A man's work had a familial character, he said, because children were born helpless and needy, requiring many years of care
from their parents. "The work of the man, the father, has a familial value because he must first of all be their provider, because their lives are his life, and
his bread is their bread."[59] Work could not be evaluated according to individualistic terms, he believed, and salaries, which were the workers' share of
the product, should not be set arbitrarily. Instead, salaries needed to take
into account the social and familial value of a given man's work, just as employers compensated greater skill with a larger paycheck.[60] Not surprisingly,
in 1932 the government passed a law making family allocations mandatory
for all employers, promoting the idea of a family wage and advancing the
notion that salaries were not simply a function of work performed, but had
to take into account a man's familial obligations.

A family man's salary not only determined how well he could provide for
his dependents, but also established his sense of self-worth and fulfillment
in life. For virtually all social critics who turned their pens to the troubles of
French families, a father's work was his most important defining characteristic as a human being and father. Madeleine Danielou believed that work
was indeed an obligation, but it was based on a fundamental human truth
in which it was man's very nature to work. "Real work is an activity in which
man realizes his whole self . . . it is the junction at which spirit is injected into

matter, the means through which man conquers and perfects the universe," she wrote.[61] A man's profession was his path to self-actualization, and it responded to his true inner compulsions for mastery and control of his environment. The novelist Paul Géraldy wrote a book titled *L'Homme et l'amour,* which takes the form of an intimate dialogue with a man as he passes through the thrills of youth to the more sensible pleasures of family life.[62] Although the dialogue revolves mostly around associations with women, Géraldy confirms the notion that work is man's most important assignment in life. "To work is to march toward yourself. Attain yourself!" Géraldy exhorts his imaginary interlocutor.[63]

A father's relationship with his children was expressed concretely in the hard work he undertook and the skills he mastered in his chosen profession. Work outside the home not only shaped the disposition of his time, but also set an example for his children and determined their status in society outside the home. Maurice Carité affirmed that a father's "professional activity exercises a significant influence on his behavior in the home," because a man was not simply a husband or father, but a complex blend of roles, with that of worker occupying a prominent position.[64] Carité believed that a father's prestige in the eyes of his children was in large part a reflection of his professional status:

> For [the children], without a doubt, he is the leader, not only because he is the father, but also because he represents power, experience, work and struggle in the world beyond the family sphere and in which he must, in order to assure the life of his family, affirm his mastery, his courage, and his spirit of initiative.[65]

Authors hoping to educate young people in the facts of family life warned of the problems a man's zeal for his profession could bring to a home, while conceding that this was a crucial element of paternal identity. Madeleine Danielou, for example, thought that men were often forced to give up a profession they loved and had chosen as youths in order to provide their dependents a better standard of living and to raise more children. "This is the masculine form of sacrifice, accepted once and for all," she wrote, "but very difficult, as Frenchmen love their vocations and exercise them with passion, especially if their work calls on their initiative and their leadership skills."[66]

Potential strains of conflict can be detected in Maurice Carité's insistence on the dynamic power of the world beyond the walls of home, however, for if a father was drawn inexorably out into society, what could keep him involved with family life? Such engaging work outside the home ran the risk of distracting a father from his family obligations. Paul Géraldy, in his urgent appeal for men to work, noted that this work could also take a man beyond love of his family. "Men work in order to conquer women," he wrote, but "their profession distracts them from love. They end up preferring the former. At forty years old, man knows nothing else but how to work."[67] Carité agreed that a man's career was increasingly captivating the more responsible and dignified his position, and this enthusiasm might encourage his withdrawal from the family scene and his neglect of those elements of domestic society that called for a father's strong hand.

If a man expended all his energy in science or politics, he would inevitably foster a "shared solitude" between him and his wife that was a trial and a menace to the household. No matter how many work-related, financial, or legal difficulties a father faced, Carité maintained that he had the responsibility to keep an even temper and not taint his home with gloomy preoccupations and a somber demeanor.[68] Furthermore, he had the obligation to dissipate the melancholy atmosphere of a close family circle where boredom and monotony could set in, particularly for the children. A father's role was to revitalize interest in family life, animating the home with news from beyond, interpreting current events and drawing on his treasury of experience and reflections to nourish the interior life of his children.[69] Madeleine Danielou warned young women that "a man is rarely tempted to limit his horizon to the walls of his home," and a wife would do well to remember that, refraining from burdening her husband with domestic trifles or trying to keep him at home. Other activities beckoned a man: his work held an important place in his life, and he made the concerns and problems of the nation his own.

The apprehension that men were loath to remain in the intimacy of the domestic circle at all times was apparent as well in recommendations to wives that they make their homes as attractive and modern as possible. The magazine *Action familiale* presented an article encouraging homemakers to visit the *Salon des arts ménagers* for a lesson in how this could be done.[70]

> Men are like children: they like new sensations and, if they are drawn to street spectacles, the cinema, and other attractions, it is because the everyday doesn't appear. Many leave their homes—the little apartment where one can hear the eruption of dirty water from the man on the third floor mixed in with the piano exercises of the young lady on the fourth who practices systematically, every night—because it's monotonous to live at home, between the predictable furniture from Levitan and the mass-produced radio. But what about those interiors one could see at the [Salon des] Arts Ménagers? Those living in such decors would never tire of seeing them, and I'm afraid they might be so beautiful that they would never go out![71]

What, precisely, would a father be missing if he *did* go out? Certainly he was to infuse the home with the benefits of his participation in the outside world, but if a father maintained a spiritual and distant relationship with his family, what were his specific duties at home?

One clearly established obligation was a father's responsibility for the education of his children. It is not by accident that associations that sprang up to fight for religious education, or *neutralité scolaire,* as they called it, went by the name of "Associations de pères de familles." In the early twentieth century, groups of concerned Catholic citizens formed in order to "maintain the cult of national traditions and patriotism in school, and to enforce respect for religious neutrality prescribed by law," according to the statutes of one association of fathers of families.[72] Fathers in these associations believed that the school was a continuation of the household, and that they had unequivocal rights to pass on their intellectual and spiritual patrimony to their children in school, a right clearly ordained by divine, natural, and French law. The authority to educate one's children according to one's own religious beliefs was a fundamental element of the authority flowing from paternity. Republican schoolteachers, who had no respect for God, country, or family, were egregiously infringing on these rights, members of these associations argued.[73] The solution to this violation was to group together and fight for paternal rights: the priest Terrel wondered whether the problems of current educational legislation didn't stem from the fact that the fathers of French families had insufficient consciousness of their responsibilities.[74] The mayor of the village of Saint-Gilles-sur-Vie noted the difficulties facing concerned fathers:

> Isolated, the father of a family can only exercise restrained action; his natural timidity in front of the *instituteur,* the representative of the State, and fear of troubles or harassment often prevent him from exercising his rights to control. It is to supplement the insufficiency of individual initiative that we ask you to gather into associations.[75]

Education was seen as a father's natural and imperative prerogative, one he was to protect and fight for in the face of intrusion from the state. Children were first educated within the home, and a father cultivated social virtues in them before the state attempted to make active citizens of them in its scholarly institutions.

Partisans of the secular schools obviously did not agree, and they fought the associations as thinly veiled reactionary Catholic gatherings aiming to undermine the Republic. Many opposing the associations called for their dissolution, citing a 1901 law that outlawed associations supporting a cause contrary to law or a goal that compromised national territorial integrity or the republican form of government. The newspaper *Rappel* of September 1908 reported that such associations tried to deceive the public into thinking that they were made up of well-intentioned citizens supervising children's education and facilitating the difficult task of the instructors; actually, however, they were motivated by a completely different goal. The article asserted, "It is essential to unmask this [goal] if only to demonstrate one more time how clericalism is expert in concealing rotten goods under a pretty label."[76] Although republicans, and the government itself, mobilized against these associations, they did not contradict the basic assumption that fathers had a right and a responsibility to educate their children. Rallying for paternal authority and the family was not problematic; it was the priests scheming in the background and their antisecular views who made associations of fathers a threat to the French republic. In principle, fathers were indeed responsible for overseeing their children's education and inculcating them with values before they entered the compulsory public education system. This fundamental belief inspired the Associations of Fathers of Families and was a common enough assumption that the courts did not in fact declare them illegal. The education of children, therefore, was an important component of a father's role within the family and constituted part of his identity in civil society as a bridge-maker between domestic and public worlds.

Other prescriptions for a father's domestic role also linked his behavior to rights and responsibilities in the world beyond the home. Just as a father was obliged to improve his family with knowledge of the world and to educate his children according to his own values, he was compelled to spend time at home reading, enriching himself with culture and information that would make him worthy of these tasks. Reading could make men into better and more active citizens, set a good example for children, and keep them off the streets and out of cabarets and cafés. Encouraging male workers to stay indoors reading was obviously politically and socially useful for paternalistic employers, but the need to create time for the *père de famille* to read was echoed in the demands of workers themselves. In the early twentieth century, reading was promoted as such an important part of home life for fathers that architectural plans provided separate spaces for the *chef de famille* to read, and illustrations in magazines and advertisements often paralleled this prescription by depicting men reading in the midst of different family activities (fig. 2.3). In publicity for such household conveniences, manufacturers suggested that a proper family life, with father at home reading, would emerge with the well-being engendered by their products.

Workers formulated their demands for shorter work hours in terms of having more time to read, and reading symbolized to their employers a constructive and safe pastime for filling up newly won leisure time. In the world of labor, a man also came forth not merely as a solitary worker, but rather as a man whose family rights and responsibilities were to be recognized by employers. This recognition surfaced in one of the pressing social issues facing France at the end of the First World War: the growing demand for the eight-hour day. The campaign for the reduction of work time was an international movement that drew France into an intense labor struggle and threatened to shut the country down with general strikes.[77] French propaganda for the eight-hour day had since the 1880s focused on familial themes in its argu-

LA SINGER 15K71 électrique
sur table N.40 se transformant au repos
en un joli meuble

185. Anonyme, vers 1925

Le dernier mot
du confort ; le
chauffage central
par chaudière à
gaz.

LA GAZETTE

Pour tous renseignements, s'adresser
au Service de Vulgarisation des Applications du Gaz, 8, rue Condorcet
qui fait examiner toutes les questions soumises et indique la solution la meilleure.

11. Une brochure du « Service de vulgarisation des applications du gaz »
met en scène Gastoul, personnage en forme de compteur à gaz.

Figure 2.3. Reading as a Paternal Pastime. *Le Plumeau, la cocotte et le petit robot* (Paris: Bibliothèque Forney, 1994), 24, 151.

ments for a reform of working hours that would better accommodate family time.[78]

According to the Union féminine civique et sociale, proper use of leisure time was one of the fundamental motors for social renovation and change, and fathers had a special obligation to take full advantage of enlightenment through books and magazines.[79] Any earnest father of a family would have the resources to subscribe to a proper magazine or newspaper that would help him to be a positive influence in his community and nation, as long as he didn't spend money at the cabaret. The Union warned wives that they should respect the need for their husbands to grow intellectually and culturally and should keep children and other annoyances at bay while father was reading. "Papa must be able to read a review article or a few pages of a book, without being interrupted, while the soup cooks and the children are away. . . ." The Union affirmed that any thrifty and sober father could build up a substantial personal library, which could be perused at spare moments by the eldest son or occasionally by his wife.[80] Reading, therefore, was not simply a convenient pastime, but a key ingredient in the formation of conscientious citizens. The way in which a man prepared to read and digested the information gathered was not unlike the way in which he participated in politics and chose to cast his vote for the best candidate.

If reading was important for the average male citizen, it was that much more so for a father of a family, who was responsible for and embodied the voice of all the members of his family. Maurice Guérin, a union organizer and supporter of the eight-hour day, was incensed by the suggestion that a good father who worked ten hours a day would have plenty of time for an ideal family and social life. In the five hours that one critic of the eight-hour day said would be left over for family duties, fathers would have consecrated "two [hours] for meals eaten together, and two more (at least!) supervising their children and overseeing their lessons, and helping the mother in certain household tasks." This would leave only one hour for these fathers to study the countless religious, moral, political, economic and social questions that their quality as citizens obliged them to examine. Perhaps, Guérin wrote, if they were exceptionally intelligent, they could learn how to read the newspaper thoroughly, but who would pretend that this was enough to shape a good citizen and enable him to fulfill his duties? Proper education required reading good books and having the time to reflect on them afterwards, as well as attending a host of other associations of a pedagogical nature. "I repeat," Guérin exclaimed,

> To do all this, a worker, a model father and a conscientious citizen, will have ONE HOUR A DAY! How do you expect him to do it all, to be worthy of his multiple tasks, to think and vote well, and to live as a complete man, with a fully human life? It is materially impossible.[81]

Reading proper books and political or social tracts of an educational nature was essential to the makeup of a model citizen and father, and Guérin believed that fathers should have more time to attend union meetings and to participate in workers' associations. Members of the General Confederation of Labor (CGT) argued that their members would use newly won leisure time in self-improvement and domestic pursuits, rather than in drinking and frequenting cabarets.[82] In a 1922 campaign to preserve the eight-hour day, the CGT also argued that men would not only lose wages with increased working hours, but would also be unable to educate themselves and their families.[83] Increased free time was the key to social reform; the eight-hour day allowed the male worker to "enjoy the pleasures of family life and to fulfill his paternal duties."[84]

Catholic advocates of the eight-hour day could support this family-centered ideology, and they also campaigned for shorter working hours for heads of households. The promotion of domestic harmony through shorter working hours and an "English Week" with Saturday and Sunday off had been a frequent component of conservative Catholic discourse since the 1890s.[85] The social-Catholic *Semaine sociale* of 1923 affirmed that the eight-hour law was essential, because it permitted fathers to be at home during certain hours when their presence was needed for the exercise of their paternal duties of authority and education.[86] Upon the victory of the Popular Front and the passage of new social legislation on work reduction in 1936, the *Revue de la famille* published a special section titled "intelligent pastimes" in which the editors pointed out that with the newly passed law establishing a forty-hour work week and paid vacations, workers had new opportunities to better themselves (see figs. 2.4 and 2.5).[87] Reading, according to Paul-Leclercq, the editor of the *Revue,* implies

> first choosing a book, composing a program of readings, and imposing on oneself a cultural effort. . . . To read is then to take the time to acquaint oneself with a work, to assimilate it, to savor it or to discuss it. To read means to have the courage to start a book and the perseverance to finish it.[88]

In order to accomplish this paternal and civic duty, a father obviously needed enough time; he also required the proper space in which to carry it out. In her study of a group of workers' houses on the Avenue Daumesnil in Paris, Monique Eleb describes the philanthropic, reformist discourse that surrounded their construction and the goals of the foundation that sponsored them. The Fondation groupe des maisons ouvrières attempted to mix together a great variety of tenants, bachelors as well as large families, workers as well as employers, in a social setting that would provide a happy compromise between a communal phalanstery and the intimate homes of the petit-bourgeoisie. In particular, the ground floor would encourage commu-

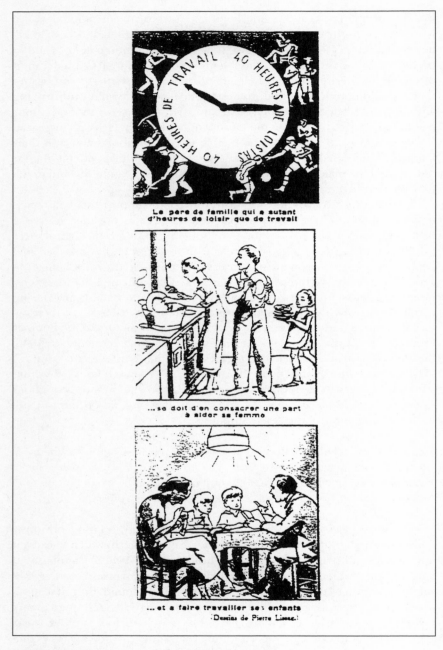

Figure 2.4. "Forty Hours." *Revue de la famille* 143 (15 March 1937): 3.

Figure 2.5. "Intelligent Pastimes." *Revue de la famille* 130 (15 August 1936): 3.

nal living and strengthen bonds of sociability and solidarity through common reading rooms and smoking rooms in which men could gather. The
promoters of the houses predicted that these reading rooms would be very
popular among fathers and young men, who would no longer spend their
evenings far away from home and would thereby afford mothers greater
moral tranquility. In addition to the communal reading room, however, the
Foundation emphasized that the units not be built according to workers'
usual demand for the most inappropriately small and cheap housing available; such modest apartments did not furnish enough space for a proper
family life. The editor of a construction magazine from Lyon wrote in 1913:

> One must not simply build cheap lodgings, but desirable *homes* [English used],
> gay and salubrious, large enough to accommodate the children separately
> and permitting, to a certain extent, the isolation of the head of the family who
> wishes to relax and who can aspire, through reading, to certain intellectual
> distractions without cramming himself into a communal room. . . .[89]

Whether or not fathers of any class always employed their leisure time profitably engaged in reading is doubtful; what is clear, however, is that reading
was projected as an important task for fathers, and architectural plans
needed ideally to take this into account. Home design was to provide the
space for fathers to read with a certain amount of privacy, just as social legislation needed to allow enough time for this uplifting paternal enterprise.

Reading was promoted as an important part of a father's role at home,
but according to moralists and family philosophers, intellectual pursuits
such as reading were to be complemented with physical pastimes that exercised the body as well as the mind. Manual hobbies, for instance, were not
only useful in building, fixing, or growing things; they also helped a father
appear as a competent and proficient leader. A child's esteem for his father
could not be dictated, but could be won over by demonstrations of his skill.[90]
Maurice Carité believed that a man could incarnate certain aspects of his paternal role through practical activities around the house, and use such hobbies to demonstrate his all-around competence. As a manual worker, for
example, he should express an interest in the intellectual pursuits of his children, and if his career was intellectual, he should be able to demonstrate
certain physical aptitudes. In this way, Carité wrote, the effective authority
of the father "will be largely facilitated if he appears as a complete being."[91]
There were always innumerable little household tasks to perform that could
occupy a father's time; furthermore, a father was likely to feel a greater attachment to a home he maintained and in which he tried his hand at *bricolage*.

The idea that men could be enticed, cajoled, or shamed into staying at
home rather than spending leisure hours out at the bistro is a persistent
theme in discussions of hobbies for the family man. The pastime that per-

haps best countered this enduring fear of restless men was the garden, the plot of land in which a man could watch his vegetables, and his aspirations, grow. A garden taught patience, discipline, and a wholesome knowledge of nature; it reminded the gardener of his country origins and provided healthy food for his family. It also, as Danielou so revealingly put it, "settled the vagabond soul of workers, formed their social consciousness, and destroyed anarchy."[92] Gardens were therefore particularly suited to the fathers of the working class, and employers, charitable groups, and government authorities often focused on promoting them as a means of raising workers from their presumed sloth and lack of foresight, and especially as a means of preventing social unrest. The Association pour la protection légale des travailleurs depicted fathers of families as especially clairvoyant and discerning citizens and suggested that a psychological study might well be undertaken to explain why fathers who worked their own garden plots had particularly keen political insights. The hope that workers' gardens offered a wholesome and time-consuming pastime that could keep men out of the cabaret and picket lines was not lost on the Association, but in the battle against social ills the father figure played a pivotal role.

> The workers' garden is an excellent element of social defense. The worker who asks us for a garden is already, de facto, a leader of a family [*chef de famille*].
>
> We want even more: that he become a conscious leader of a family, that he be proud of his family, and that in active struggle, he decide to defend the principles of the rights of the family.[93]

The Association's mingling of concerns for social defense with the seemingly banal act of gardening demonstrates the disparate ways in which fathers could be credited with merits and capabilities that were politically useful. At the *Semaine sociales de France* of 1919, held in Metz, César Chabrun spoke on the merits of gardening in highly paternalistic terms, asserting that legislators had left their work only half done by granting workers more free time while not protecting them from unhealthy sloth. Every worker's home should be surrounded by a garden, Chabrun believed, because tilling the soil brought the family together to work and was at the same time a pleasant activity.

Gardens not only kept workers off the streets; they were particularly suited to fathers who were burdened with family and could not run off to the playing fields or organize a weekend trip, as bachelors could. A father's garden could enhance his sense of worth because he was providing food for his family in his spare time, working for them without having to toil in an inhuman factory. On the occasion of the 1937 Exposition internationale des arts et techniques dans la vie moderne, held in Paris, a special guidebook was published to lead the visitor through the Pavilion of Solidarity, which housed an exhibit on workers' gardens. The guidebook suggested that gardens offered fathers a precious kind of liberty:

> The *père de famille* loves his garden because of the benefits he reaps from its cultivation, but even more so because nowhere else does he feel more free than in this little domain. In the garden, there is no other master, except the one imposed on every gardener because only He can make the sun shine and the rain fall. The worker's garden is really the "land of liberty."[94]

Gardens, therefore, were a healthy and highly recommended pastime for fathers and an important outlet for their time spent at home.

Philanthropists and employers certainly believed that gardens could preserve social peace, but the appeal for a return to the soil was not simply a function of early twentieth-century labor relations. The years after World War I were marked by a profound nostalgia for rural life, an idealization of the peasantry, and a sense that France had lost all direction, spurning its roots in a relentless pursuit of urbanization and industrialization. Peasants seemed to bear a disproportionate share of the losses from World War I, but it was "peasant tenacity" on the land as well as on the battlefield that many French credited with the victory at Verdun, and peasant tenacity that would lead France out of its postwar torpor. By the mid-1920s, more French citizens were city-dwellers than were rural inhabitants, but belief in the regenerative powers of the countryside denied the reality of the rural exodus.[95] The deep regret for rural life and for the virtues of the farm laborer shed light on important social and cultural trends in the interwar period; they were powerful themes not just in France but also in Nazi Germany and in fascist social ethics generally. Extolling the virtues of gardening was more than the province of paternalistic employers; it was an ideological blueprint for the future of society.

The movement to encourage workers' gardens gained momentum after the law on the eight-hour day of 1919, but in a decade when France desperately needed regeneration and renewed productivity, all French citizens could join in the cultivation of French soil rather than squander their time with urban entertainment. In the 1930s, Frenchmen longed for a return to the ancient virtues of practical country folk through a return to the land, and one minister of agriculture declared his wish that every Frenchmen could own a field, whatever his profession.[96] Fathers could enhance their authority at home by manual tasks that made them appear as complete beings, and they could achieve liberty, self-respect, and productivity working for the renewal of France on their garden plots. A father undertook an apprenticeship in the wise ways of the peasant when he worked the soil, and he fulfilled part of his paternal duty of providing food for his family.

Gardening was an emblematic activity of the ideal *père de famille,* and the organic metaphors many commentators used to extol its benefits were closely related to another important prescription for fathers as great creators of life. The ideal father was distinguished by his unrelenting courage; he was not afraid to bring abundant life into the world, confident of his ability to provide for his own. Giving life and taking care of it was the *père de famille*'s own form of heroic patriotism, just as selfishly restricting births was not a personal decision but a crime against the nation. In 1936, according to the April 15 issue of the *Revue de la famille,* France needed a special kind of moral courage, rather than diplomatic alliances, to maintain peace as menacing neighbors hovered around her borders. One month before, Hitler had taken a particularly bold step in the dismantling of the Versailles Treaty, sending 12,000 troops into the demilitarized Rhineland. On France's southern border, elections in February had polarized the Spanish nation and war between competing factions seemed inevitable. In light of these alarming events, the editor of the *Revue* declared that men needed to have the courage to father children, and the courage to raise their sons in a virile manner, inculcating them with love of discipline and country (see fig. 2.6).

A father was particularly accountable for moral courage in the face of trouble, as it was his role to lead his family boldly into the future, even if there were sacrifices to bear. Family life, however, according to one Catholic observer, was characterized more and more by the avoidance of effort and an abhorrence of duty. Malthusianism was the best example of this loathsome fear of life. In restricting life, a man demonstrated the same cowardice that extended to all other areas of his life: "restricting life, restraining production, fearing enterprise, avoiding risk, not earning but economizing, this is the malthusian mentality that is leading us to inertia and to death," wrote Eugène Duthoit. Such fainthearted behavior on the part of a father could only lead to parasitic, lazy descendants who believed they could simply save instead of achieving their own lives. Duthoit believed that this spirit would "propagate the bureaucrat and kill the colonizer," making French influence around the world a shameful remnant of what it had been.[97] French fathers needed to be more like brave colonizers, Charles Peguy's "great adventurers of the modern world," than like timid civil servants afraid of engendering families.

This impulse to give life was so essential to the definition of a model father that even men who were sworn to celibacy and would never "establish a family" could be revered as fathers, as long as they shared this common courage and esteem for life. The Catholic clergy, often the most vocal spokesmen and supporters of the French family, were particularly sensitive to the potential criticism their celibacy could incur, but they managed to get around this inconvenience by stressing the spiritual rather than the physical nature of fatherhood. Monsignor Lavallée accused of superficial think-

Figure 2.6. Preconditions for Peace. *Revue de la famille* 124 (15 April 1936): 3.

ing those who thought that each celibate priest had essentially diminished French vitality. Celibate priests, by not having children of their own to distract them, could guide and protect other families and act as their servants, as had Saint Vincent de Paul. "If one had to raise a statue to the saint of paternity, the honor would fall to Saint Vincent de Paul, because he alone gathered, saved, and offered more children to France than hundreds of fathers," Lavallée wrote.[98]

This seemingly paradoxical conviction that single and childless clergy could also be authentic fathers came up frequently in social-Catholic discussions of the family. The Abbé Viollet was one of the most active and influential advocates of the family, founding numerous family associations and neighborhood parents' leagues in the 1920s and 1930s. At the Congrès annuel de la Confédération générale de familles et des Associations familiales de France in December 1937, Abbé Viollet addressed this problem in his speech, indicating that he belonged to a "race" that would be mistrusted by such an assembly: the "race of *célibataires*." Yet parents, he explained, often needed the assistance of single people to help with the many arduous tasks associated with raising a family. Furthermore, some unmarried people had even more of a family spirit than married people did themselves. He exhorted the audience not to condemn the many *vieilles demoiselles* without their own children, as these old maids often took better care of a child than the child's own mother. Single people with family spirit were necessary to every modern society, the Abbé contended, because they gave up marriage to devote themselves completely to the families of others.[99]

These selfless single people were serving the family cause in France even though they were not increasing the number of its citizens; another group, however, the *vieux garçons,* who remained single purely for pleasure, were a different breed altogether. If the ideal father gave of himself freely and generously, the bachelor jealously guarded his time and his fortune. The animosity toward bachelors in France extends far back in time and cannot be seen exclusively as a function of the chaos of the interwar years. Nonetheless, with the conjunction of social conditions emanating from the Great War and anxiety about depopulation reaching a feverish pitch in the 1920s and 1930s, the *célibataire* came to embody all that was most corrupt and decadent in France.[100] Novels in the 1920s were rife with allusions to distress over the "emasculation" of France after the war. Many contemporaries believed France had lost its manliness and virility because it no longer produced as much as it consumed and because it had become an economically impotent nation.[101] Bachelors were attributed a hypersexuality that was indiscriminate and selfish, but their sexuality was not the "virile" kind, for it produced no legitimate children. The single man's life of debauchery, in fact, weakened young men by producing physical and psychiatric problems and gave rise to serious social problems such as prostitution, abortion, and pornography.[102] In the tense postwar environment, no figure seemed to evince the troubles of France more thoroughly than the effeminate, pacifist, pleasure-seeking, and sterile *célibataire,* often coded as homosexual. Even if all these labels did not apply, the bachelor became an important rhetorical symbol for a wide variety of causes, and most importantly, he was the negation of everything the ideal father should be.

In 1929, as the crash on Wall Street drove the United States and eventually the world economy into depression, Georges Ferré published his *Chroniques des temps d'après-guerre,* a text that might serve as a sort of manifesto of the *célibataire.* The preface warns the reader that Ferré is especially fond of the innovations of the postwar years: "mechanization, a taste for profit, cocktails, speed, violent exercise, mass-produced elegance, serialized pleasures, anti-sentimental love, and Americanism . . . all haunt the pages we will read," it cautions. Indeed, Ferré describes the pleasures of immoderate behavior, the thrill of fusing with one's automobile and becoming one, like a centaur, and most importantly, the excitement of a new morality that was nothing more than "enjoy yourself" (*jouir*). The new world, according to Ferré, required a new kind of man, one who was not imbued with solid traditions of bourgeois wisdom, carrying out a monotonous life of steady effort and Sunday promenades. Such an old-fashioned man would not amount to much, would never become the man of the hour with a right to public acclamation and fame. He would be mocked in such terms as these:

> "I present to you, ladies and gentlemen, Pierre Dupont-Durand, an honest young man of thirty-five, son of a blacksmith, who taught himself to read by the light of his father's forge, who clawed his way up to an enviable position and currently is raising ten children who will all be just like their father."

This would surely not make the grade, Ferré wrote, and he advised a young man who sought ready honor and public acclaim to go about it another way.[103] Easy pleasures, therefore, and an avoidance of slow, steady effort seemed essential to the life of postwar bachelors as Ferré described them; they were also characteristics that inspired biting criticism from family supporters.

The *célibataire* was not just admonished for his frivolous and selfish lifestyle; many social critics were outspoken in their indignation that he should have so much political power. The current suffrage system was a travesty because elections among so many unmarried male citizens ensured that candidates of their kind would be installed in all the corridors of power and governmental committees. The maxim "male celibacy rules in France" was a favorite among supporters of the family vote, as was the assumption by these supporters that all bachelors reasoned with the mindset of *après moi, le déluge,* unconcerned as they were for the future of France. Bachelors not only failed in their patriotic duties by refusing the burdens of raising a family; they were also social outcasts who were unfit to govern:

> Society, which is a collection of fathers of families, has slid into the hands of men who have few or no relatives, who at a young age detached themselves from their domestic circle, or never frequented it at all, or who were estranged from the primitive altar of home. . . . [Such men] were not governed by a family, and they have no family to govern; they never knew its purifying worries, its perpetual preoccupations, its precious restraints and its noble sorrows; [they] have lived without God and without children.

The upsurge of selfishness among bachelors, according to the lawyer André Toulemon, only accentuated the destructive individualism of the age and placed French democracy at risk. Ignoring the *célibataire*'s tenacious grip on politics could have ominous consequences. Toulemon reported that journalists covering the elections of 1933 in Germany saw single people as responsible for Hitler's popularity and the dangerous polarization of German politics: "It is the combination of male and female bachelors that provoked the fatal eradication of moderates and the triumph of extremists," he wrote.[104]

Georges Ferré's description of the freewheeling bachelor life was probably only within the reach of the relatively well off, but *célibataires* of all classes were mistrusted and viewed as social misfits, whether they were portrayed as homosexual or merely indiscriminately oversexed. Some industrialists hoped that single workers could be re-educated and reformed through constant contact with a normal, honorable French family. In a housing project for unmarried workers, employers imagined that a reputable family could lodge a relatively small group of young men, sharing daily meals and chores with them. The *célibataires*, it was hoped, would soak up a healthy atmosphere that would "penetrate them unawares . . . the example of the family they live in also has the salutary benefit of pushing a bachelor to start his own family."[105] Moralists discussing the scourge of *célibataires* believed that it was in fact the secret desire of many single people to marry and start a family, but their instincts were repressed under layers of self-seeking thoughts and egotistical behavior developed in modern times. For supporters of the traditional family, being unmarried was not simply a matter of personal choice, but a problem to be corrected and the manifestation of a warped attitude toward life itself.

The fierce hostility facing bachelors in France in the postwar period continued throughout the 1930s, and it comes through very clearly in the letters sent to President Edouard Daladier as he promulgated the *Code de la famille* of 1939. Many supporters of the Family Code believed that it was an important first step toward the redemption of the French family, but much still had to be done about "voluntarily sterile" individuals who imperiled the future of France. The treasurer of the association La Plus grande famille from the town of Nevers, for example, asserted that bachelors should be taxed at higher rates in order to make up for their irresponsible shirking of family charges.[106] He wrote to Daladier:

> It is indispensable for the salvation of the nation that the household obligations these individuals evade be *imposed* on them. It is profoundly unjust that they continue to lead a selfish life, plunging France into a deadly torpor. Carry out the reform and you will see that everyone will support you![107]

The issue of assessing single people with additional taxes came up frequently in anti-*célibataire* tirades, seemingly without any allusion to the tenuous justice of such a practice. Justice, in fact, was the main motive many saw in levying an extra charge to make bachelors pay their "fair share" of societal burdens, and a tax was included in the provisions of the Family Code of 1939.

In France in the 1930s, raising a family was a matter of state interest and a duty of national consequence. The most important way in which a *célibataire* differed from a *père de famille* was in his refusal of this sacred charge. Fathers, after all, were givers of life, and according to some contemporaries, vitality was the very essence of paternity, in that it sustained both physical life and the life of the mind. The lifestyle of a bachelor was egotistical and mean, while the ideal father's life was an exercise in sacrifice and self-effacement. A professor at the Catholic University of Lille expressed this definition most succinctly:

> Paternity is an education in magnanimity. A father repudiates all selfishness in love; if he asks for a child from his wife, it is because in his eyes the satisfaction of an instinct and a fleeting moment of passion cannot be an end in itself . . . egotistical passion says "take a woman": as for [the father], he does not want to take, he wants to give.[108]

A crucial characteristic of a father, therefore, was a demonstration of largesse with respect to life and the future that burdened him with grave responsibilities. A *célibataire* mocked such ideals, thereby scorning his national duty and imperiling the future of France itself.

At his most basic, a father had certain definite rights and responsibilities toward his family and society that helped citizens of the Third Republic define his status and shaped his own sense of the paternal rights he possessed. A father was to be the director and initiator of life; mirroring divine authority in his own home, he served as undisputed leader and counselor for his dependents. He was therefore accountable for the number of children he fathered, and he was responsible for providing his family with food and shelter. In order to accomplish this, a father's main duty was to work tirelessly for the good of his family, earning enough that his wife could fulfill her proper role in the home, devoting herself to the numerous children allowed for by his salary. The obligation to feed a child was central to the judicial understanding of paternity: failing to provide food meant that he had legally abandoned his family, whereas feeding an illegitimate child could be a *de facto* admission of paternity. Philanthropists encouraged working-class fathers to enhance their ability to provide food by promoting the benefits of gardening. The responsibility to initiate life extended to the duty to prolong and enrich it through education, another obligation central to the definition of a good father. Catholic associations of concerned fathers gathered to protect the right to direct the education of their children, which they perceived to be threatened by the secular republic. The *père de famille* was to enliven his household with knowledge from society, and he had therefore to spend a certain amount of time reading at home, sharpening his mind with newspapers and good books. Finally, a father was to expend himself generously for his family and for the nation, in all circumstances distinguishing himself clearly from the selfish, pleasure-seeking *célibataire*.

Alongside this exaltation of paternity and rhetoric about regeneration, Third Republican legislators and philanthropists were trying to deal with the problems generated by fathers who were anything but ideal. Nevertheless, these quintessential characteristics of a proper father were not only discernible, but also apparently consistent across class lines. Certainly legislators often attacked working-class fathers in particular with charges of alcoholism; yet as publications such as the *Revue de la famille* demonstrated, even a man of modest income could create a happy home environment by avoiding intemperate arguments with his wife and resisting the lure of the café (fig. 2.7).

Furthermore, it was the small-minded bourgeois habits of stinginess and prudence that drew criticism from supporters of the family, and certainly moralists who decried the immoderate sexuality of the times did not exclude men of means from their critique. As we have seen, certain family activists drew attention to the fact that even among the ruling elite of the nation there were too many "sterile" or "partially sterile" men taking charge of state affairs. Neither was the high estimation of the *père de famille* simply a function of reactionary Catholic rhetoric; even staunch secular republicans supported his rights and privileges. Radical Republicans, for example, whose political passions often sprang from visceral anticlericalism, advocated strengthening paternal power in the face of demands for greater rights for women.[109] Communist leader Maurice Thorez argued in favor of a supplemental salary for fathers of large families.[110] For many Frenchmen across class and religious lines, a proper *père de famille* was an embodiment of the most committed, caring, and capable citizen. Because the arduous task of

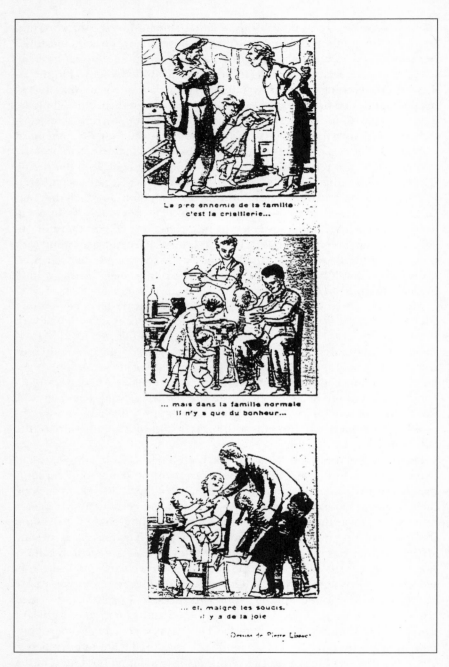

Figure 2.7. "What Joy!" *Revue de la famille* 172 (1 and 15 July 1938): 3.

raising a family had trained him in a superior way, a father was simply a better citizen, more fit to govern others and to legislate for the nation than any other less accomplished man. All of these attributes made the *père de famille* a key protagonist in the struggle against the alarming degeneration that seemed to afflict postwar France, and for many made him an essential figure in their hopes for the revival of the nation.

3

Building on the Family

The National Revolution in a World at War

In June 1940, the French army suffered a disastrous and humiliating defeat. In a few short weeks, more than 300,000 soldiers were dead or wounded, almost two million had been taken prisoner, and Hitler's forces had overrun two-thirds of France. The French nation had been crushed militarily and humbled politically as Marshal Philippe Pétain took over as head of state and requested an armistice with Germany on the 17th of June.[1] In France this cataclysmic defeat provoked despair, soul-searching guilt, and a fierce indictment of the Third Republic, but at the highest governmental levels Pétain set the tone by calling for a National Revolution, an ambitious program of social renewal, to remedy the errors of the past that had led to France's shocking humiliation and to set France once again on the path of greatness.

The Armistice agreement signed at Rethondes on June 25 brought about a revolution in France's external relations; the process of internal transformation wrought by the defeat continued over the next four years, however, and went far beyond the dictates of German demands. As Robert Paxton points out, nothing obliged France to undertake such a change, but "to an extent unique among the occupied nations of Western Europe, France went beyond mere administration during the occupation to carry out a domestic revolution in institutions and values."[2] France's collapse in the summer of 1940 ushered in a new order on both international and domestic fronts. Under Vichy, officials sought to negotiate with Germany to safeguard a place for France in the new Europe, but they also strove to bring about a new France from *within* through an ambitious program of reform at all levels of society.

Fundamental to this revolutionary program was a set of convictions and policy directives related to the French family, confirmed in the nation's new motto, *Travail, Famille, Patrie*. In Vichy ideology, the family was inextricably linked to the political and social fate of the French nation. To many conservative social critics, the war was a divine punishment for the decadence of the Third Republic and its mistreatment of "natural" societies such as the family. From his first days as the leader of the new French state, Pétain proclaimed the family as a primordial concern of the nation, and claimed for himself the role of national father, assuming the position of *paterfamilias* who would protect his family from misfortune.[3] He assured radio listeners in early July that their families would have the respect and protection of the nation, even as husbands, sons, and brothers languished in German camps.[4]

Far from being deterred from their goals, Vichy administrators set about the process of renewing French families in the absence of thousands of fathers and husbands held as prisoners of war. The heads-of-household detained across the Rhine became, in fact, a celebrated theme for propagandists at Vichy, not only justifying the regime's acquiescence to German demands, but serving as standards of moral virtue and pretexts for state assistance. Despite the extreme hardship and dislocation caused by the occupation, leaders of family associations heralded the Vichy era as a golden age for France's families, a time when the individualism of the past decades would be corrected by the sometimes unpalatable but necessary medicine of social reform. Defeat strengthened the resolve of zealous family activists, who interpreted the war as a moral parable that only underlined the seriousness of the work to be undertaken on behalf of French families.

The rhetoric of conservative critics who saw the defeat as an opportunity must be evaluated against the backdrop of a very real war that raged on with little regard for Vichy's propaganda. France's failure to hold out against the German onslaught cannot be simply explained away as the problem of a low birth rate, as Marshal Pétain himself summed up the situation. The events of the summer of 1940 arose more from the shortsightedness of generals and the universal dread of another long, drawn-out bloodbath than from the demographic figures publicized by alarmists throughout the Third Republic. French family policy must be set within a specific social and political context arising from the war, where the Germans were omnipresent even as Vichy administrators looked myopically inward to focus on the rebirth of a stronger and "truer" France. The first part of this chapter, therefore, outlines the historical context of the French defeat and explains how specific groups such as veterans and fathers of families were to act as an elite in the new Vichy regime.

Yet the war and the German occupation did not impose alien concepts of family policy on a reluctant French population. The "strange defeat" gave credence to the ideas of conservative critics who had for the preceding several decades made ardent appeals for a social revolution of the most fundamental nature.[5] The ideals of the National Revolution were ultimately homegrown, and the new government in Vichy did not have to look to National Socialist Germany or fascist Italy to invent a new discourse on the family.[6] Although focus on the family intensified under Vichy, the leaders of the National Revolution did not concoct politically useful metaphors out of nowhere or borrow them from abroad. Vichy officials drew on a rich French heritage of symbols and beliefs related to family life that had been at the center of public debate since the Revolution, as is described in the first two chapters of this volume. Whether positive or negative, this heritage provided fertile ground for the social imagination of the new leaders. The images associated with and the prescriptions for paternity in the interwar years provided a perfect starting point for debates on the reconstruction of society and were immediately implemented by Vichy leaders, who took up the cause of the French family.

Within the Vichy framework, "building on the family" implied returning to time-honored traditions of family life with clearly distinct gender roles and hierarchical relationships. Women were to return to their "natural" roles as mothers, and men were to reclaim authority over their wives and children, working selflessly and courageously to support as many children as possible for the renewal of the nation. Fathers in particular were held up as the key to reestablishing proper order and discipline in the nation, as representatives of Marshal Pétain, the country's true father and savior, in their own homes. Mothers were celebrated as the reproducers of French greatness, long-suffering guardians of the home who were the last to succumb to the evils of the Republic and the first to express their gratitude for the Marshal's new plans. Despite the very difficult and at times radically new reality of family life in Vichy France, it was precisely an "ideal" family of strong paternal authority, numerous children, and traditional gender roles that obsessed Vichy propagandists, and to which they returned at every level of public discourse.

Why was the concept of the family so important to Vichy administrators, who passionately debated the minute details of policy initiatives, even as the world was burning all around them? As legacy of a brilliant past and guarantor of a strong future, the French family was at the very center of Vichy ideology. The regime's propagandists attributed France's former glory to its strong families, the denigration of which during the past 150 years went a long way toward explaining the catastrophe of June 1940. Furthermore, Pétain's traditional model of the family seemed to promise an end to the divisive partisan warfare and class conflict of the Third Republic and an ideal for relations between the state and its citizens. In Vichy ideology, the family served as a universally appealing abstraction that propagandists hoped would heal the wounds of defeat, foster unity among France's divided population, and lead the nation into greatness and virility once again. In political terms, the metaphor of the traditional family also served as a potent metaphor of obedience and submission; it promoted relations of hierarchy between the state and its citizens that would supersede the individualism of the discredited Republic. The importance of *la famille* grew in proportion to the demands placed upon it: for Vichy administrators, no problem was without relevance to the family, and likewise no solutions could be reached without careful attention to the needs of France's first "natural society."

In the aftermath of June 1940, prophets of the French capitulation were easy to find, many holding up the "decadence" and ineffectiveness of the Third Republic as a major cause of defeat. Nothing seemed lost in 1939, however, and the accords signed by Edouard Daladier at Munich in 1938 did not appear to contemporaries to be the cowardly acts of appeasement later historians have understood them to be. Daladier, in fact, was greeted warmly upon his return to France at the end of September, for the Prime Minister's capitulation to Hitler's demands coincided with a significant pacifist movement within France and widespread opposition to another disastrous war.[7] Even for the skeptics who believed war was unavoidable, Munich had the advantage of postponing the inevitable conflict until France was better prepared militarily and had undertaken more serious rearmament.[8]

The hopes that another major war might be averted dimmed as it became clear that Hitler's expansionist desires would not be satisfied with the incorporation of the Sudetenland. In March 1939, Hitler defied the Munich accords and German troops marched into Czechoslovakia and occupied Prague. Hitler then demanded that the Poles return the port of Danzig to German control, and as the announcement of the Molotov-Ribbentrop Pact stunned the world, the prospects for peace seemed distant indeed. France had entered into an alliance of assistance with Poland and was therefore committed to war; the French people accepted this with an attitude somewhere between resolution and resignation.[9] When asked whether French forces were sufficiently prepared, military leaders responded that there was little choice—France would honor its commitments to Poland, and the two chambers voted to increase military credits in order to face the current international crisis.[10] France reluctantly declared war on Germany on September 3, 1939. Despite the widespread desire to avoid armed conflict over Poland, Daladier faced little opposition to the declaration of war, for it seemed clear that this was a fight to be undertaken with "head held high and a pure conscience."[11]

If the rather tenacious myth of widespread demoralization among the French population in 1939 is misleading, it is true that images of the slaughter of the Great War held many to a defensive, "wait and see" mindset. Militarily, the French had prepared for future protection against Germany through the construction of the Maginot Line, an immense system of fortifications that stretched from Switzerland to the Belgian border. The Maginot Line became a poignant symbol of the entrenched, defensive attitude of the French high command, as troops clung desperately to their positions beyond all strategic reason. In addition, the declaration of 1939 came just twenty years after many of the mobilized soldiers and generals had last fought to defend France's eastern borders, and memories of the bloody and senseless slaughter of those times tormented these *poilus* and their sons. For many, therefore, the eight months of inactivity and anticipation that became known as the phony war, or *drôle de guerre,* was both a reassuring respite from combat and a period of profound anxiety and disquiet.[12]

Disillusionment and a sense of foreboding undermined the troops' morale during the winter of 1939–1940, and as the months of waiting wore on, the irresolution of the French government also eroded confidence in Prime Minister Daladier. Caught between determined pacifists who continued to believe that a fight might not be necessary and supporters of more forceful action against Germany, Daladier's government fell in March 1940, and Paul Reynaud succeeded him. When the uneasy peace was shattered on May 10 by a German attack through Belgium and Holland, Reynaud responded by summoning seventy-three-year-old General Weygand from Syria to take over as Commander-in-Chief.[13] He also appointed the eighty-four-year-old Marshal Philippe Pétain as his personal military advisor and deputy prime minister. Pétain, the decorated World War I veteran, had long since retired from active military duty, but he had been serving since 1939 as the French ambassador to Franco's Spain. Even though he had led one of the bloodiest and costliest battles of the Great War at Verdun, his opposition to offensive tactics had earned him a reputation as a great preserver of French lives. Reynaud had a more bellicose resolve to stand up to the Germans than had Daladier, but he surrounded himself with defeatists like Pétain who were both disenchanted with the Republic and eager to salvage the honor of the French army through an armistice.

The French high command had failed to anticipate the German *blitzkrieg.* Resolutely fixed on the defensive tactics of the First World War, French leaders soon discovered that the key to victory lay in mobility and in the use of tanks and aircraft.[14] The defeat came with stunning speed as German forces smashed through Belgium and France and made their way to the English Channel. The government abandoned Paris for Tours and then Bordeaux, and as General Weygand ordered a general retreat on June 12, millions of people from Paris and other northern cities took to the roads on bikes, carts, cars, and foot in a mass exodus southward. The Germans entered Paris on June 14, and Prime Minister Reynaud resigned two days later, angered by General Weygand's demand for an immediate armistice in defiance of his own wish to fight on. Philippe Pétain, the hero of Verdun, took over as prime minister, and on June 17 he sent out a general appeal to French forces to cease combat. France had capitulated, the forces of defeatism having won out over those few parliamentarians inclined to fight on.[15]

The debacle of 1940 was, indeed, a strange defeat, and the disintegration of the political, social, and physical landscape made an indelible impression on the thousands of citizens who feared or fled from the German advance. Although some were quick to blame the army's failures, French forces in fact fought valiantly and well, inflicting significant losses on the Wehrmacht.[16] As for the military high command, generals such as Maxime Weygand fervently denounced everyone they considered responsible—the troops, the English, the politicians—without, of course, considering what was essentially a failure within the army leadership to respond appropriately to German tactics. The first weeks of June, however, were catastrophic not only because of casualties on the battlefield; incompetent leadership left hundreds of thousands of men stranded and out of communication, simply waiting to be swept up by the advancing German army. Of the estimated 1,850,000 prisoners captured during the war, almost 1,100,000 were imprisoned after June 16, when direct combat had officially been suspended.[17] Nearly 50,000 soldiers continued to fight on after the armistice went into effect, and many thousands persisted in their defense of the Maginot Line until early July, when they were forced to surrender by explicit orders from Weygand. Although Weygand and Pétain protested Reynaud's decision to fire top military leaders in early June, a significant portion of the responsibility for the debacle does lay at the feet of military commanders who made costly strategic errors.

Both Pétain and Weygand were intent on concluding the war as quickly as possible, and they argued into the night of June 16 for an armistice. This bitter disagreement led Reynaud to resign, and President Albert Lebrun named Pétain as the last prime minister of the Third Republic. Having concluded that further resistance would be futile, military leaders were intent on salvaging the army's honor. Weygand insisted that the government responsible for declaring war should also request its conclusion, and Pétain asserted that the French people needed to have the prestige of their army intact to lead the spiritual renewal of the nation after the shock of defeat.[18] According to Weygand and Pétain, to continue the fight against the Germans from North Africa or any other locale would have been to leave the French people, including the prisoners across the Rhine, at the mercy of the invaders. Pétain's envoys at Rethondes held out for only two concessions from the Germans in the armistice "negotiations": that an independent French state should continue to exist, and that the French fleet be spared from German expropriation.[19] The French army was reduced to a modest occupation force of 100,000 men; General Huntziger saw this as a precious concession, but in reality it spared Hitler the costs of occupying all of France and freed German troops for deployment elsewhere.[20]

Why was the prestige of the army such an important consideration for Weygand and Pétain? Nervous French officers feared that in the face of perceived parliamentary opposition to the military, the very existence of a professional army would be called into question if it became apparent that the French nation could continue to function without a multitude of military officials guarding the peace.[21] In addition to addressing the fundamental question of professional survival that many officers faced in 1940, the armistice force was also held up as an essential leavening agent for the vigorous and socially conservative society Marshal Pétain envisaged for the future. One notable concern military leaders expressed was that without an army France would be convulsed by the kind of social revolution that had terrorized the country in 1871. Weygand in particular was obsessed by fears of another Paris Commune, which pushed him to demand an armistice in the first place. With thousands of displaced persons on the roads, severe economic hardship, and rumors of a Communist Party uprising in Paris, Weygand firmly believed that conditions were propitious for such an upheaval. General Huntziger, the newly appointed head of the armistice army, thought that the army was essential for domestic order *within* France and that it would be called upon to intervene in the coming months.[22]

Above all, the army was crucial to the project of refashioning French society according to the outlines of the National Revolution. General Weygand, head of national defense in the first eleven weeks after the armistice, expressed this idea in a note in which he blamed the old order—that is to say, "a political regime of Masonic, capitalist and international compromises"—for the defeat. Within the army, he called for a veneration of that practical and worthy ideal that "can be summed up in these few words: God, Fatherland, Family, and Work," a direct anticipation of the National Revolution.[23] Soldiers were to play an important role in the work of moralizing and restoring the nation, providing an example of integrity and virility to their compatriots and setting themselves apart through perfect loyalty to the Marshal.[24]

Pétain envisaged that soldiers would also make up the solid backbone of the National Revolution through affiliation with the Légion française des combattants, formally established in August 1940.[25] A veterans' association such as the Légion would be the most fruitful means of linking Vichy leaders to the public, Pétain believed, more effective and less contentious than a single political party. Vichy administrators saw that some kind of consultative body was necessary to disseminate the ideals of the National Revolution among the public at large. Veterans, alongside fathers of large families and peasants, were part of that noble elite upon whom Pétain could count to lead the country in the difficult task of moral renewal.[26] The Légionnaires acted as intermediaries between individuals and the authorities in their efforts on behalf of prisoners of war cut off from their families in Germany. The veterans' tireless campaigns to raise money for food, clothing, books, and other essentials for prisoners and their families were among the most successful and widely appreciated actions of the Légion.[27] Both veterans and sol-

diers, reorganized into cadres of faithful apostles of the National Revolution, were to function as "intermediate communities" between the nation
and its families.[28] According to Vichy propagandists, such collectivities
grouped citizens together around the noble goals of social renewal and
counteracted the isolating individualism of the Third Republic.

No community better exemplified the association of individuals in meaningful and distinctly hierarchical groups than the family. If the French people were to consider themselves as indivisible parts of a larger national
family, there was no doubt who the country's father was. Marshal Pétain described the Légion française des combattants as "a family, the prolongation
of the great family of the front. Every Légionnaire should know that he has
in me a father and a friend."[29] During each of his radio addresses in the first
months of the Vichy regime, Pétain spoke from the perspective of a father.
In October 1940, for example, he advised his followers: "Let every mother,
every wife and every son [of a prisoner], know that my thoughts never leave
them, that they are also my children, that every day I struggle to ameliorate
their existence."[30] Vichy propaganda infantilized the French people, and
Pétain's tone of paternal authority underlined the fundamental dynamic of
power and dominance that would thereafter mark relations between the
Vichy regime and its "citizens."[31]

Paternity had become the perfect emblem and tool for state control; authority over the family was perhaps the only kind of power that had not been
swept away in the calamitous defeat.[32] Pétain's prestige as the hero of Verdun and his status as the symbol of courage during *La Grande Guerre* was bol-
stered by a familial association that defied the reality of his childless personal
circumstances.[33] The Marshal had lost no sons to the German Wehrmacht,
nor had he struggled to raise a large family; but he linked his legitimacy as
Head of State to legitimate fatherhood and deliberately cultivated all the devotion and obedience his paternity afforded him.

During the summer of 1940, Marshal Pétain *did* enjoy an unparalleled
level of veneration and respect. As a great war hero, he embodied the ideal
of a wise and prudent leader, in sympathy with his followers yet keenly aware
of the need for discipline and order within the ranks.[34] His sacrifice in offering France the "gift of his person" on June 17, 1940, was a Christ-like
atonement for the sins of his people.[35] Beyond reproach and immune to the
criticism of the Republic, Pétain held himself up as a shield protecting
France. He had led her out of the disaster of Verdun, and many believed he
could lead the French from the ruins of another war with Germany. In his
tours of the provinces, women knelt at his passage and begged him for the
"balm" that would render France great once again.[36]

Such idolatry seemed even to extend to France's parliamentarians, the
elected officials whose duties ostensibly included upholding the laws of a republican system that had been in place for nearly sixty years. Politicians of

the Third Republic were not generally marked by enthusiasm for a continued fight with Germany, even in revised form.[37] Bereft of many of their social and political points of reference and traumatized by defeat, they found
themselves eager to pursue the solutions proposed by minority leaders such
as Laval, and anxious to hand over the reins of government to the Marshal.
On July 10, in a spectacular act of collective suicide, the Chamber and Senate voted to grant Pétain exclusive and virtually unlimited executive and legislative powers. Only 80 Deputies and Senators voted against this proposal;
20 abstained, but 569 parliamentarians voted in favor of a governmental
decree that effectively signaled the death of parliament and the end of the
Republic.[38] Philippe Pétain thus came to power legally in July 1940, and as
the redeemer, legislator, and guide of the French people, he was willingly
charged with powers far beyond those of any previous president or prime
minister.

As a charismatic leader, Pétain's legitimacy as head of state rested on personal appeal and a self-conscious development of the cult of *"maréchalisme,"*
which demanded complete loyalty from its adherents.[39] Pétain's personal
"sacrifice" was well rewarded by the allegiance of French citizens and by the
last leaders of the Third Republic, who granted him supreme power. In one
poster issued by Vichy's propaganda division, citizens inclined to question
the legality of Pétain's authority were asked to reflect: "Are you more French
than he is?" (fig. 3.1). It seemed clear that a majority of French men and
women were relieved to see Philippe Pétain take over a confused, defeated,
and occupied France. Furthermore, they were willing to entrust him with
the task of resolving what Jean-Pierre Azéma describes as the profound and
humiliating crisis of identity in which the French nation found itself in
1940.[40]

Part of Pétain's appeal surely lay in the fact that he appeared to his followers to be an impartial and pragmatic leader, a hero above the fray of partisan warfare with no particular political ax to grind. Pétain himself
cultivated this impression, and using the language of sacrifice, suffering, and
irreproachable patriotism, he projected the image of a wise and judicious
counselor gently chastising his people. Yet to believe this illusion was to misunderstand the Marshal's goals completely. Pétain sought nothing less than
a social revolution, a regeneration of the fabric of French life along radically
different lines than had existed under the Republic.[41] A bitter anti-parlia-
mentarian and ardent critic of the "decadence" of modern society, Pétain
instrumentalized the defeat in order to bring about his own National Revolution. This misapprehension of Pétain's goals was twofold: first, he was not
simply "entering the way of collaboration" as a means of buying time against
the Germans; and second, his solution to France's disintegrating social foundation was not merely a "balm" but the imposition of a clearly defined cultural revolution.[42]

When Pétain took over full powers as head of state, he was convinced that

Figure 3.1. "Are You More French Than He?" Reprinted from Robert Frank, "Guerre des images, guerre des symboles," in *Images de la France de Vichy* (Paris: La Documentation française, 1988), 217.

he, and he alone, was the legitimate leader of the French nation, and that his top priority was to bring to fruition his ideas for the National Revolution. The Vichy government was certainly not a monolithic unit, espousing only one political ideology or advocating only one course of action. Much has been written about the heterogeneous makeup of the regime, and the often discordant agendas of Catholics, Maurrassians, traditionalists, and techno-crats who populated Pétain's administration.[43] Yet considering that Pétain himself underwrote or sanctioned every major act of policy from June 1940 until August 1944, Vichy must be first and foremost considered the Vichy of Philippe Pétain.[44] For Pétain, the concerns of domestic politics took prece-dence over negotiations with Germany and external relations with the rest of the world still at war. He hoped collaboration, a term he coined, would offer the Vichy regime the space and authority to bring about a domestic revolution and install the reactionary, authoritarian state that was so dear to his heart.[45]

Pétain and other conservative social reformers were struck in the summer of 1940 by what they saw as a tremendous opportunity for transforming the French nation. Devastated by defeat, the French people were more respon-sive to the criticism traditionalists had for the past 150 years been leveling against the republican system. The profound trauma had in turn given rise to hopes for a new utopia; in the fall of 1940 it seemed as if France could be reconstructed anew, and that this forsaken society could be redrawn on a clean slate.[46] Capitalizing on the defeat that discredited the parliamentary Republic and on the enormous prestige the Marshal enjoyed in the summer of 1940, the Vichy regime did in fact profit from an exceptional window of opportunity in which the ideas behind the National Revolution gained more impetus than they might have enjoyed at any other moment of French his-tory.[47] The Vichy regime's repeated emphasis on the degeneration of the population and the corruption of the Republic all gained credibility in face of the capitulation, and politicians who had mocked the "eternal truths" of family, work, and fatherland seemed fatefully compromised in light of the judgment of the war.

From June 1940 until the decisive turn of November 1942, the top priority of the Vichy regime was the elaboration of a revolution in domestic values and structures of power.[48] Pétain's early speeches were grouped together in a brochure published during the occupation, constituting the essential core of his domestic policies. Family activist Georges Bonvoisin maintained that every Frenchman should have a copy of the small tricolor brochure at his bedside table and should immerse himself in the truths Marshal Pétain re-called "with the most paternal tone of authority." Everyone would be in-spired, Bonvoisin believed, by the advice he offered "in the name of the most clairvoyant affection."[49] What were these ideas, imparted with such pater-nal divination, and how was the family to play a part in the National Revo-lution?

Fundamental to the ideology of the National Revolution was a reexami-nation of the role of the family in the past, present and future of the French nation. From his first days as the leader of the French State, Pétain pro-claimed the family as a primordial concern of the nation:

Let's start at the beginning, with the family. . . . The rights of families are, in effect, anterior and superior to those of the State, as well as to those of the individual. The family is the essential cell; it is the very foundation of social structure. It is on the family that one must build; if it weakens, all is lost; as long as it endures, all may be saved.[50]

Even if resounding defeat at the hands of Germans had humbled France, the nation could still be saved through its families, whose demise was held up as a major cause of the debacle. For Pétain and the Vichy administrators assigned to promote the cause of the family at every level of the government, addressing the concerns of the family was the first step toward national renewal.[51]

Beginning with the family was essential because Pétain and other family activists found important roots of the disaster in the ruin of France's families. If soldiers had not been up to the task of facing the German Wehrmacht, perhaps it was parents who should be held accountable for their failure to raise decent men. According to Vérine, the founder and president of the "School of Parents and Educators," parents had been tried in the court of public opinion and found wanting:

The verdict was severe, but just: French families must take a great part of the blame for the crisis of conscience that brought about our defeat; a great number of them failed in their mission, which consists not only of *creating* men, but also *shaping* men. *Quantity, Quality, everything was missing.* In consequence, the Family is bound to repair the ills it has committed by action, omission or ignorance, because *it is in families that France is made.*[52]

In his address to the nation on June 20, 1940, Pétain himself echoed the idea of familial responsibility when he declared that "too few children, too few weapons, and too few allies" caused the French defeat.[53] Although misguided military leaders and feckless allies might be held responsible for the latter two, individual men and women were to examine their role in France's demise through their own self-interested limitation of births.

The Vichy regime addressed the issue of limited births at the highest level of government and made family concerns central to the administration. During the first months of the occupation, several different offices and administrators tackled the problem of promoting the family, until in September 1941 the General Commissariat on the Family was created. Under the leadership of Philippe Renaudin, the Commissariat enjoyed direct access to Pétain and was authorized to monitor acts of legislation and policy emanating from other ministries that pertained in any way to family life. The Commissariat's main duties were the development of family policy within the regime and the dissemination of pro-family propaganda throughout the nation.

In its propaganda, the Commissariat on the Family evinced no doubt about what was the "most essential problem of the hour" facing French citizens. In a brochure distributed to would-be Scout leaders and their troops, the anonymous author from the Commissariat addressed the question of France's most pressing need:

> The response is simple. It has been dictated by reality itself. What France lacks, more than anything else, is children—and children capable of establishing, tomorrow, solid households that rely on healthy family traditions.[54]

In the eyes of Vichy propagandists, the reality of France's defeat was commensurate with the nation's demographic situation and the lack of children in French families. Yet the intense focus on the French family represented more than a simple desire for higher population figures and greater military strength, for their role in shaping the nation far surpassed concerns of army size. Babies would obviously not, in and of themselves, have made a difference on the battlefields of eastern France, but children were nonetheless symbolic of the shortsighted refusal of life that family activists saw as responsible for the nation's military defeat. They were also the most precious and essential resource for the reconstruction of the devastated fatherland (fig. 3.2). Children were an obvious link between the nation's past and the future, both of which the Vichy regime tried to master and mobilize for the defense and legitimation of the new government. The cataclysm of defeat offered social reformers an exceptional opportunity, a caesura in the usual flow of political and social events that made radical change seem possible. It also, however, created an atmosphere of timelessness and transition in which proponents of the regime struggled to give the new administration a foundation beyond the extraordinary events of the summer of 1940. Officials at Vichy needed to find ways to link the newly established government to meaningful and potent symbols of the French past as well as to a better future, in order to secure the authority and legitimacy of Pétain's powers. One obvious way in which this process occurred was in the myth of the Marshal himself, a hero whose life spanned all three of the preceding century's major conflicts with Germany and whose valiant efforts at Verdun were constantly brought to the fore in Vichy propaganda. The Vichy regime also found an invaluable means of linking the legitimacy of the government to a glorious French past, and a promise of future greatness, in discourse and propaganda on the family.

The family was instrumentalized first and foremost through education. French history was harnessed in service of the regime through a new law, enacted in March 1942, that made demographic education obligatory in all French primary, as well as secondary, schools.[55] Through a series of promotional brochures, the General Commissariat on the Family attempted to

Figure 3.2. "You who want to rebuild France . . . First give her children." Centre historique des Archives nationales, Atelier de photographie. 72AJ 1233.

enlighten school instructors on the ways in which demographic and familial topics could be introduced into regular school lessons at all levels. In
mathematics, for example, teachers were to offer their pupils calculations
that pertained to family life or to problems of comparative population size.
One brochure suggested that laws on social assistance, with their various sub-
sidies, could lead to the most "picturesque" math problems, such as what the
family of the forester Petit Poucet might have bought had he been eligible
for a large-family bonus.[56] In the arts, instructors were admonished to take
advantage of the fact that most children enjoyed drawing houses when given
free artistic rein. The children could be prompted to include familial scenes
such as children's games, family celebrations, and voyages in their illustrations, all of which would have a most salutary effect on their character.[57]

The most important subjects in which the lessons of demography and family life could be transmitted, however, were literature and history; the trans-
mittal would be through evocation of a glorious French past. *Instituteurs* were
encouraged to bring to light the grandeur of French civilization through
texts exemplary not only of the nation's remarkable literary heritage, but of
France's great familial traditions as well. When studying the literature of the
sixteenth century, a teacher might compare the writings of the Huguenot
Agrippa d'Aubigné, whose memoirs attest to a keen interest in continuing
his family line, with Montaigne, whose observations on marriage and family
life also attested to a profound attachment to community and continuity,
even while seeming to downplay familial sentiment. Vichy officials thought
both writers treated familial themes deftly, offering lessons from former centuries that could be profitably impressed on young minds in secondary
school.[58] The association of great literary figures with the cause of the family enabled the Vichy regime to ground its own ideology in an illustrious and
traditional past, free of the taint of present-day concerns.

Vichy propagandists were most explicit about linking the familial ideology of the National Revolution with a distinguished past in their recommendations for history lessons. A brochure titled *L'Université devant la famille*
encouraged educators to introduce two much-neglected concepts into their
history curricula—namely, *family* and *population size*. Beginning with the
Germanic invasions of the third century, instructors could demonstrate that
a growing population and strong family system led to expansion and conquest, whereas a failing population was always marked by "anemic troops"
and societal decadence. The Vichy text noted that "the familial institution
would be the principal element of moral and social progress in the West,"
the armature of the new world. The Roman Empire was said to have col-
lapsed in ruin thanks to the dissolution of familial institutions.[59]

Great figures such as Joan of Arc—"who never would have existed if her
parents had only wanted four children"—as well as Henry IV, Sully, and Col-
bert were all examined in light of the inexorable link between national

greatness and population size. In the seventeenth century, the booklet addressed to Scout leaders asserted, France was the most populous nation in Europe. This coincided with Louis XIV's promulgation in 1666 of an edict in favor of marriages that considered a family to be "numerous" only after the birth of the tenth child.

> At that moment, French culture imposed itself on all of Europe. The French language was spoken in all the courts, as the premier diplomatic language. . . . But then France had 20 million inhabitants, whereas Spain and England together had only 13 million. A century and a half later, Napoleon was at the helm of Europe because we were still, after Russia, the most populous nation.[60]

In the eyes of Vichy administrators, the direct causal relationship between French greatness and population size was an essential lesson to be impressed on young minds. Students were to be made aware of the fact that luminaries of the French past would not have been as powerful, or might never had been born at all, if individuals had acted as short-sightedly as their parents were behaving in present-day France.

Nor was this idealization and simplification of history limited to brochures of the propaganda agencies; newspapers emanating from family associations also used the past to justify pro-familial policy and establish its importance. The newspaper *Familles de France* carried a front-page article in 1943 titled "When One Could Marry at the Age of Three," describing famous aristocratic marriages in which children were married off at a very young age. Noting that this custom was at odds with the mores of twentieth-century society, Paul Vincent asserted that many of these marriages were nonetheless marked by great love and enduring fidelity. The article lauded both Jeanne of Bourbon and Isabelle, daughter of Charles VI, for their precocity and their important role in securing political alliances for France through their prepubescent marriages.[61]

Conspicuously absent from these acclamatory reflections on the French past was the Revolution of 1789, that decisive event to which many traditionalists in the Vichy regime pointed as the beginning of France's long descent into republican equivocation, individualism, and societal decay. The Revolution was associated with the destruction of strong families based on paternal authority, and it was used primarily as a negative example in the selective history of greatness brought to light by Vichy's educational materials. Thus the past Vichy officials mobilized was a carefully edited past, one that included notables with suitably "traditional" family values and natalist politics rather than figures who elicited reflection on the democratic traditions of France over the last century and a half. This selective commemoration helped the Vichy regime to fix its own ideology within the context of an established tradition and to ground its authority through association to the likes of Louis XIV.

Perhaps the Vichy regime's attempts to harness the past were best exemplified in a distinctly ahistorical children's fable produced by the Commissariat during the early years of the occupation. The fable, titled "Il était une fois un pays heureux," was written by Victor Dancette and was complemented by a series of original illustrations.[62] It told the story of France's demise at the hands of false prophets, "modernists" who preached a gospel of easy pleasures and loose morality. At the beginning of the tale, the people of the fortunate land were living rich, peaceful lives of earnest effort; the men were "healthy and vigorous: the purity of their souls was apparent in the azure of their eyes, their wives were beautiful and their children, adorable." Soon, however, strangers claiming to be at the forefront of progress led the people astray, teaching them laziness and avarice with their motto of "ever-increasing pleasure for ever-decreasing effort" (fig. 3.3).[63] Naturally, Dancette continues, "this people that no longer wished to be great and had ceased to be happy no longer wanted children. And this was the decisive step in its unhappiness." In its final descent into morbidity, the people began to ignore the family, and egotism, vice, and disorder became the law of the land (fig. 3.4).

All was not lost for the hapless denizens of this thinly disguised French nation, however, for in the midst of the torment a voice of truth rose up from the confusion.

> It was the voice of a patriarch, with a serene spirit, who spoke with simple language that even the most humble could understand:
> "Turn back," he said, "you have been deceived, you have been lied to. . . ."
> "If you wish to see the sunlight of liberty illuminating your granaries abundant with harvest, put an end to the barrenness of cradles!"
> "A legion of only sons never saved its country. . . ."

The patriarch had spoken, and the people understood; the cradles began to fill up once more, and birds, as well as mothers, began to sing again.

Dancette's fable illustrates the considerable effort Vichy propagandists went to in order to master and elucidate a past that seemed in many ways unmanageable. In a remarkable march through time, the story attributes the destruction of France's traditional, "happy" state to ill-defined foreign elements intent on destroying the procreative values of the nation. No reference was made to the Germans or to the disastrous reality of war, but credit for the salvation of the nation was offered up to the great patriarch, Marshal Pétain, who alone was capable of seeing through the deceit and setting France on the right course once again. In this allegory of the National Revolution, neither the World War nor the Revolution of 1789 even exist; the

Les hommes des villes se laissèrent tenter les premiers. Et sans doute, sans ce vent de folie qui devait dévaster cette terre enchantée, eussent-ils convenu très vite de leur déception. Car le plaisir ne peut remplir une vie et la recherche de sensations nouvelles laisse un vide que rien ne peut combler.

Figure 3.3. "In Search of New Pleasures." Victor Dancette, "Il était une fois un pays heureux." Images de P. Baudoin. Office de publicité générale, n.d. Fonds actualités, Guerre, 1939–45, BHVP.

only constants are the soil, hard work, and, of course, the providential and restorative powers of the family.

Mastering the past, however, was only one of the challenges facing Vichy social reformers. If the family was key to the nation's former glory, it had to be given a significant role in building a future in which families would constitute the very foundation of society. Such was the task family advocates set out to accomplish in projects for a new constitution that were drafted even in the first months of the occupation. As mentioned previously, the National

Dès l'instant où la Famille n'est plus le fondement de la Société, c'est la Société qui s'écroule. L'égoïsme devient roi. La vertu se cache et le vice s'étale. Le désarroi est partout. Les meilleurs s'interrogent devant le triomphe du mensonge et de l'immoralité. Les plus sages y voient les signes avant-coureurs de la ruine et de la décadence. Mais leur voix n'est plus entendue. C'en est fait. Il est trop tard. Ce peuple marche à l'abîme.

Figure 3.4. "March toward the Abyss." Victor Dancette, "Il était une fois un pays heureux." Images de P. Baudoin. Office de publicité générale, n.d. Fonds actualités, Guerre, 1939–45, BHVP.

Assembly granted Pétain full powers to draw up a new constitution for the nation, a license that far exceeded the immediate demands of the armistice arrangements and that effectively obliterated republicanism in France. In his radio address of July 11, 1940, shortly after the British attack on the French fleet at Mers-el-Kebir,[64] Pétain explained to the French people how he would use these expansive powers. Describing the moral framework for the new state, he affirmed:

> Your family will have the respect and protection of the nation. . . .
> French families are still the depositories of a long and venerable history. They have the responsibility to maintain, across the generations, the ancient virtues that make a people strong. Family disciplines will be maintained. . . .[65]

French families were invested with the honor of a glorious past, and the strength of this history was to be reflected in the esteem families were offered in the new French constitution.

Family activists insisted that the new constitution be crowned with a preamble that would outline the rights and responsibilities of families, providing all that followed with the proper orientation. Paul Leclerq, editor of the *Revue de la famille,* wrote to Vichy authorities who were reviewing the constitution and suggested that since the Marshal, in his "genial lucidity," had proclaimed that the country was to be rebuilt on the basis of the motto *Travail, Famille, Patrie,* the constitution needed an opening statement that would recognize the primacy of the family unit over civil society. He went on to offer the following proposals for such an introductory statement:

> The French nation itself is nothing more than the community of French families, whose continuity and work ensure its existence . . . in addition . . . the neglect of the rights and responsibilities of families led France into defeat and nearly brought about the very destruction of the French nation. . . .
> [N]o one is a good citizen unless he faithfully fulfills his familial responsibilities.[66]

Thus in the midst of an increasingly devastating worldwide conflict, French social reformers turned their minds to drawing up a new constitution that would safeguard the rights of families. The new constitution was not, in fact, to be concerned primarily with the rights of the individual citizen; rather, it was to consider the family as the original unit of social organization on which the state was built.

This was the premise of the important Gounot Law of December 1942, another step in the Vichy regime's attempt to codify the rights of families and define their importance in the future. Within each commune and region, a large family association was to be formed, its leaders elected by family suffrage and authorized to take part in a national federation of family associations with consultative powers and representational rights within the government. This was the first time the family was not only assisted and protected by the state, but also entered into the domain of semipublic law, with a right to representation within public institutions. One of the most original and enduring of Vichy's innovations in family policy, the law was upheld, in slightly modified form, after the Liberation.[67] The Gounot Law was considered a "preconstitutional law," one which Philippe Renaudin, General Commissioner on the Family, said would form the basis for the new French state. The family was, therefore, not yet explicitly a part of the constitution, but it would be given a special role in considering texts for such a document in the future.

In an article titled "Building on the Family" in *L'Actualité sociale,* Georges Bonvoisin averred that the importance of the law of December 29, 1942, could scarcely be overestimated.[68] He noted that it was without doubt the first time in history that the family had been legally inserted into the political framework of the nation.

> It is a sign of the times that such a reform could come to light in France, a country of strong family traditions, in the aftermath of a disaster without precedence, of which the primary cause can be attributed to the abandonment of the family spirit and of the virtues that it implies. May this return to one of the surest sources of social regeneration mark the beginning of the renewal of our nation.[69]

In a government memorandum, Commissioner Renaudin agreed that the law held immense possibilities for the role of families in the new French state. "It would truly be a national revolution if we could give [the law] the life it contains," he wrote.[70] Within Vichy's National Revolution, therefore, the family was gaining legal ground, and the ideological drive to endow this "natural" unit with constitutional powers was manifest in the concerns of both family activists and government administrators.

Such reformers believed that the family was a unit endowed with a "moral personality" and as such took precedence over individual persons; it was therefore the unit through which all state power was to be directed.[71] In preparatory texts for a constitution, one internal Vichy document pointed out that questions might be raised about the necessity of family associations at the communal and regional levels, as the state was, after all, simply a larger version of a family association: "Is not the State itself, by definition, the unique and compulsory association for all families?" The memo conceded that no matter how "familial" in character the state was, it would nonetheless be forced to deal with other concerns in the domain of economics, war, and foreign relations that were not strictly familial. Therefore it was necessary to maintain a system of separate familial associations so that "the voice of authentic family interests could be heard without cease" by public authorities.[72] The fact that administrators needed to call attention to the fact that state politics might not always turn directly on family affairs attests to the wholly symbiotic relationship many reformers imagined between families and the state.

Yet in the very midst of the occupation and the strategic political bargaining the situation required, family policies and French policies could be acclaimed as one in the eyes of zealous National Revolutionaries.[73] Family activists envisaged a new society in which relations between the state and the family would be reciprocal and reactive; the promotion of the latter contributed directly to the grandeur of the former. "Strong families make strong countries: when the family fails, the country wavers. France has just been cruelly reminded of this fact," proclaimed a booklet from the General Commissariat on the Family on relations between the commune and its families.[74] The booklet went on to explain that the prosperity of the nation and its communes was directly proportional to the well-being of families, and that fiscal policies motivated solely by the desire to economize were disastrous to the life of a community. Calling attention once again to history's lessons, the text cited Baron Louis, a Restoration minister, who proclaimed that good politics led to good finances. In the twentieth century, French mayors were exhorted to recognize that good *family* policy created prosperous communities and municipal wealth.[75]

In the ideology of the National Revolution, the interactions between families and the state were not simply a matter of numbers; families also embodied an important relationship of hierarchy that was to become the cornerstone of the new regime. This system of authority was underlined in a manual on fatherhood written by Vice Admiral de Penfentenyo, a high-ranking military official who had been captured by the Germans and imprisoned in Königstein. As a father of fourteen children, the Vice Admiral used his time in captivity to author the *Manuel du père de famille,* addressing it to his son François on the occasion of his marriage. Pétain himself wrote a preface to the book, expressing his wish that the booklet be distributed as widely as possible to all those "who had the noble and difficult mission to restore France."[76]

In the introduction to the manual, Penfentenyo claimed that while political or military leaders might be partially to blame for the disaster of 1940, a country had only the government or leaders it deserved. France had been overrun by a spirit of selfishness, cowardice, and disrespect for authority at all levels of society. As a consequence, the Vice Admiral maintained, a total lack of authority in the state and within families had led to a betrayal of obligations in the familial, professional, and electoral arenas. A chapter titled "The Reciprocal Duties of a Father of a Family and the State" explained that families and the state were part of the same organic whole, the two collectivities having a duty mutually to support one another in both the moral and the material domain. As for the father of a family, his role was to support the state by offering "an example of discipline, respecting the decisions of the responsible authorities, and ensuring the proper execution of these decisions in everything that concerns the family."[77] For a regime that sought a child-like obedience from its citizens, the evocation of the father was both an appropriate and an emotionally powerful symbol for the hierarchy that would subsequently mark relations between a strong, centralized French state and its "citizens" deprived of a real political voice. As Pétain took on the public mantle of national fatherhood, the metaphor of the traditional family based on paternal authority served to reproduce this power dynamic at more intimate levels of society. In the context of total French capitulation, this message was of course politically useful, and the projection of such a family model served to "naturalize" the submission of French society as a whole.

The use of familial metaphors also served another crucial purpose in the ideology of the National Revolution: that of unifying a fragmented and bitterly divided population. The family was held up as a national cause around which all members of society could rally, for who would object to the comforts and gratification of the family hearth in a world turned upside down? Philippe Renaudin, the Commissioner on the Family, expressed this attitude at a widely publicized public lecture at the Sorbonne:

> In the coming months, and in those we are living now, family policy has the chance to bring about the unanimity of the nation; it can be a point of crystallization of energy, a point of application for common efforts. . . .
>
> Uncertain of the future, hesitant about the present, the Frenchman is more apt to reflect on his past and receive the lessons of his forefathers. The family is reclaiming its meaning.
>
> The French people need a clear, constructive task that is easy to comprehend, and one that finds an echo in its profound aspirations and in its history. The restoration of the family responds to these needs. . . .[78]

Thus the family not only embodied the hierarchical structure of the new French state, it also provided a focus and a goal on which to reflect, contributing lessons of the past and generating energy and enthusiasm for the projects of Pétain's new regime. Pierre Taittinger, President of the Municipal Council of Paris during the occupation, gave a speech before town councilors and city leaders asserting that there was no issue that resonated more deeply in Frenchmen's souls than the issue of the family. "It is the consummate French problem," he said, "one that encompasses and conditions all others, because it portends, for us, equal chances of a rapid recovery, or *alas!* definitive decadence."[79] An emotionally resonant and seemingly apolitical concept, the family was to solidify support for the National Revolution in a manner that any less passionate symbol could not. As the "most general fact" and the "basic element" of life, Vichy officials claimed that unanimous sentiment and centuries of history had confirmed the family as the source of all vitality.[80]

Despite the ostensibly obvious importance of the term, however, Vichy officials made every effort to detail just *how* essential the family was to the regeneration of France and to explain its status alongside such words as *Travail* and *Patrie*. Elaborating on the motto of the National Revolution at the same meeting before city leaders at the Hôtel de Ville, Philippe Renaudin explained that Marshal Pétain had thrown out a life preserver to the nation in the form of three great principles—Work, Family, and Fatherland. Yet in certain milieus, he noted, "Family" was an unexpected term, one that elicited no unfavorable prejudice, but, if truth be told, seemed comparatively less potent.

> It seems to many that the family was discovered on the day after the disaster, and that the word doesn't have true roots in our history or a profound resonance in our people. Was it therefore an accident or a miracle that it emanated, in June 1940, from the lips of one who took the overwhelming responsibility to forge a new path of life for a dying country?[81]

Renaudin went on to affirm that attention to the family was far from being the result of any "spontaneous generation," and was far more than a "benign concession to some virtuous aspiration."[82] Long before the war, profound guilt had led the French nation to reflect anxiously on these issues.

Despite the Commissioner's protestations, however, it was evident that the term "family" was not so transparent as to elicit the unanimous approval and acclamation for which social reformers might have hoped. Renaudin reiterated that the nation's leaders would hardly have made the family a quintessential element of national policy had it been reducible to petty or archaic concerns; one was compelled, however, to "break open the word in order to discover its secret." Reconstructing the state on the basis of the family meant to find in this entity

> a stable force, a belief in expansion, an equilibrium, an educational resource, a social virtue, an aptitude to understand and satisfy national needs, a moral shield and a spiritual impulse that make up an essential and unique element of renovation.[83]

The family represented all that was good and vital in the French nation, the unit through which the difficult task of reconstruction would take place. Lest skeptics question the appropriateness of this theme in the midst of a military occupation, Vichy's family administrators were equipped to sing its praises and unfold its many "secrets."

To further enhance its role as a national unifier, Vichy officials proclaimed the need for a "mystique" surrounding the family that would bind citizens together in a quasi-spiritual quest. Family associations set out to restore a family spirit in the land, while government officials outlined plans to encourage the healthy and robust elements who were already doing their part by raising large families. According to Juliette Droz, a writer who took up the cause of the family, "the family spirit is capable of all transformations . . . and brings about, every day and without fanfare, all sorts of miracles."[84] The General Commissariat on the Family also pressed for a revival of a "familial mystique" that could spur national renewal. Raymond Postal, the director of a major publishing firm, declared that the "soul of the National Revolution will be a mystique," a powerful collective sentiment that lifted people out of themselves and complemented the coherent and thoughtful doctrine that stood behind it.[85] A country was no greater than the men who made it up; their bodies assured its physical permanence and its defense, but it was the souls of men who could make of *La Patrie* a spiritual creed.[86]

Such spiritual fervor was to be applied to one of the most important celebrations of family life under the Vichy regime: the commemoration of Mother's Day. Despite difficult political circumstances and the material privations wrought by the war, Vichy administrators announced that Mother's Day would be celebrated with all the national recognition and flourish it deserved. While Mother's Day had been officially celebrated since the 1920s, the General Commissariat instructed local officials to honor mothers of numerous children with medals and public praise, schoolchildren were urged to write special poems and make drawings for their mothers, and people were generally encouraged to reflect on the virtues of motherhood. The Commissariat had discovered through a series of opinion polls that many citizens questioned the appropriateness of the holiday in light of the absence of so many husbands, brothers, and fathers detained in Germany. Nevertheless, the members of the Commissariat asserted that no time was more apt for the celebration of motherhood, as mothers assured the permanence of the homeland by maintaining their households and raising children in the face of ever-mounting difficulties.

Vichy officials hoped that through the fervor of their tribute to mothers, Frenchmen could learn to set aside the political differences that divided them. Addressing the propaganda campaign for Mother's Day 1943, one administrator wrote:

> This action aims, through the homage offered to mothers, to foster the unanimity of Frenchmen. It calls for the participation of all social milieus and the liveliest of the country's personnel in order to make the last Sunday of May into a national holiday that enters more and more profoundly into national custom.[87]

The Vichy regime struggled to find suitable holidays and days of commemoration that could rally the public and link the new administration to significant events in the past. The 14th of July, Bastille Day, was inappropriate because of its obvious republican and Revolutionary significance, but so was the 11th of November, Armistice Day, which was outlawed by the Germans. May 1 was a potentially contentious observance that Pétain adjusted to represent a glorification of work rather than a symbol of struggle for workers, and it was observed with mixed success.[88] Mother's Day, however, was the national day of honor for the family, a holiday upon which Vichy administrators pinned their hopes for domestic reconciliation.[89] To this end, mayors, regional councilors, leaders of family associations, and schoolteachers were all called upon to help orchestrate a national campaign exalting mothers. The post office included Mother's Day in its yearly almanac, radio stations devoted all their programming on the last Sunday of May to the celebration, and priests were encouraged to pay homage to mothers in their sermons. The Commissariat instructed mayors to complement the traditional religious and award ceremonies with theatrical and musical performances, games, and "flowery parades." Posters were mounted in every village of more than a thousand inhabitants, in the railway stations of Paris, in large stores and public administration buildings, and in all schools. Pierre Laval himself wrote to the regional prefects asking for their firm and unanimous support in the successful celebration of Mother's Day.[90] The national holiday would be both spontaneous and orderly, but it would above all manifest the unity of the French people.

The pursuit of unanimity was also a significant consideration in the discourse surrounding French prisoners detained in Germany. The welfare of the prisoners, and bargaining with Germany for their return, posed a key political dilemma for Vichy. Pétain used the issue to justify the regime's existence, addressing the plight of the prisoners at every opportunity and indicating that their return was essential to the goals of the National Revolution.[91] There was no logical connection between the prisoners and the moral renewal of France, but they became conspicuous media subjects for the regime, patriots whose suffering made them particularly qualified to lead France to redemption.[92] Because the cause of the prisoners and their families generated widespread support, the Vichy regime hoped to capitalize on these universal sympathies and make of the captives apostles for the new regime.

It was in fact their very absence that made prisoners of war such effective symbols for the ideology of the National Revolution, and most particularly for propaganda concerning the family. Although the prisoners seemed unlikely heroes for the family movement and were by definition separated from their own loved ones and homeland, they occupied a crucial place in the

Vichy constellation as vessels of the prescribed hope, longing, and concern for the family. Through the evocation of their homesickness and patriotism, those in France who would neglect the rights of the family could be put to shame; their reputed attachment to the goals of the National Revolution could also be used to spur greater advocacy on behalf of these same goals. In a brochure dedicated to the prisoners and disseminated in German camps, the Commissariat on the Family proclaimed:

> Attached to their families by every fiber of their saddened hearts, [the prisoners] will feel some consolation in knowing that their family is saved, that they themselves are not forgotten—even more so in that every clairvoyant Frenchman is counting on them more than ever for the necessary work of national reconstruction through the family.[93]

The brochure exhorted prisoners to reflect on "family questions" during the final period (still undefined) of their captivity, discussing them with fellow inmates and possibly even setting up informative displays and exhibits within the camps.

Upon their homecoming, the prisoners would then be highly qualified to intervene in local government affairs as advocates of the family and to promote the ideals of the National Revolution at every level of society. "Prisoners," the brochure read, "the cause of the Family is counting on you. Tomorrow you may speak to the nation with an authority that belongs only to you: *the authority of suffering and sacrifice.* Put this authority to work for the Family!"[94] Negotiations for the welfare of the prisoners were intimately linked to the legitimacy of the Vichy regime in the eyes of the French public. The prisoners were also a crucial repository for the social agenda the Vichy regime wished to import alongside their much-anticipated physical return. Discourse on the family thus brought French prisoners of war into a national dialogue Vichy officials could control and turn to their advantage, unlike the negotiations on the same subject conducted with the Germans.

Familial themes were also used to foster a sense of unity by discrediting political opponents and social adversaries of the regime. Jean Guibal, a veteran and conservative family activist, discussed the important integrative benefits of family policies in his booklet, "The Family in the National Revolution." Guibal wrote that "nothing brought people together like shared sorrow," and he went on to describe the ways in which family policy could serve to create a grand communion of the French people by reordering value systems and national laws. Quoting Léon Blum, he expressed disgust at what he called the former Socialist leader's notion that the family was a most dangerous collectivity because it bound people with "ties of shared affection and mediocre happiness" that hampered the free development of the individual. This, according to Guibal, was what had thrown the country into such disillusionment and disaster. Paraphrasing liberally, Guibal juxtaposed Blum's supposed idea that "the family is salutary . . . I wish to deprive you of it" with Pétain's assertion that "the family is salutary . . . I wish to guarantee its rights."[95] The French family had finally found its voice in the venerable Marshal, who believed he had simply put into words the inchoate demands of the great majority of French citizens.

Other social reformers asserted that family policy was a more effective means of addressing the concerns of workers and the lower classes than was a broad labor policy. According to one internal Vichy memorandum, attracting the worker through his family meant rooting him firmly within a wider national context, instead of isolating him as an individual. The family was, after all, the primordial unit of social organization. "It is therefore battling directly against the proletariat by suppressing it," the report stated.[96] Class enemies as well as political enemies could be subdued by the all-encompassing and corrective powers of the family. In a society as conflict-ridden and bitterly divided as France was during the years of German occupation, the family functioned as an essential balm that could heal the wounds of division and humiliation and foster the unity of a revitalized nation.[97]

The notion of *La Famille* was therefore a cornerstone in the ideology of the National Revolution, and certainly worthy of its place alongside *Travail* and *Patrie* in the new triptych of the land. In fact, the case can be made that of these three guiding principles of the Vichy regime, "Family" was the most substantial and readily promoted ideal, and the one least obviously compromised by the dictates of an inherently humiliating armistice agreement. Certainly the Germans were less strategically concerned with what Vichy officials said and did with respect to the French family than with their actions vis-à-vis the compulsory labor system initiated in February 1943 or the resources of the French empire and fleet. Yet family policies were not a secondary concern for Philippe Pétain or the administrators who surrounded him, and German directives on social or population policy were not needed to convince Vichy officials to seek the answers to national reconciliation in this primordial "natural" community. Interest in the family under Vichy was the legacy of a rich French heritage of debates on family life and spoke to long-standing concerns for the status of families that drew on, yet far outreached, the exigencies of the war.

It is certainly true that Vichy officials were not alone in proclaiming the family as a cornerstone of society or in initiating policies that explicitly linked population size and vigor with national strength. In the 1930s and 1940s, many other European nations contemplated the connections between the intimate sphere of family life and policies of national defense and political reform; some even proclaimed the family as the key to a radically different future based on a conservative social revolution.[98] In both fascist

Italy and the Third Reich one can point to policies and ideological orientations toward the family that appear remarkably similar to those apparent in Vichy France. Victoria de Grazia notes that in his speech of May 1927 Mussolini declared that policies in "defense of the race" were fundamental to fascist domestic goals. Italy's reproductive policies included measures such as tax exemptions for fathers of large families, marriage loans, and family allowances, all provisions that were also at the heart of French family activists' policy visions.[99] Chiara Saraceno points out that while husbands and fathers in Italy were awarded a breadwinner's supplement from the state to defray the costs of paternity, men were also held responsible for the failure to marry, as it was bachelors, not unmarried women, who were taxed. The male head of the household was favored in a series of other measures including marriage bonuses and advantages in professional recruitment and advancement.[100] Fascists in Italy followed the French example of rewarding fathers of large families with tax exemptions for dependent children, but these entitlements were, according to Sophia Quine, much less in reality than they were in propaganda. Despite this discrepancy, the family and the demographic campaign were central to fascist rule in Italy and were linked to the larger political and social aims of the regime.[101]

German family policies in the Third Reich offer something of a contrast to those of France, as the Nazis were more unequivocal in their support for the head of the household than were French administrators. Fathers were privileged over mothers, for example, as family allowances were paid to men instead of women. Since the 1930s, conservative middle-class women had argued for a restoration of privileges to the male head of household as a way of binding the man to his family.[102] Gisela Bock asserts that it was fatherhood, not motherhood, that was glorified as "nature" and promoted as an unambiguous concept in Germany—a marked contrast to the contradictory and ambivalent treatment of the nature of paternity in France.[103] Although this support might imply greater support for the father of the family, Nazi ideology did not focus on the rights and responsibilities of men within their families, and such discourse about a *père de famille* was absent. Issues surrounding fatherhood were eclipsed by discussions of men's vital role as fighters rather than family men, as German fathers had their own battlefield to fight on, far from the domestic sphere.[104] Unlike the French prisoners of war who were called on to render ill-defined help to France's families upon their return, German fathers were ideally military men who were advancing the family cause by protecting the nation itself in war. Nazi propaganda focused on fathers as warriors, *führers* in their own households, certainly, but not as intimately tied to the internal life of the family, as Vichy propaganda made French fathers out to be.

Two of the most significant differences between French policies with respect to family life and those originating in Germany or Italy were the comparatively fewer references to "race" in French debates and the absence of forceful sterilization campaigns and physical violence against "undesirables" that shaped German population policy.[105] The concept of "breeding" between racially fit Aryan partners loomed large within Nazi ideology, where the goal was not so much the propagation of ideal families as a "racial revolution" producing the most genetically desirable offspring. According to Claudia Koonz, "The war accelerated Hitler's determination to establish an entirely new social order based on race and sex, with the ideal couple at its core: not a husband and wife, but a soldier and his mother, obedient to Hitler, the patriarch *über alles*."[106] In the Third Reich, the *père de famille* was not a compelling figure, whereas fighting men and their devoted mothers occupied center stage. In France, at the first meeting of the Superior Council on the Family in December 1943, Minister Raymond Grasset indicated that "a racial policy requires conditions that are, at the moment, unattainable, such as the regulation of immigration."[107] Disagreements arose between French social reformers about the desirability of encouraging workers in the cities to have large families, but such conflicts were more shaped by the presumed value of a particular type of family than by their biological ancestry.[108] In Germany, however, the "racially fit" characteristics of the *kinderreich* families distinguished them from the "genetically inferior" and therefore undesirable *Grossfamilien*, who were merely large.[109] While it is true that French family activists looked anxiously to German pro-natalist policies and drew up stark comparisons of population size, such ideas did not need to be imported from across the Rhine, for French policy initiatives found substantial support and a rich heritage within the hexagon itself.

Most importantly, the family was elevated to an unparalleled status in Vichy ideology because it responded to particular needs for unity and legitimacy emanating from the occupation. The symbolic exaltation of the family sprang from very French traditions that linked the family to the rejuvenation of a stronger, more hierarchical and authoritarian society. Discourse on the family provided a means of linking the Vichy regime with both the past and a legacy of French greatness, as well as with a future that included a place for France in the new, Germanic Europe. Focus on the family was therefore far from being a safe theoretical distraction, an impractical philosophy propagated by Vichy officials whose hands were tied. Nor was it animated solely by a desire to spur indiscriminate population growth. In the midst of a continuing war of devastating consequence, Pétain and other leading Vichy officials turned to the family because it offered hopes of unifying a fragmented nation, dissolving long-standing political conflicts, and drawing in the thousands of soldiers left to the mercy of German captors. Vichy officials made the family the cornerstone of the National Revolution because, they believed, it was the only way of explaining the calamity of June 1940, and the only means to make France great once again.

4

Modeling the New Man

Images of Men and Family under Vichy

In late December 1940, an article titled "Are You Men?" was published in the virulently anti-Semitic newspaper, *Réveil du peuple*. Its author, Henri Vibert, asserted that it was the physical, social, and economic "emasculation" of Frenchmen that had caused the recent military catastrophe. He declared that men no longer wanted children and had forgotten how to perform as "males." After a scathing review of the faults of his fellow citizens, Vibert ended with the exhortation: "Frenchmen, be males! Frenchwomen, become mothers!"[1]

Although Vibert's politics and the ideology of the *Réveil* cannot be taken as representative of public opinion in wartime France, his invective underlines a crucial tension Vichy policymakers faced as they attempted to model a society organized according to the directives of the National Revolution. What would fathers look and act like in a regenerated France, and what kind of new man was needed to fill this role? Vibert's rallying cry is telling, for while women were admonished to become mothers, men were called on not to become fathers, but to be more "male," more the virile and effectual beings whose duties presumably included siring more children, but for whom paternity was not the primary component of their identities. This call to adventure and manliness, in the end, contradicted Vichy's own perception of what fathers were supposed to do and to be. While motherhood was presumed to be self-explanatory and all-encompassing, distilling the essence of fatherhood and promoting it proved difficult for Vichy propagandists. If fatherhood was an ideologically important part of Philippe Pétain's designs for a new nation, who exactly were the new fathers, and how would they perform their duties?

Those concerned with the problems of family life in occupied France frequently quoted the Catholic philosopher Charles Peguy. Peguy christened fathers as "grand adventurers of the modern age," an aphorism that was repeated *ad infinitum* in the prefaces to books, quoted in countless articles, and used in speeches by Vichy officials and family activists alike. Although the adage strikes modern readers as odd, apostles of the National Revolution set out to fulfill precisely this dictum by emphasizing the taste for risk, the leadership skills, and the virility that would be required of the new men of France. In addition to "grand adventurers," fathers were called on to be *chefs,* or leaders, in their homes, communities, and professions. As masters and true leaders, fathers would eschew the narrow and petty mindset of the *fonctionnaire,* or bureaucrat, who sought only to promote his self-interest and who avoided strenuous effort of any kind.

The rhetoric of the *chef* was most apparent in new projects for the education and formation of young men that sprang up in the early years of the occupation. Although not wholly a product of official government initiatives, these movements, such as the Chantiers de la jeunesse and the École nationale des cadres d'Uriage, emphasized the physical and moral instruction of a new group of elites who could lead France in a "Revolution of the Twentieth Century." Many of the youth associations and the leadership-training schools organized in 1940 had important links to social-Catholic movements that had been powerful before the war, and their association with the Catholic church continued through the formative years of the National Revolution, up until November 1942. Such groups shared a common belief in the need for a "new man" faithful to principles of honor and loyalty, of sound body as well as sound mind, and committed to fighting against the decadence of parliamentary democracy and individualism. As such, the education of the emblematic man of Uriage paralleled a larger transformation in ideals of masculinity and bodily representation that marked the early twentieth century in Europe.[2]

As vital and robust specimens, the new men of the National Revolution also shared many traits with the ideal fascist man embodied in Nazi propaganda and Italian fascist rhetoric.[3] Ideals of masculinity in Germany and Italy, however, were not primarily focused on fatherhood and family per se, whereas French rhetoric was infused with both a long-standing tradition of interest in the family and a new desire to reinstate familial "traditions" as a template for the new state. While French authorities put the discourse of virility to use in defining the new men needed by the National Revolution, they struggled to make the link between the modern, antibureaucratic superhero and the promotion of the *père de famille,* a project dear to the hearts of many family activists and certainly to Pétain himself. Unlike a pure fascist archetype, French men were defined through their willingness to demonstrate initiative and zeal in fathering children, a task at once both clearly defined and hopelessly vague.

Under the Vichy regime, the increased attention to strong models of masculinity and discipline did not correspond to increasingly well-defined visions and rehearsals of the performance of paternity. In fact, Vichy administrators struggled with increasing manifestations of doubt and uncertainty about the importance of fatherhood, even as they ardently proclaimed official projects for its rehabilitation. Despite frequent public affirmations of the role of fathers in the new French state, Vichy officials faced the same ambiguities of goals and methods in crafting family policy as had confronted legislators of the Third Republic, even with Pétain himself at the helm as national father. Ideologically speaking, it was easier to advertise visions of untainted youth, long-suffering mothers, and honest peasants than it was to advance powerful images of real-life fathers.

In part, the conditions wrought by the occupation and the absence of so many who were languishing as POWs in German camps made proclaiming any archetypes of French independence and fortitude a difficult task. Yet Vichy officials were not merely hampered by the exigencies of war; they actively disseminated an irreconcilable message of fathers as alternately strong and dependent, indispensable and absent, courageous and resigned. This paradoxical discourse accentuated images of inadequate fathers even as it hoped to associate them somehow with the virile and self-sufficient creatures supposedly minted by the National Revolution. Compelling images of real fathers were difficult to find within the projects of family activists, Catholic reformers, military personnel, and government administrators for whom paternity was a concept that remained more theoretically than actually important.

In the summer of 1940, one of the most pressing questions facing the newly organized Ministry on Youth and the Family was what to do with the thousands of young men who had been called up to fight but who were now left idle by the catastrophic military defeat. The armistice agreements allowed for only a small domestic force, of some 100,000 men, leaving military leaders to determine how to reintegrate almost three million recruits in a country where order was rapidly disintegrating.[4] In July, newly mobilized men, incompletely outfitted and in poor health, were forced from their camps in the invaded territories and led on foot to an uncertain fate in the southeast. The army then called on one of its leaders, General Paul de la Porte du Theil, who had been active in the scout movement, to take charge of this rag-tag group of young men and to enlist them in the fight against what he labeled "the frightening decadence of the nation." By a decree issued July 31, 1940, the recruits were dispersed into several camps for six months of service making charcoal and doing forestry work. By the end of January 1941, the General had received permission to make of the Chantiers de la jeunesse permanent institutions, "instruments of the National Revolution." A mandatory eight-month period of national service was inaugurated for all young men of twenty years of age, whom Marshal Pétain praised as "the fortunate youth for whom work has become once again a source of satisfaction."[5]

According to de la Porte du Theil, something had to be done with these young men whose state of moral and physical depression made the idea of sending them directly home untenable: "From the first day the goal I set for myself was a moral one: taking in hand all these dispossessed young men who had just experienced a terrible shock, who were mostly bitter and ruined. . . ." The General quickly realized the national interest inherent in this mass of young men who were "available, trained, directed, devoted to their leaders. . . . I hoped that before long the day would come when I could launch these men into decisive action." Although the idea of maintaining a force of trained young men for future resistance activities weighed heavily in de la Porte du Theil's account after the war, the primary goal of the Chantiers put forward in 1940 was the moral re-education of these ex-soldiers, for whom hard work and communal life in camps would help combat the supposed individualism of the age.[6]

Close to 400,000 young men participated in the various camps and work sessions of the Chantiers de la jeunesse until they were officially closed in 1944.[7] Developed along much the same lines as the scout camps of Lord Baden-Powell before the First World War, the Chantiers grouped together young men in rustic chalets and tents and tried to inculcate in them a sense of duty and obedience to their own leaders and to the new leaders of the French state.[8] Creating the "culte du chef" was an important component of the trainees' eight-month session, and the general commissioner of the Chantiers wished to

> develop . . . the veneration of the leader, to prevent any disputes with superiors. He condemns any sign of disrespect towards a leader, even if he deserves it, because he defines each leader as a being "covered with a partially sacred character, recipient of a portion of the State's authority, which is also itself sacred because it is a reflection of the authority of God."[9]

Part of the role of the Chantiers was to facilitate acceptance of the new political realities of the occupation and to animate the cult of *maréchalisme*. Youth leaders insisted that devotion to authority would do nothing to diminish the desired sense of initiative and ingenuity in young men, but rather would encourage such instincts because they would unfold in an orderly and disciplined environment.[10]

Another way in which the Chantiers and other youth groups elicited support for wider Vichy aims was through propaganda and games that emphasized France's imperial power. French colonial possessions were a key bargaining chip both for General de Gaulle, who hoped to bolster his standing with the British and Americans, and for Vichy officials, who until 1942 believed that possession of the empire could win concessions from Hitler.[11] In the context of youth activities, imperialism provided both a source of inspiration for future *chefs* and a wealth of adventure games in which boys could relive French colonial feats. One propaganda tract emanating from the Ministry of Youth stated that the creation of the Empire was the work of hardened and powerful personalities: explorers, soldiers, and colonists were all authentic *chefs*, and the Empire now provided a limitless field of expansion for young men's creativity. "Their young strength, their audacity, their taste for effort will all be profitably put to use. . . . The youth of the twentieth century will realize the Empire."[12]

Other youth leaders suggested games that could be played in scout troops around colonial themes. The leaders of the Éclaireurs unionistes de France, a Protestant scout organization, suggested that colonial adventures offered scout leaders the "attraction of the unknown, the taste for mystery, the energy strained toward success, unflagging optimism," and many other benefits for their followers. Encouraged to delve into France's history to find a suitable hero, the Chefs éclaireurs were advised to use their imagination to adapt the story and reenact the events in a grand outdoor adventure. Reliving the colonial experience would help transform untested and hesitant young boys into the audacious and virile men needed to maintain control over the French empire in the twentieth century.[13]

The colonies themselves became a stage for the showcasing of French virility as well. Eric Jennings shows that in French Indochina, the Vichy sympathizer Decoux promoted parades of the Légion française des combattants as a means of expressing French solidarity and strength in front of the "natives." The Indochinese were prohibited from becoming de facto members of the Légion; here the spectacle emphasized the virility of the French colonizers, obviously eager to reaffirm French legitimacy in the eyes of colonial subjects.[14]

Virility was a particularly important concept for the directors of the Chantiers and for all those wishing to transform French men into new apostles of the National Revolution. Leaders of the Chantiers described their mission as one of initiating a new "virile order" in France, a "moral" order being necessary but insufficient and a "bourgeois order" being nefarious. According to Vichy propagandists, "virility" was based on three words: man, virtue, and force. It meant leading "a man's life, a forceful and virtuous life. . . . What is opposed to the virile? The feminine, which is complementary, but different. The infantile, which is incomplete. The senile, which is weak." A virile man was defined by both exterior and interior qualities: he was to have a free demeanor, head held high, a clear expression, and "frank gestures."[15] In addition, his spiritual makeup would include a sense of responsibility, an attraction to risk, a sense of honor, and strength.[16]

Although the moral attributes of the new masculine ideal were the subject of frequent commentary, there was no doubt that a man's corporal self and his physical gestures were to adhere to a new standard of dignity as well. To be avoided above all was an attitude of *suprême désinvolture,* a casual, offhand manner of indifference.[17] Such lassitude had cost France the war, and now a new style of bold candor was required of young men. In a government brochure intended for future *chefs,* the author proclaimed that first and foremost boys needed to acquire an inclination for the simple and healthy life:

> You will have no trouble, I know by experience, in developing this taste among sixteen-year-old boys. You will heap ridicule upon those decadent youths with wavy hair, preoccupied with dancing and with the black market. France has always known, following its defeats, movements and fashions that embodied the moral weakness of a society out of kilter. These derisive young men represent instances of weakness, and the shame of a beaten France. . . .

One innovative scout leader from the Île-de-France had helped his boys to understand these principles in a more concrete form. Borrowing a mannequin, he decked it out in the latest fashions and most current hairstyle of the "youth of the bars" and set it up in the main room of a youth center, where it was a huge success. "When celebrating authentic values, there is nothing like showing everyone a tangible example of their opposite" (fig. 4.1).[18]

The idea of physical virtues balancing out the moral qualities essential to the new male was echoed in a brochure on the university written by Paul Haury, Inspector General of Secondary Schools and vice president of the National Alliance against Depopulation. Haury blamed teachers and professors for wanting to educate minds rather than people, for producing thinking machines rather than flesh-and-blood human beings.[19] Through the illusions wrought by parliamentary democracy, the French had come to believe that they had done enough if they merely talked a lot. The terrible judgment of June 1940 demonstrated that not only did French citizens have to educate their minds; they also had to act and achieve in the physical sense. Virility, the essence of "frank" and efficacious action, was to be inculcated in schools, youth groups, the Chantiers de la jeunesse, and everywhere young men were called to be agents of the National Revolution.

Another key component of the National Revolution's curriculum was educating young men in the challenging science of family governance and fatherhood. Paternity was such an important commission that its instruction could not be left to chance, nor was it easily fathomed among young people who had grown up amid the decadence of the Third Republic. The principles of harmonious family life and the Marshal's material efforts to render honor to the families of France were the subjects of lectures and *causeries*

Figure 4.1. The Fop. Commissariat général à la famille, *Le Chef et la famille.*

within the Chantiers and other Vichy youth gatherings. Chef Cassou, for example, taught his troops that the family was the primary cell of society, a community of parents and children. "The father is the leader, and therefore he has the responsibility and the burden of the family."[20] Other youth leaders discussed family allowances and benefits for large families in their seminars on bodily hygiene, the French peasantry, and the inner life of the *chef.*[21]

The General Commissariat on the Family tackled the problem more directly, detailing the ways in which boys might be won over to the family cause and instructed in the art of paternity. Alerting its readers to the dangers of sermonizing, the Commissariat nevertheless directed future *chefs* to evoke a love of home and an understanding of women among the young people in their care. Admitting the difficulties of transmitting such values to adolescent boys, some of whom came from broken families or had no family at all, one brochure stressed:

> One must play up the enthusiasm, the taste for greatness and adventure—all of this resonates with young men. They will have a fresh start, those who have understood because of their sufferings. They will try to construct the ideal home, solid and warm, lively and numerous, but open to light, action, risk, to the call of great deeds near and far that all men of good will desire.[22]

Integral to the program of the National Revolution was a rendition of home economics for young men in which the new ideals of masculinity were put to use in the cause of the family.

Although such familial sentiments were often difficult to convey to adolescent boys, the Commissariat suggested that mockery of only children and ridicule of their selfishness were also effective means of communication. Besides derision, however, youth leaders were encouraged to awaken an instinct of paternity and a love of children through their own paternal demeanor with the boys (see fig. 4.2).[23] The *chef* was directed to exercise that affectionate and understanding authority that gave birth to truly filial sentiments among its recipients. The brochure claimed that "too often today's fathers are simply pals," but this went against the development of proper relations of respect. Paternity could be taught through imitations of hierarchy within the group, rather than sermons on family life.

This was also the perspective offered to schoolteachers by the journal *Éducation*.[24] Teachers were advised by the journal that hierarchy was an essential characteristic to accentuate in their lessons about the structures and principles of family life, and lessons were to make clear who was in charge. Under the category of "Father," children were to understand that he was "the leader of the family, he is in charge of everyone; everyone must obey him." The sample lesson plan continued with questions to be asked about the father, such as: "Is he at home all day?" The answer, of course, was negative, for he was to be out working in order to maintain his wife and children.

Children could then be asked *when* their fathers were at home, which was usually at dinnertime, Saturday afternoons and Sundays. While at home, he "tinkers, he works in the garden, he reads, he helps mother, he looks after the children." When asked for a physical description of their fathers, children were to respond with the appropriate gender stereotypes: "He is big, and strong; he has a powerful voice; he punishes the children when they are naughty, but he is happy when they are good; he can like sports, the arts, collecting, manual work. . . ."[25] Questions about mothers elicited much different responses: she was smaller, more gentle, at home most of the time, and had little time for distractions such as reading. Through well-structured discussions, children could be reminded of the distinct roles and obligations of each of their parents. The physical and social attributes of a father were clearly laid out, and even if some children found themselves without a father at home, every child was to know what a proper one looked and acted like.

As to the more delicate questions of fatherhood involving sexual relations, Vichy propagandists acknowledged that there were differing perspectives on how to guide young men and set a proper example. After all, a true *chef* wanted to mold "real men, not a group of choir boys. What is most important to us is a virile conception of life." Yet it was precisely in the sexual domain that young men could exercise moral restraint and physical hygiene, eschewing the depraved pleasures that were part of typical adolescent ritual.

avec les Compagnons de France…

Agence Tranqus

Figure 4.2. Pétain Visits the Compagnons de France. Fonds actualités, Guerre, 1939–45, BHVP.

Knocking down the myths about gratuitous pleasure was an important first step in advancing the cause of honorable paternity.

> Here again, one can use ridicule and disdain. The man degraded by debauchery—whose children are feeble or depraved beings—doesn't he appear as a failure, beside the robust, healthy and virile boy, who will establish a normal household, founded on the only love worthy of that name, where beautiful children he will be proud of will grow up?[26]

The proper father was a virile man whose potency was channeled in appropriate ways; virility involved, above all, action—and healthy children were the natural outcome of such energy.

If teaching virility was an important component of the program in the Chantiers de la jeunesse, the École nationale des cadres at Uriage brought its instruction to perfection. The École d'Uriage was established in a chateau near Grenoble in December 1940, where its founder and director, the cavalry officer Pierre Dunoyer de Segonzac, offered exceptional young men an education in the moral, spiritual, and physical qualities needed to lead France into a new era.[27] Originally intended as a leadership school for the *chefs* of the Chantiers de la jeunesse, Uriage soon became much more, aspiring to develop a new breed of French elite capable of bringing about profound changes in France. Uriage was not only an avant-garde community living the "twentieth-century style," but also "the most innovative and prestigious think-tank of the National Revolution."[28] Here, the principles of "virility" and "efficiency" were elevated to an art and a code of honor for a man's existence.

Some experts on the Uriage school maintain that the young men trained at the Chateau Bayard were not would-be fascists, imitating the models of Nazi Germany or fascist Italy.[29] It is clear, however, that the themes reiterated both at Uriage and in the Chantiers de la jeunesse bore some striking similarities to the motifs of fascist movements elsewhere. Key to the ideology of the SS or the Hitler Youth, for example, was a common glorification of the male body and an emphasis on physical beauty and strength as a vehicle to "genuine" experience and "natural" truths.[30] In addition, the emphasis on male bonding and homosocial friendships that were an important part of the Uriage "style" is reminiscent of the community of men embodied in the Männerbund of the Third Reich or the Arditi in Italy.[31]

The strength of such male communities generated fears within Nazi Germany that men could eventually shun marriage and family life to devote themselves wholly to their brothers—a fear that was reiterated, as we shall see, in the *causeries* and programs of Uriage.[32] Nationalism and fascism served to redirect men's passions to a higher purpose than the inherently "anti-social" lower concerns of family and sexuality. In Germany, exalted notions of manliness often came into conflict with the family ideal, leading some to believe that "society was carried upon the shoulders of unwed males."[33] French reformers, however, made a concerted, if ultimately unsuccessful, effort to link virility directly with fatherhood and family life. In the programs at Uriage, Vichy ideologues went to great lengths to try to describe how this new breed of men should fulfill its familial obligations.

Fascism in Italy and Germany often developed as a continuation of the community created on the western front in World War I and attempted to perpetuate the state of war into peacetime.[34] The French defeat made this focus on militarism and violence less practical, and the Chantiers tried to turn defeated soldiers into men whose virility was expressed in other ways. The young *cadres* at Uriage were selected from among demobilized officers, but also from Catholic and other intellectual movements whose goals had little to do with the camaraderie of the trenches. Uriage instructors were comparatively less concerned with racial theories or biological conceptions of the new elite, explaining, for example, that Charles Maurras's ideas had to be interpreted within the framework of Christian values.[35] Thus although the models of masculinity promoted in Vichy's schools for *cadres* found resonance in fascist archetypes, they cannot be considered identical in practice or in theory.

For all its uniqueness, Uriage's influence undoubtedly extended far beyond the walls of the Chateau, and its alumni included such important figures in the postwar world as Emmanuel Mounier and Hubert Beuve-Méry.[36] The École nationale des cadres d'Uriage therefore provides important insight into the ideology of the National Revolution and the goals of political and military leaders who wished to shape a new mode of social existence. As a training ground for the nation's elite, it offers an exceptional opportunity to analyze the ideals of this social revolution as they were enacted in the seminars and physical endurance tests of Uriage. Although Uriage was certainly the most famous of the national schools, another training center was established for young women at Ecully-lès-Lyon, and by 1941 as many as sixty state-run regional schools had been set up to train youth leaders for the Chantiers.[37]

Uriage has benefited from a rich scholarly interest, partly because of its equivocal relations with the Vichy regime. A fervently Pétainiste institution in 1940, the leaders of Uriage were nonetheless providing false papers for Jews and hiding fugitives from 1941 on. After the Allied invasion of North Africa and Germany's total occupation of France in November 1942, Dunoyer de Segonzac, who had been convinced that Pétain and Weygand were playing a double game and waiting to launch an army of liberation, was threatened with arrest. By December he had joined the Maquis along with several of his staff. Although the history of Uriage's attitudes toward the Vichy regime and its links to the Catholic church are important themes for the history of Vichy and of modern France generally, crucial to the subject at hand is the way in which Uriage attempted to model a new man, both physically and spiritually, to lead France into another age. Uriage was a "laboratory of civic and social research" devoted to contemplating and enacting the goals of the National Revolution.[38] *Travail, Famille,* and *Patrie* were not mere slogans for the interns of the school, but principles to live by and carry out within a community of like-minded leaders-to-be who all shared a common distaste for parliamentary democracy and the decadence of republican France.

Living the National Revolution meant following a rigorous curriculum and program of action that included both intellectual growth and physical development. According to Dunoyer de Segonzac, "the most beautiful revolutions are without value if they are not followed by constructive acts." Too often, he complained, university students and other idle intellectuals had appeared with "long, greasy hair, generally stringy, pimpled and untidy."[39] The *cadres* at Uriage were to manifest a balanced and complete personal development: in the school's journal, entitled *Jeunesse . . . France!,* P. Reuter described the mission of Uriage as being one of "synthesis" and of "organic continuity between thoughts and deeds, a sense of efficiency."[40] Intellectual pursuits were to be undertaken with a rigorous vitalism, just as sports and physical labor were to be infused with principles of honor and spirituality. As Dunoyer de Segonzac himself proclaimed, "the intellectuals of the National Revolution must be chosen without further delay: let us opt for the intellectuals in good physical condition, good fathers of families and those capable of jumping into a moving streetcar."[41] Above all, the young men of Uriage were to shun the incomplete, enervated demeanor that had cost France the war: the attitude of "*à peu près*" or "good enough" was antithetical to the *cadre*'s way of life.[42] Instead, the *cadre* was called to give fully of himself: this was not an affected virtue, but rather the "normal mode of life for a rich-blooded nature that is incapable of 'doing things halfway.'"[43]

For the rich-blooded young men of Uriage, education in family life was also an important component of living up to the high standards exacted by the National Revolution. Here, however, the case for "se donner à fond" was more difficult to make, for the new elite could not afford to be wholly immersed in domestic life and family concerns. In her article on "the conjugal community" in *Jeunesse . . . France!,* Mme Brunet alluded to these complicated influences pulling Frenchmen away from their families, a paradox that is discussed in greater detail later in this volume. She noted that male love and female love were of two distinct yet complementary natures:

> Once born in the female heart, love takes a much more substantial place than in the male heart. It absorbs everything and banishes all that cannot be assimilated to itself.
>
> The entire feminine personality is polarized by love, but a virile nature

maintains all its power of action; love is not a dominating presence for a man—other interests can impassion him without the depth of his attachment being diminished.

A man's role was essentially one of self-affirmation, of creative force, and mastery of the universe. His aptitudes, therefore, corresponded to this mission. Suggesting a dialogue that might constitute the basis for greater marital harmony, Brunet scripted these words for the young husband:

> Do not resent me for looking elsewhere, beyond your own vision. I sense your peace and sweetness, but they should not put me to sleep. Look at this world that belongs to us and its hostile forces to be conquered; it is for this that I am taut and strong. Could your offspring live if I didn't bend nature to my will? I am here to expand your vision.[44]

Far from impoverishing a man, female love enriched his person through a natural complementarity. Since love itself was not inherently "efficient," however, a young *cadre* needed to be wary of excessive tender thoughts and to reserve the better portion of his self for virile pursuits and manly action.

Lesson plans intended for the education of future *cadres* beyond the walls of the Chateau d'Uriage also focused on the need to make family life a stepping-stone to greater civic and social responsibility, rather than a drain on the imagination and spirit of adventure of the *père de famille*. Decrying the degeneration of the French soul, one tract warned that Frenchmen had listened for too long to accounts of how one must sacrifice for the family, when it was rather the family's creative and aggrandizing qualities that were emphasized in the National Revolution.[45] In another tract, titled "My Rights and My Responsibilities," young leaders were taught that the father of a family had the duty to "raise his children in a solid and virile manner," and he had the right to the material and moral support of a government that pursued a truly familial policy. Furthermore, *pères de famille* had the right

> to be respected by all as the true wise men and benefactors of the fatherland, because through their populous households they give the fatherland all its assistance. . . .—to intervene, in the proper way and according to a sensibly familial legislation, in civic government, in proportion to the number of souls within the household.[46]

Young Frenchmen were to learn the important role of family life in molding their individual selves and defining their responsibilities within the national community. Within the social and civic laboratories of Uriage and other youth centers, men were carefully instructed on how to bring the National Revolution home with them.

There was another, more ominous laboratory established under the Vichy regime that also aimed to reform men and the French population in general. Established by decree in November 1941, the Foundation for the Study of Human Problems (or Fondation Carrel) was the brainchild of Alexis Carrel, a Nobel Prize winner and the author of the international best seller, *L'Homme, cet inconnu*.[47] Carrel had for years attempted to found an institute for the scientific study of man, focusing on diagnosing the ills of modern society that had led the French population into such degeneration. An admirer of Colonel de la Rocque and Jacques Doriot, Carrel profited from the interest Vichy authorities demonstrated in eugenics and natalism to set up the Foundation. He hoped to contribute to the psychological, physical, and moral amelioration of the French population in a newly revitalized nation.

Carrel's eugenics were based on the idea that out of great quantity, quality will necessarily emerge. Rather than preventing the reproduction of those less genetically fit, if the "strongest" and "most gifted" were encouraged to reproduce, a new and superior French elite would come to the fore. With an annual budget of 40 million francs, the Foundation benefited from the support, both ideological and material, of the Vichy government. Although Carrel himself turned down an opportunity to become Minister of Health in 1942, the Foundation enjoyed close ties with Vichy and was instrumental in developing legislation on the prenuptial certificates and school health certificates required by the regime.[48]

The specific means by which Carrel hoped to raise the physical and mental standards for a new elite were never clearly spelled out, yet the Fondation Carrel was not the ephemeral project of a lone theorist.[49] Transformed into the Institut national d'études démographiques (INED) in 1945 under the direction of Alfred Sauvy, the Fondation Carrel was symptomatic of a widespread dismay at the health of the French population and a belief in the progress possible through the scientific application of energetic measures against "decline." Carrel's philosophy echoed the disgust for deficient male bodies witnessed among the *cadres* at Uriage and the scouts of the Chantiers de la jeunesse: all were convinced that through the imposition of a new, vigorously masculine elite, the nation would reclaim its dignity and cease wallowing in mediocrity and humiliation.

During the occupation, the idea of designating a new French elite was a recurring theme among those concerned with the renovation of France, from the radical fascist leader of the Parti populaire français, Jacques Doriot, to the more pedestrian newspapers of family associations (see figs 4.3 and 4.4).[50] Along with fathers of families, Vichy propagandists singled out one group in particular to play an important role in the nation's renewal: the prisoners across the Rhine. As we have seen, the prisoners served vital political and rhetorical purposes for the regime, providing a justification for the government's negotiations with Hitler and acting as patriotic blank slates upon which the goals and ideology of the National Revolution could

CHEFS DE FAMILLE

Prenez conscience de vos RESPONSABILITÉS, de vos DEVOIRS

VOUS ÊTES UNE ELITE

sur laquelle le Maréchal compte pour refaire la France

VOUS AVEZ DES DEVOIRS
PLUS GRAVES QUE LES AUTRES :

MAINTENIR les traditions : simples, saines, fortes, que nous ont transmises nos ancêtres ;
ÉLEVER vos enfants dans la fidélité à ces traditions, dans l'amour du pays, dans l'effort et la loyauté, dans la confiance en l'avenir ;
ASSURER la vie de ceux dont vous avez la charge ;
DONNER l'exemple d'un foyer peuplé, discipliné, heureux.

VOUS AVEZ DES DROITS QUE LA FRANCE NOUVELLE S'EFFORCE DE CONSOLIDER OU D'ÉTENDRE :

RESPECT pour la Famille et les valeurs qu'elle représente ;
EDUCATION des enfants selon votre conscience ;
RESSOURCES matérielles nécessaires pour assurer l'existence de la Famille dans la dignité ;
POUVOIR de faire entendre officiellement la voix des Familles et de participer même à la gestion des affaires publiques.

SOYEZ DES ANIMATEURS !
MIEUX VAUT CONSTRUIRE QUE REVENDIQUER !

Ne vivez pas repliés sur vous-mêmes, mais

UNISSEZ-VOUS

pour que triomphe la CAUSE FAMILIALE qui est CELLE DE LA FRANCE

ADRESSEZ-VOUS : au Délégué Régional à la Famille (Préfecture régionale)
ou à l'Association Familiale de votre résidence.
COMMISSARIAT GÉNÉRAL A LA FAMILLE

Figure 4.3. "Heads of Families!" Commissariat général à la famille. Propagande en faveur de la famille. Bibliothèque de documentation internationale contemporaine.

be drawn. It was not only the firm-fleshed *cadres* of Uriage who took on the mantle of virility; the administration also constantly referred to the prisoners as France's new elite and heaped upon them all the hopes and expectations of a humiliated nation.

In one brochure issued by the General Commissariat on the Family, administrators suggested that reflections on France's future and projects for its renewal were premature until all the prisoners had returned home. Some of the best men in France were held in barracks in Germany, and through their long exile they had contemplated the causes of the current situation:

Ce solide gars, père de cinq enfants, qui mène sa moissonneuse-lieuse, n'est-il pas le symbole de cette élite française qui refera le pays malgré les intrigants et les politiciens ?

L'ÉLITE FRANÇAISE

Figure 4.4. "The French Elite." *Familles de France* 10 (15 August 1943): 1.

How could one plan the future without them? Their sufferings give them the right to speak. Their reflections, ripened by this ordeal, are of an exceptional value. With them, a light will return to us, without which it seems that we will always be more or less hesitant about which road to choose. . . .

The Commissariat on the Family went on to affirm that all the prisoners who had meditated on the miseries of the fatherland had arrived at the same conclusion: "France will only truly and durably rise up again when first the French family rises up again." It was precisely this young and powerful elite imprisoned in Germany that was to take responsibility for the resurrection of France:

This elite undoubtedly will, when granted their freedom tomorrow, respond to the call of a country that wishes to live, and can only live through the family. . . . Elite, it must preach through example. For it is all French youth that must be moved to the salvation of the Nation through the family.[51]

The brochure was intended to convince the men of the camps of the importance of their mission upon returning home. It also designated a new elite, which, being essentially without voice or agency, was a perfect mouthpiece for the dissemination of the ready-made voice of the National Revolution.

There was, however, a less exultant side to the discourse on prisoners that complicated their role as leaders of the family revolution and ultimately undermined their status as a new elite. Alongside the triumphal affirmations of the qualities of these captive men in Vichy propaganda came an obsession with their absence from their families and a profound anxiety about their successful reintegration into the national community. Prisoners could be hailed as apostles of the National Revolution in brochures destined for the Stalags and the work camps, but in the books, brochures, and articles intended for their wives and families at home, the message was far more ambiguous. Here the *père de famille* appeared as an outsider, a symbol of defeat and humiliation, a pity-inspiring yet ultimately inconsequential adjunct to France's process of renewal.

Despite the Vichy regime's assertions that the suffering they had endured granted prisoners special rights and a privileged voice in the new nation, this suffering was often, in fact, portrayed as pathetic and powerless in the descriptions circulated about the prisoners' lives. One such booklet, titled *Femmes d'absents,* displayed a grim scene of camp life in which French men gathered around a rough table playing cards, with laundry strung prominently overhead (fig. 4.5).[52] "Have pity on me," the caption read, "at least those who love me." Further along in the same booklet, another picture depicted a cold and preoccupied prisoner sitting down to his meager rations

Figure 4.5. "Have Pity on Me. . . ." *Femmes d'absents.* Série "Fêtes et saisons."

(fig. 4.6). Here the caption explained that while letters and packages were eagerly awaited in the camps, the prisoners expected something else, something less concrete and yet far more important: "do not let us become strangers in our own homes by dint of our absence."[53] Although the booklet encouraged wives deliberately to save a place for their distant husbands in their hearts and at their tables, such depictions emphasized the want of these men and the humility of their condition rather than any redemptive and Christ-like suffering.

The prisoners' condition, in fact, flew in the face of precisely those characteristics supposed to define the new man of the National Revolution. The much-vaunted attribute of "efficacy" was directly contradicted by the men's imprisonment, where they were forced to wait passively on other soldiers and the political machinations of the Vichy regime to liberate them, or on their captors to put them to work for Germany.[54] While the General Commissariat on the Family could announce that "Action" was the key to France's regeneration (fig. 4.7), such a proclamation had to ring false for the prisoners for whom such effectual action would have been impossible.[55] Instead, the captives were forced to wait on a distant future that was depicted as luminous, but was separated from them by heavy barbed wire and isolation from their families (fig. 4.8).[56] In the context of the German Stalags and Oflags, the prescriptions for a new, virile masculinity capable of uniting thoughts and deeds in the pursuit of concrete action would have seemed both impossible and cruelly impractical.

In fact, one of the only ways in which French men, including the prisoners, could act in the decisive and masculine fashion suggested by the National Revolution's propaganda was through labor, forced or ostensibly voluntary, in the Third Reich. As early as 1940, the Germans had sought out French workers for its plants and factories, and about 70,000 French men and women had left voluntarily to work in the Reich. Between 1942 and 1944, however, the German General Commissioner of Labor and Employment, Fritz Sauckel, inaugurated a new and more brutal period of labor requisition, demanding close to two million French workers. In the face of such demands, Pierre Laval attempted to maintain the fiction of a sovereign Vichy state in the summer of 1942 through the publicity of a new system know as the Relève, whereby for every three workers who went voluntarily to Germany, one prisoner would be released and returned to France.[57]

The Relève was a total failure, clouded with misunderstanding and miscommunication that left only acrimony among those frustrated families who longed to see their loved ones return home. Although widely publicized by the regime, the few prisoners able to return were usually notorious collaborators rather than rank-and-file soldiers.[58] Under pressure from mounting German demands, Laval instituted the Service du travail obligatoire (STO) in February 1943, requisitioning young men mobilized for the army into

CLICHÉ FÊTES ET SAISONS

Figure 4.6. Do Not Let Us Become Strangers in Our Homes. *Femmes d'absents,* 17.

forced labor.[59] The inauguration of the STO was decisive in turning French public opinion thoroughly against the Vichy regime and the politics of Pierre Laval, as well as against the German occupiers. Not only would the STO affect most French families, who risked losing a son, brother or uncle to the dangers of work in the Reich, but it also eliminated one of the few ostensible reasons for the existence of the regime in the first place: the protection of the French population from excessive German demands.[60]

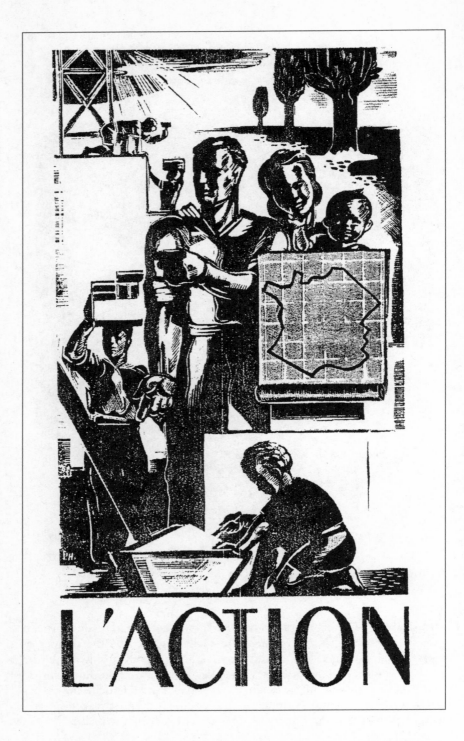

Figure 4.7. "Action." Commissariat général à la famille, *Les Prisonniers et la famille*, 59.

Figure 4.8. "The Future." Commissariat général à la famille, *Les Prisonniers et la famille*, 71.

The conflict that arose between a regime that professed ardent reverence for the family and a state-enforced law that took fathers and other male relatives away from their families to work for a victorious occupying power was obvious. Despite the contradictions inherent in this policy, Vichy officials nonetheless attempted to make forced labor into both the grand adventure and the proper fulfillment of paternal role that coincided with the regime's gender prescriptions and political needs. In one propaganda poster advertising work in Germany, a young man protects his wife and child from the claws of the Soviet bear, warding it off with a shield and hammer in the manner of the warrior he is supposed to be (see fig. 4.9). Many posters in favor of the Relève and the STO emphasized the noble and manly nature of those workers who heeded the call of their country and their imprisoned compatriots to work across the Rhine.[61]

Other propaganda actually played up the familial nature of the work these Frenchmen were called to do. Rather than attempting to mitigate the obvious pain of separation facing the workers, one poster celebrated a father's departure and monetary gain by depicting a joyous mother and child for whom the "bad days" of poverty and scarcity were over (fig. 4.10). Once again, the worker himself is depicted in the triumphal pose of strength and victory, an agent of his own destiny and the embodiment of paternal duty. Here his absence is portrayed as a noble act of self-sacrifice and productivity rather than as a deficiency of domestic life.

Yet the image of a mother and child rejoicing at the departure of a *père de famille* had profoundly unsettling implications for a regime that intended to rebuild the nation on the basis of its families. For even while "sacrificing" for family and country, he was, unmistakably, absent—and what would become of his paternal authority, and indeed his very role in the family, when he was gone? If the state itself was encouraging such a truncation of families, was the *père de famille* really an essential member of the family community? While focusing on the integrity and productivity of fathers out of political expedience, Vichy authorities were at pains to integrate this image with the desired ideal of a stable, unified family firmly under paternal control.

Vichy propagandists attempted to circumvent this predicament in a variety of ways. One such effort entailed a letter-writing contest for children whose fathers were working in Germany, with prizes for the "most beautiful letter," ranging from 50 to 3,000 francs. Written by children up to the age of fifteen, the letters were to be judged by professors at the Sorbonne, and were collected by a group known as the "National Committee of Friends of Workers in Germany." These letters, preserved in the archives of the Rector of the University, were, if not fraudulent in their origins, certainly the product of vigorous coaching, for they contain certain stock phrases and themes that seem unlikely to have come from the pens of children. The two winning letters in the under-ten category, for example, both report that the child au-

Figure 4.9. "Worker!" Centre historique des archives nationales, Atelier de photographie. 72AJ 1424.

Figure 4.10. "The Bad Days Are Over!" Centre historique des archives nationales, Atelier de photographie. 72AJ 1422.

thors had asked their mothers to "buy another baby" to make father happy when he finally returned home.[62] Other letters dwelt on the suffering of prisoners, the regeneration of France, and the nobility of the Relève, all of which topics seem coincidentally to echo propaganda for the National Revolution more than they express the preoccupations of fatherless children.

The letter-writing contest did signal an attempt to bridge the distance between fathers sent to work in Germany and the families they were forced to leave behind. The letters also included, amid the adulation of Vichy's policies, the expected terms of endearment and sentimental expressions of longing for a father's return. Yet often such emphasis on the missing *père de famille* and reports on life in his absence only accentuated the sense that fathers were marginal beings, both literally and figuratively on the periphery of the family's life.

In the state-sponsored celebrations surrounding Mother's Day, for example, schoolchildren were instructed to write a composition in the form of a letter to their father imprisoned in Germany. In the letters, they were to describe the work "their mothers undertook to replace them" while assuring the moral and material life of the home. One composition retained in the archives of the Academy of Paris read: "sometimes we go off together to cultivate the garden where the imprint of your clog has been erased." All that is left of the father's presence is a photograph on the buffet, adorned with a bouquet of violets, not unlike a grave. The author, Henry, concludes by reporting that "to her sensitivity and feminine gentleness, Mother has added courage and a virile energy. Be reassured of our fate: you are incarnated in her."[63] Rather than emphasizing the paucity of life without father, the story focuses on the heroic efforts of the mother that make his absence less difficult.[64] The father has been reduced to an effigy adorning the furniture, and his very footprints have been erased. The masculine virility with which he suffused the household has been incorporated into the mother's own nature.

Similarly, another story circulated in the *Almanach de la famille française* accentuates the ephemeral nature of the father's presence even while it attempts to assuage the suffering of those who miss him. In a vignette titled "New Year's Day," a family celebrates the first New Year without their father, who is imprisoned in Germany. The mother takes her three young children to his photograph, where they proclaim: "'Happy New Year, Daddy!' The children's mouths administer big kisses on the cold glass. The glass gets fogged up; one can barely see father anymore."[65] Although the tale ends gaily with the arrival of a letter from Daddy, it nonetheless calls to mind images of paternal inconstancy and intimates that the father's image may be in some manner "erased." As stories intended to recognize and mitigate the effects of a father's absence, these anecdotes nonetheless carried with them an unsettling preoccupation with paternal estrangement and loss.

The potential obliteration of the *père de famille* was also a recurrent theme appearing in advice to wives of prisoners awaiting the return of their spouses. Alongside recommendations to women to keep themselves well-groomed, their houses clean and their dispositions cheerful, prisoners' wives advised each other to speak frequently of their husbands to the children, so that "upon his return he is not the unknown '*Monsieur*,' but rather the Daddy who is known and well-loved." Only the persistent efforts of the mother could overcome the alienation of the father from his own children. In the illustrations surrounding these *simples conseils,* the fears of the prisoners' wives are depicted graphically: in one scene, a child runs in fear from the figure of his father appearing in the doorway (fig. 4.11).[66] In another drawing, a child has taken the photograph of a man (presumably his father) from its frame and broken it over the child's own head. While intended to prepare wives for the imminent return of their husbands, the sense of disaffection and loss of paternal recognition in these messages is palpable.[67]

The problematic reintegration of the father is underlined in another brochure written by wives of prisoners at the very end of the war, upon the return of thousands of husbands and fathers. The booklet details many of the things that were not to be said to the returnees, such as comments on their healthy appearance or questions as to their loyalty to Marshal Pétain. In an article titled "La Flamme du foyer," one wife described the very real problem of disappointment and disillusionment upon the return of the prisoners, on whom so many hopes and expectations had been projected. This was a great danger for children, in particular, who may have been too young in 1939 to know their father much at all: "The children have grown up and have changed; a father must get to know them, and even win them over to a certain extent. He can start by being their mother's husband, then a friend, then a dad. . . ."[68] Here again, paternity was no longer an essential fact to be taken for granted; it had to be won back gradually, its recognition undertaken in gradual steps.

Another article aimed at children addressed such problems of disappointment and misunderstanding even more directly. After years of waiting and mindful reverence of "the Absent one," the article warned, this was the hour of truth:

> Your father is before you. His arrival surprised you: you didn't recognize the man of your reveries when he appeared; despite his open arms, you felt a mild shock at having to call this man, or rather this stranger, "Daddy."[69]

In his absence, a child might have become the mother's confidante, the man of the house, and would have taken part in important household decisions. Now, with the return of their fathers, children felt displaced and even hostile at the intrusion of this outsider with whom affections were to be shared.

Figure 4.11. Father's Arrival. *Femmes d'absents*, 29.

Despite the temptation, however, children were admonished not to tolerate any tractability or submission on the part of their fathers. If the prisoners' intense suffering had made them meek-natured, children were told, "Do not accept nonsense, and the devirilization of your father!"[70] Similarly, adolescents were cautioned that five years of war would naturally have drawn them closer to their mothers, with whom they had shared many experiences, while the life of the prison camp would seem strange and forbidding. This isolated the *père de famille* even more, the article warned: "Who knows whether solitude might once again surround the Man of the Barbed Wires? . . . What a dangerous development for all concerned!"[71] In this paradoxical approach, children were encouraged to be "virile" and independent themselves in order to guard against the potential emasculation of their fathers. The returning prisoners seemed perpetually in danger of slipping once again into obscurity if their status as fathers was not carefully supported.

In the *Almanach de la famille française,* the authority of the *père de famille* was also portrayed as imperiled by the neglect of his own family. The "sick families" of France needed strong guides to lead them from the depths of egotism, individualism, and excess. The father was called to be a *chef,* but

> We have so disregarded his authority and diminished his prestige in the eyes of the children. Even if he is absent, let us guard his place—his whole place. When he sees that he has remained the respected and popular *chef,* he will regain awareness of his responsibilities.[72]

If a *père de famille* did not take charge in the appropriate manner, mothers and children would have to help salvage his authority and hold him accountable for his duties. Although the advice offered to wives of prisoners constantly reminded them to give their husbands back the reins of household and family management, such insistence betrayed both an ambiguity about the source of domestic power and the threat of implied paternal forfeiture.[73]

Despite grand proclamations of a new age of virility and of the adventures of parenthood, returning prisoners reeked of failure, for they had lost the war and had been reduced to impotence during the occupation. While the prisoners' suffering served as an important rhetorical device in Vichy propaganda, it was considerably more difficult to draw connections between their fate and the robust, effective *chefs de famille* who would lead a newly regenerated nation. The war had not made them better fathers, nor had it made them more manly. In fact, it had engendered serious doubts on both these accounts in the minds of anxious wives and distant children. Yet returning men were called precisely to these tasks by the insistent propaganda of the Vichy state that both idolized their affliction and demanded they overcome it by becoming ideal and powerful fathers. The manner in which this transformation could occur was left vague, but the insinuations that they might fail at their duties were conspicuous enough. An air of ambiguity surrounded returning prisoners, therefore, as they were both objects of solicitude and authors of possible humiliation at both the national and the familial level.

It was, in fact, much less complicated to venerate mothers rather than fathers in propaganda for the National Revolution. While fathers were often absent, potentially enfeebled, or even resigned, within Vichy ideology mothers were obviously productive and properly feminine by virtue of their motherhood. Miranda Pollard notes that in Vichy's sexual politics, French women "were 'there' symbolically and actually to be exhorted, mobilized, and controlled in a way that men were not."[74] The maternal role was portrayed as so straightforward that there could be no question of failure for a woman who followed the proper gender role assigned to her by "nature."[75] The call to motherhood within the Vichy regime was women's own form of mobilization, a "blood tax" payable through childbirth.[76]

Mothers, along with other voiceless emblems of state propaganda such as the prisoners, were the heroes of Vichy propaganda, and they were honored each May with elaborate government-sponsored events. Their intrinsic powerlessness only heightened their value for the rhetoric of the National Revolution. Unlike fathers, mothers did not need to be independent, effective, or virile in order to fulfill their "natural" destinies, and the joys of motherhood could be celebrated during the occupation without major ideological contradictions within Vichy thought. This is not to say that real mothers experienced fewer difficulties under the very difficult circumstances of the occupation. This loud public acclaim was projected above a reality in which most women could not possibly afford to be stay-at-home mothers due to the economic exigencies of the war. Francine Muel-Dreyfus demonstrates that the darker side of this celebration of motherhood was a system of constraint that outlawed married women's work in an effort to promote the "career of motherhood," even as this work was often essential to the family's survival.[77] The General Commissariat on the Family, however, focused on exploiting this perfunctory veneration of mothers in magazines, films, radio programs, communal events, and school assignments. If fathers were not always the model heroes the Vichy propaganda machine needed, mothers could easily be molded to fit the bill.

In celebration of Mother's Day 1943, the General Commissariat produced a film titled "The Cult of Heroes," which documented the "everyday heroines" one encountered on the street and in village squares. The film reminded viewers that many cultures celebrated their dead war heroes, but there were living heroes all over France who could be distinguished from other women by the "reflection of joy in their faces . . . and a common name,

'Mommy.' " The film, produced in documentary style with "grand music" and "an authoritative tone," encouraged French citizens to "tell their Mothers 'thank you' at least once a year," for "you certainly are still indebted to her for all she has done for you."[78] Mothers could be thanked, simply, because they had already performed their national duty and were prohibited from demanding greater rights or responsibilities in the new French nation.[79]

Fathers, however, could not be so easily thanked. What were the compelling images of fatherhood that could appear in a laudatory film recognizing their service and praising them for their heroism? This omission was all the more obvious when taken in the context of catastrophic military defeat. Perhaps dead war heroes could be celebrated, but what about modern fathers, especially those imprisoned by the Reich? Vichy propagandists did their best to draw out the "heroic" implications of fatherhood and to portray it as a "grand adventure" whenever possible. The General Commissariat on the Family asked numerous journals and newspapers to take part in its campaign, "Alerte à la famille," in which familial themes would be treated in special articles and editions. The magazine *Sciences et voyages* was one of the few to take up the issue of fathers, in contrast to the multitude of events surrounding celebrations of Mother's Day. In its special edition dedicated to the family, *Sciences et voyages* dealt with falling birth rates in France, the fertile French Canadians, the Indochinese family, and many other topics of both domestic and international concern.

As expected, the introduction quoted Charles Peguy, who,

> speaking of fathers of families, called them "the great adventurers of the modern world." Creating a family, isn't it essentially entering into [*pénétrer*] the most passionate adventure of all? A person is created where nothing was before, and a world of possibilities opens before his eyes. Creating a being of this kind, giving him life in an almost divine manner, isn't it a responsibility that demands of man more greatness, more seriousness and at the same time more optimism, that intellectual optimism that Nietzsche spoke of?

It is unclear here exactly what dimension of paternity is being celebrated. Is it essentially the physical act that gives paternity its grandeur, or are the other requirements of majesty, gravity, and enthusiasm more important still?

In any case, Frenchmen had lost this courageous spirit, and the author complains that for more than half a century, fathers had failed to heed the call to adventure: "this taste for risk has been succeeded by a cowardice and a concern for tranquility which is nothing else than a fear of life and a dread of death." The introduction concludes, "one can hope that the spirit of adventure will be reborn among Frenchmen. There remain, in spite of the defeat, immense possibilities."[80] Even in an homage to paternity, therefore, praise of fatherhood came inextricably linked to its failure, its deficiency, and the burden of missed opportunity. There was *possibility* in fatherhood, not actuality. Paternity could be induced or assumed, but it was not the tractable given that motherhood was, and all too often it was a disappointment to Vichy propagandists who needed simple images, compelling emotional scenes, and powerful symbols to represent the goals of the National Revolution.

One prominent family activist, William Garcin, attempted to deal with this problem head-on in an article titled " . . . Et les pères?" Garcin noted that "since the family has been in the limelight, everyone has spoken of mothers. Mother's Day, Mother's Awards, etc., etc. . . . What about fathers?" Fathers were more than simply the wage earners that enabled the family to live, he asserted; they were essential to the equilibrium and health of the entire household. "All those who never knew their father, or those legions, alas! for whom he was simply at home 'for appearances' will understand." In an effort to draw out the different, yet essential characteristics of paternity, Garcin went on to enumerate some of the father's gifts. Fathers taught "virile virtues," and their own morality sustained the family. Yet Garcin concedes: "one must admit that the paternal sentiment has nothing of the dramatic, irrational and spectacular love of maternal love." Rather, the first contact between father and child was usually negative, and only after babies grew up a bit and were capable of play could the bond between the two be cemented. Despite these initial false notes, however, fathers who had watched their children grow up would be convinced that they had taken part in the magnificent work of creation. "It is children who make fathers eternal. To make oneself comparable to God, that is truly the highest human enterprise, the most magnificent task of man."[81]

Family activists and government administrators did continue to try to portray fatherhood as a magnificent enterprise, using, for example, the occasion of a family exposition set up in the Mairie of the fifth *arrondissement* in Paris. This exposition, organized by the General Commissariat on the Family, ran from the end of May to the end of June 1943.[82] Originally the Commissariat had intended to organize one large exposition for all of Paris, but because of various technical complications had to settle on several smaller exhibits organized in the town halls of the various *arrondissements*. The exposition then traveled to several locations in France, including Bordeaux, Caen, and other cities in the north. Organizers from the General Commissariat compelled students from the lycées of the fifth *arrondissement* to attend, and it is in the communication between these school officials and the administrators of the exhibition that the content of the *Exposition de la famille* comes to life (see fig. 4.12).[83]

The exposition was set up in the Salle des fêtes of the Mairie on the Place du Panthéon in Paris. A map of the room indicates that upon entering, vis-

EXPOSITION DE LA DÉFENSE
DE LA FAMILLE FRANÇAISE

MAIRIE DU Vᵉ ARRONDISSEMENT
DU 22 MAI AU 20 JUIN 1943
EN SEMAINE : 13 h. 30 à 19 h.
LE DIMANCHE : 14 h. à 20 h.

Figure 4.12. The Defense of the French Family. Fonds actualités, Guerre, 1939–45, BHVP. Notice the way in which the girl's position is reminiscent of Marianne, whereas her placement on the medieval tower associates her with Joan of Arc.

itors were confronted with a "dramatic panel" describing the demographic and familial crisis in France. These panels included illustrations on bachelors, households without children or with only one child, and the general aging of the French population. From this section, titled "La France en péril," the visitor moved along the wall to discover the "Chaîne des fléaux," or Succession of Scourges, that afflicted French families. First was the slum, where dirty children and dreary interiors pushed men out onto the streets and into neighborhood bistros. Then the second panel on alcoholism took over: the exposition offered statistics of alcohol consumption in France, in Paris, and in the fifth *arrondissement,* including photographs. There was also a diorama presenting the nefarious effects of drinking and the evils of bistro company (see fig. 4.13).[84]

After this sensational illustration, the visitor moved along the chain of scourges to discover the themes of "Immorality and Debauchery." Here prostitution, pornography and venereal disease were brought to light with statistics, drawings and photographs, which also depicted antidotes to such immorality with pictures of open-air stadiums and sound moral education. Next in line were family abandonment, divorce, and free unions, with lamentable pictures of abandoned and illegitimate children. The series of familial enemies ended with a panel on egotism, "the origin of all ill."

At the end of this progression, set up on the stage and covering one entire end of the room, was the section titled "Restoration of the Family." Here, three large panels dominated: "Joy," "Strength," and "Audacity."[85] Under "Joy" and "Strength," pictures of happy familial celebrations were interspersed with those of strong and numerous families from France's past. Under "Audacity," the *chef de famille* came to the fore. The responsibilities of the father of the family were evoked through photographs and artwork as well as through descriptions of the family as a school of discipline and an education for true leaders.[86] The *père de famille* appeared, surrounded by his numerous children, probably in a manner not unlike other illustrations from the General Commissariat (figs. 4.14 and 4.15). Once again, paternity was presented as a bold and daring exploit, a gamble undertaken by the authentic leaders of the new France.

The Exposition ended with practical information on family associations, state assistance, and public health initiatives of both government and private origin. It also focused on concrete recommendations for ameliorating one's home and lifestyle with the benefit of insights gleaned from the exhibits. One of these panels announced that in the clean, pleasant, and flourishing household, in which the mother was the soul of the home, "the husband finds contentment and stays at home." Despite the optimistic tone of the panel, there are also hints of recurring doubt about paternal adequacy evident in the illustrations and captions. Is the household perpetually in peril of losing its *chef* to the distractions of the street? The man, who is en-

Jeune Français

prends garde...Tu peux devenir un alcoolique sans le savoir. Mais tes enfants, eux, le sauront. Et ce seront eux, les innocents, qui porteront le poids de ton alcoolisme. Jeune Français, si tu veux fonder une famille heureuse avec des enfants sains et robustes, Souviens-toi qu'un homme ne doit pas absorber plus d'un litre de vin par jour.

Un homme digne de ce nom
doit savoir se discipliner

Figure 4.13. "Young Frenchman . . . Drink No More than a Liter Per Day." Fonds actualités, Guerre, 1939–45, BHVP.

Figure 4.14. The Father of a Large Family Turns Away from Degenerate Pastimes. Commissariat général à la famille, *L'Université devant la famille*.

Figure 4.15. The Family Outing. Commissariat général à la famille, *La Commune, rempart de la famille.*

gaged in the appropriate pastime of reading (see chapter 2), is not even named as "father"; rather, he is the "husband." The mother, the spirit of the family, is obviously properly maternal, but the man's distance and ambiguous paternity brings to mind the *Réveil du peuple*'s exhortation for Frenchmen to "be males" and Frenchwomen to "become mothers." The various faults of men were portrayed vividly in the exposition: alcoholism, debauchery, and venereal disease. When redeemed and brought back into the home, however, what were the positive images of "audacious" and daring fathers?

In fact, Vichy's conception of paternity was incompatible with its own exhortations to virility and adventure.[87] This was a fundamental problem facing the social reformers and propagandists of the regime, one that led only to more questions and more fervent protestations that the *père de famille* could be both a father and a *chef*. The newspaper *Familles de France* attacked this issue directly in its September 1943 issue. The author, André Fabre, asked readers: "Is the Father of the Family a Leader [*chef*]?"

When Peguy exclaimed, "the father of the family, the grand adventurer of the modern world," I have known some to snicker and laugh. But they are not among those who have risen to the challenge. The father of the family is no longer the fearful bourgeois, feet in his slippers, neck protected with countless scarves, and whose soft and pampered life inspires both a feeling of envy and of disgust. Image of the past.

Today's father is an adventurer, the "conscious and organized" adventurer. At every moment of life he protects his children as Chanticleer protected his chicks. He protects them from wind and rain, from the hardships of life and from its ignominy. He struggles the livelong day, physically, morally and socially.

The article goes on to describe the father's encounters with the world, his place in the social order, and his status as the "best of citizens." Fathers must have their feet firmly planted in reality—children help do that—yet they must also see farther, "from a more serene and pure point of view." Finally, their call was to be true *chefs*, epitomes of masculinity who were grounded in the real, yet who "dominated it with daily action." The article ends, however, not with a rousing confirmation that the father is, indeed, all these things, but with more of a suggestive platitude: the "*père de famille* of today has the vocation of a leader."[88] Had he fulfilled this prescription? Were readers left with the image of Chanticleer, or with the image of a timid bourgeois foremost in their minds? Once again, images of an asocial and potentially foolish father battled it out against lofty ideals of a superman with children.

Rather than images of noble Gallic roosters, the General Commissariat on the Family chose icons of a completely different sort to represent the fathers to whom it addressed one of its many propaganda posters. In an edition of

1943, titled "Leaders of Families, Here Are Your Rights," stick figures with blank, round faces designated the *pères de famille,* while their children lined up, in descending order, by their sides (fig. 4.16). Rather than grand escapades, the poster spoke of wills, family allowances, and retirement pensions. Fathers could benefit from reduced-fare train tickets and tax exemptions instead of colonial adventures and pitted struggles against nature. In the final frame, the poster proclaimed: "the State has done a great deal for you, it will do more still, but in order for France to be reborn, you must think of your duties as you claim your rights, and give your support to family associations."[89] This appeal fell more in line with a request to the plodding bourgeois than with the enterprise of a risk-taking *chef.*

Even those social reformers most committed to the principles of paternal ascendance in the new France questioned whether the vocation of *chef* was compatible with the social obligations and changes in perspective incurred through fatherhood. Within the scout movement, for example, we have seen how apprenticeship in parenting formed an integral part of the scout's curriculum. Yet even in this context, some scout leaders were uncomfortable with the conflicts that arose between the will to lead and the stultifying call of marriage and family. In the Protestant scout journal *Le Lien,* one leader complained that:

> We have few troupe leaders who are married. News of an engagement of a leader . . . well loved by his boys generally plunges them into consternation:
> "He's going to get married, it's all over for us! Now he's good for nothing but becoming a commissioner" . . . often the end of bachelorhood marks the end of work with the boys, marriage is the extinction of the scout life.

The article went on to suggest that there were some ways in which the vocation of *chef de famille* could be reconciled with the active and spontaneous life of the scout movement, but only with careful attention to the burdens of his family life. The deciding argument in favor of the concord of these roles, however, was not an affirmation of the excitement and adventure of paternity, but rather the idea that both vocations came from on high: "there is no incompatibility between the calling of *chef* and marriage if both are envisaged as ordained by God." This heavenly allusion helped to transcend the difficult question of how two very different images might be purposely combined into one compelling icon; if there was antagonism in these impressions, perhaps it was simply due to human ignorance and misunderstanding.[90]

Similarly, there was human misunderstanding in the realization of domestic authority, for fathers seldom benefited from the unquestioning loyalty their positions demanded. Some family activists continued to remind French citizens that the authority of the *chef de famille* was of divine origin and that their mission was to be "collaborators with God." Yet in the turbu-

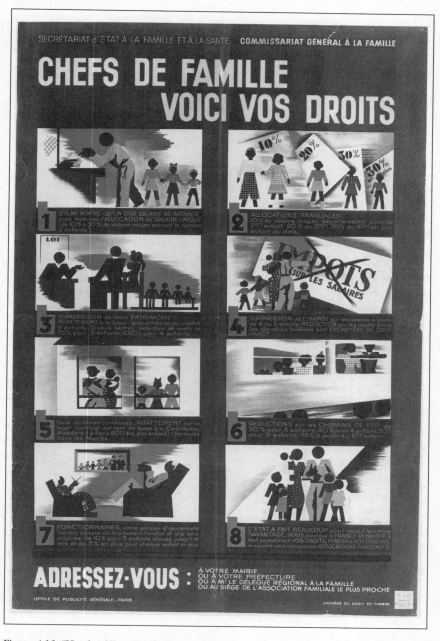

Figure 4.16. "Heads of Families, Here Are Your Rights." Centre historique des archives nationales, Atelier de photographie. 72AJ 1238.

lent war years, fathers were finding their authority more and more questioned:

> When a badly raised young man . . . asks his father, "with what right do you command me?" it happens that the question is pertinent and the answer often embarrassing. Many of our contemporaries no longer have firm ideas on the matter, alas, and that is why we see so many abdications, and so many abuses as well, in the government of families. Fathers and husbands no longer know why they possess familial authority.[91]

The author went on to describe the way in which domestic authority was to be properly maintained and effectively implemented in order to bring about joyful obedience among all family members. Abusing authority only led to its degradation, and "insubordination and insurrection most frequently are the result of the errors and faults of the *chef*, rather than the subordinates."[92] Even in an article ostensibly concerned with fortifying the status of paternity, the father was scrutinized and called into question. At every turn, the same rhetoric that set fathers apart for special consideration also served to cast doubt on their abilities and to render their positions more equivocal.

The question of domestic authority was raised frequently in discussions of the family under Vichy, and all too often it was raised with a question mark. Etienne Videcoq, for example, wrote an article titled "Who Should Lead the Family?" (seemingly a natural step in the progression of " . . . Et les Pères?" and "Le Père de famille est-il un Chef?"). Videcoq argued that whenever two or more people live together under one roof, someone must be responsible for decision-making in order for there to be peace. "For all times, French law has conferred this prerogative on the husband. Has this been wrong, has this been right? Some dispute this, but most people admit that it should be so in the laws of nature." From a position of quasi-Divine authority, the father and husband's status was now reduced to a vague majority opinion that was nonetheless disputed.[93] Although the Vichy regime did further reform laws on domestic authority (see chapters 1 and 5), the issue was a contentious one, and it seemed that once again questions, rather than firm pronouncements, were the determinants.

Ambiguity and conflict implicit in the discourse on paternity during the Vichy years were often a matter of insinuations and inferred criticism of fathers in the fulfillment of their duties. Such doubt about the *père de famille* came aggressively to the fore, however, in an article titled "Le Père, ce méconnu."[94] This piece, appearing in the newspaper of the Fédération des associations de familles nombreuses de France, merits quotation at some length, because it encapsulates the sense of alienation and disappointment apparent in the portrayal of the very fathers who were to lead their families to a new age for France. The author, Jean Bergeaud, wrote:

In the family Trinity of Father, Mother, Child, let us admit that he [the father] is the one who "has not succeeded." I am only scarcely exaggerating when I say that he interests no one. The mother, with her self-sacrifice perpetually offered to the family, and the child, who represents growing life, both attract more contemplation and hearts than he does. Because he creates in a moment of joy, whereas a woman creates through suffering, it seems as if, unconsciously, society gets back at him by offering him a lesser place. One becomes emotional about mothers, or enthusiastic about children. The father, he is not interesting.

As if this were not damning enough, Bergeaud continues to explain that men themselves may be faulted for this lack of interest, for they are responsible for withdrawing from their own homes:

Very quickly the household will contain "Man, the unknown" [*l'homme cet inconnu*]—that distant, hurried father with his furtive tenderness, his annoyed reprimands or those without measure, who abandons his children to their mother whose affection they take refuge in against such abandonment. [This father] becomes "Man, the disregarded"[*l'homme, ce méconnu*], for he is severed by his own fault, most of the time, from participation in the family community, cut off because he himself so imprudently cut himself off.[95]

Instead of proposing solutions to such a startling and dangerous accusation, Bergeaud tries only to outline the problem. Many young fathers, he writes, were preoccupied with the state of affairs in 1944. How could fathers regain their proper place in the Trinity of the Family? Did this question animate Francis Poulenc, who, also in 1944, contemplated the role of the husband in *Les Mamelles de Tirésias,* a man who gives birth to 40,000 children in one day?

Here, neither the Vichy regime nor scores of concerned family activists could offer much practical help. For all the rhetoric emanating from the General Commissariat on the Family and from family associations, the men of Vichy had failed to demonstrate just how fathers were important in the construction of the new state, and how they were to be transformed from the lead-footed civil servants they were into the robust and stalwart male specimens they needed to be. Despite repeated assertions as to the significance of fathers to the National Revolution and to the very essence of the French nation, zealous family advocates were unable to enforce the link between familial obligations and national duties. Fathers were indeed essential to the ideology of the Vichy regime, but they were not necessarily vital or even present in the midst of families that the regime instrumentalized to further these political and social convictions.

Vichy authorities could furnish very few positive images of paternity in their expansive discourse on the reciprocal obligations of family and state. They had not responded adequately to the question of what, exactly, the new father would look and act like as he led his family into another era in the history of the French state. Instead of compelling images of real-life *pères de famille,* propagandists could offer only isolated and pathetic prisoners, defeated returnees who were strangers in their own homes, distant and authoritarian domestic tyrants, or, worst of all, gross degenerates crawling from one bistro to another.

Through projects such as the Chantiers de la jeunesse or the École des cadres d'Uriage, the regime attempted to delineate and actualize a new kind of virile and confident masculinity capable of combating the decadence of the Third Republic. Yet these archetypes, which shared much in common with the ideal fascist man of Nazi Germany or Mussolini's Italy, were not convincing models of that supremely French preoccupation with the *père de famille.* Although family advocates did their best to associate the new fathers with such "grand adventurers," it was, in fact, a tenuous connection, and one that might well have made people smirk. The *père de famille* was indelibly marked by doubt, absence, and resignation. Little wonder, therefore, that Henri Vibert would call on women to become mothers, but for men, a grand exhortation to paternity rang false.

5

Bringing Social Reform Home

The Incongruity of Vichy Family Ideals

Throughout May and June 1940, the French watched with horror as the front pages of daily newspapers graphically illustrated the German military advance into French territory. A growing stain suffused maps of the hexagon, depicting the ever-increasing proportions of territory occupied by the Germans. In October 1941, a new representation of France appeared on the pages of the newspaper *Familles de France*. In this map, the hexagon was divided up into traditional *départements* instead of two military zones. Here there was no blot of defeat, and the darkened crosshatched regions represented only those few *départements* in which there was as yet no family association that had joined the Federation of National Family Associations. The caption to this illustration of a unified and strong France read: "The Federation already represents a considerable force. . . . If all the heads of families knew how to unite, this force would become irresistible." Family associations, the newspaper indicated, had "spread out and radiated to all the corners of the national territory. They surpass the frontiers of the metropole. One finds them in North Africa, in Algeria, in Tunisia and in Morocco."[1] According to this optimistic assessment, family associations were reconquering the fatherland and the colonies, knitting the nation back together in the wake of division and disaster.

The history of family associations in France is both unique and exceptionally important.[2] These associations evolved from disparate groups of concerned Catholic citizens in the late nineteenth century to become significant political action groups in the mid-twentieth century, and they continue to function to this day. Family associations were part of the new apparatus Pétain hoped to use to bring about changes not only in family policy, but also in the very character of the nation. Such groups of like-minded *pères de familles* were to be important catalysts in bringing about a new position of honor for the family in the administration, in law, and in society as a whole.

Family associations were one link in a chain of administrative structures designed to promote the interests of the family from the smallest community to the highest echelons of government. From the first days after Pétain's accession to power, family activists within the Vichy regime set about reorganizing ministerial structures and reformulating laws in order to vouchsafe the family's rightful place in the nation. They struggled to implement and to adapt the provisions of Daladier's *Code de la famille,* and, as we have seen, they launched a massive propaganda campaign in favor of the legitimate, hierarchical, and traditional family. How effective were these efforts to make *la famille* the basis for a new nation? What innovations did the Vichy regime actually make, and to what extent did they succeed in the eyes of the French public and in the judgment of history?

As with so many other examples of policies enacted by the Vichy regime, family policy during the years of German occupation was rife with contradictions and inconsistencies that make any assessment of "success" a difficult undertaking.[3] The administrative mayhem and legal discrepancies surrounding social reform, not to mention the inconvenience of a continuing war, made the Marshal's goal of prompt, vigorous action difficult to carry out. Furthermore, the creation of social policy was not a one-sided process in which family experts, or Pétain himself, dictated new laws to the population.[4] Concerned citizens, many of them members of the pro-natalist movement or of national family associations newly endowed with a political voice, lobbied for specific reforms and pressed the government to grant concessions they had sought for many years. Vichy officials were caught between the desire to harness the energy of these tenacious groups, on the one hand, and the desire to maintain ultimate control over the direction and implementation of family policy, on the other.

Despite the immense effort and cost social reformers undertook to disseminate and promote new ideals for family life, the lofty images of propaganda were frequently tarnished by the harsh realities of wartime life, which could make expenditures of paper and other essential materials on such campaigns seem particularly irksome. Oftentimes the very reforms that were intended to generate solidarity and greater redistributive justice among families only led to conflict and antagonism as individuals and groups battled over definitions and benefits. Although a precise assessment of attitudes toward social reform in occupied France would be hard to come by, the numerous letters, requests, and denunciations sent in to Vichy administrators offer some understanding of the hopes for, and disillusionment with, family policy in the new regime.[5] Considering the popular demand for state assistance to families and the lengths to which officials went in proclaiming a new age for the French family, the impact of Vichy's policies appears less than spectacular.[6]

If the fortunes of the family were not an unalloyed success under the Vichy regime, those of the embattled *père de famille* were even more equivocal. Although some laws were passed favoring fathers—for example, in employment opportunities or in tax rebates—many other new provisions continued to cast doubt on the worthiness of fathers and went so far as to prosecute them with renewed vigor for offenses committed against the family. All the contradictions that had made it difficult to promote the father as a keystone of the National Revolution were rendered more concrete in laws that at best offered financial remuneration for a certain number of offspring, and at worst simply underlined the indistinct nature of paternity. Most laws passed under Vichy protected not the father but the *family*, preferably of numerous children, as defined by government authorities and an assemblage of other interested groups.[7] Although pro-natalists were more concerned with a growing population than with gender roles and in the end even the Vichy regime did little to support a return to a powerful paternal role, it was not a foregone conclusion that "the family" as a unit would win out against efforts to reinstate a traditional family hierarchy. Rather, family activists, whether in the government or in familist and pro-natalist pressure groups, clung tenaciously to traditional views on gender roles, but these became irreconcilable with the desire to direct resources to and administrate for children and families.

Despite the Vichy regime's professed desire to enhance the role of the father in political, economic, and social terms, strong fathers were, in fact, inconvenient and even threatening to a state that wished to promote the interests of families, and especially those of children. Although powerful fathers were appropriate emblems of the traditional, hierarchical society social reformers strove for, they were not fitting accomplices in the process of state intervention in family life that increasingly marked social initiatives under the occupation. Just as family associations vied with the administration for control over state representation and resources, fathers were symbols of competing authority over the nation's families, children, and civic virtue.

Establishing a locus for family and population concerns within the government was not an innovation of the Vichy regime, but a process that had begun decades before under the Third Republic. The Conseil supérieur de la natalité, a consultative legislative committee, was set up in 1920 after the losses of the Great War made pro-natalist concerns a pressing national priority. As mentioned in chapter 1, the government of Prime Minister Edouard Daladier brought such preoccupations to a new height with the creation of the High Committee on Population in February 1939. The Committee comprised the Prime Minister; representatives of the Ministries of Finance, Interior, Labor, Agriculture, and Public Health; and five additional "specialists" in the field of family and population.[8] The *Code de la famille*, which was promulgated on July 29, 1939, and was set to take effect on January 1, 1940, came out of the deliberations of the High Committee. With the outbreak of war, implementation of some of the *Code*'s provisions was hindered, yet many other measures were taken up by the Vichy regime as it strove to respond to the numerous complaints and petitions for action that poured into its offices.

Following the dissolution of the Third Republic, finding a permanent administrative home for the family was a significant concern for family activists within the new government. Several administrative changes took place in the first two years of the occupation, as personnel was shifted and offices were renamed in an effort to streamline the legislative process and to grant directors of family policy greater autonomy.[9] The General Commissariat on the Family was finally created in September 1941, with Philippe Renaudin at its head. The General Commissariat was at first under the direction of the Secretary of Health and Family; then it was relocated to a position of relative independence directly under the authority of Marshal Pétain. Therefore, despite the changing administrative structures of the first months of the regime, the supervision of family policies fell within the purview of mainly one body, the General Commissariat on the Family, and one leader, Philippe Renaudin, from September 1941 until 1944.[10]

The General Commissariat on the Family was responsible for promoting the interests of the family at all levels of government. It took the initiative in developing laws specifically related to the family and also had the power to revise laws created in other ministries that had important repercussions on the family. The Commissariat supervised the application of laws and suggested measures for improving their impact. In addition, the Commissariat was to support the work of all other private or governmental groups that served or promoted the family. Finally, and perhaps most significantly, the Commissariat was in charge of propaganda relating to the family, encouraging a "familial mystique" among the population at large that would make the motto *Travail, Famille, Patrie* a reality.[11]

It would be impossible to determine precisely the impact of this propaganda on the population of wartime France. Yet the Vichy regime was intent on determining the efficacy of the thousands of posters, brochures, radio programs, and films that were intended to convince a beaten public of the need for its own brand of National Revolution.[12] In this effort, the regional prefects played an important role as barometers of public opinion, sending in monthly reports to the Secretariat of Information on the public's reaction to state propaganda. Often these reports were remarkably frank, and they must have greatly distressed the orchestrators of publicity at Vichy. The Prefect from the Drôme, for example, stated quite bluntly that

> Despite the activity of the departmental delegate, the propaganda gives the impression of having run out of steam. It is clear that . . . the public is very difficult and remains skeptical of official propaganda that never reaches the great majority of people and only finds an attentive and agreeable ear amongst those who are already convinced.
>
> In regards to this, it must be said that propaganda in the form of tracts and brochures, at a time in which the scarcity of paper is felt everywhere, is commented on in a very negative way.[13]

The regional prefects had little good news to report, and time and again they relayed criticism of official propaganda, often about the Service du travail obligatoire that threatened to tear families apart, or about Franco-German collaboration. It seems likely that many French citizens found Vichy's propaganda overblown, immoderate, and out of touch with the realities of their everyday lives.[14] As the Prefect of the Aveyron wrote, "I cannot insist enough on the virtues, with respect to the Frenchman, of presenting propaganda which is discreet, measured, avoids vulgar insults and offers logical arguments."[15]

Yet if state propaganda on the family often struck a false note, it is clear that the issues and problems facing families during the war years were real and commanded a considerable amount of interest. The notion of state assistance to families met with widespread consensus in the French population, whether in regard to the immediate plight of impoverished prisoners' families or to long-term concerns about falling birth rates.[16] Judging from the number of letters that poured into the Marshal's office pleading the case of the family in specific or general terms and the intense activism of family associations, it is reasonable to assume that it was not the message but the medium that made the public wary of propaganda issued by the General Commissariat.[17] The Vichy regime recognized the necessity of supporting the propaganda with real action on behalf of the family. In a confidential note within the General Commissariat, one administrator noted that "such publicity must be immediately followed up with tangible applications and reforms, otherwise it will disappoint and irritate the public."[18]

Part of the apparatus intended to help with the concrete application of concern for the family was a network of regional familial delegates established in September 1940, who were to serve as liaisons between the government and individual families. The role of these twenty-three regional delegates (the number eventually rose to sixty) was to oversee all familial action and legislation at the local level. In coordination with the regional prefects, they were to deal with problems of housing, home economics, aid to families in towns under bombardment, expositions, and conferences, and they were to coordinate all measures in the application of the government's family policy. According to a contemporary commentator, Pierre Sauvage, "the regional delegates therefore have a very expansive mission, for there is scarcely a social, political, religious, economic or even athletic or artistic activity that does not concern the family."[19] The regional delegates met twice a year with Renaudin, the General Commissioner on the Family, and their role in realizing government directives for family policy was considerable.[20]

Another administrative body was established in June 1941 whose origins may be traced to similar consultative bodies in the Third Republic.[21] The Comité consultatif de la famille was intended to play an advisory role similar to those of the Conseil supérieur de la natalité and the Haut comité de la population, and the archives of these inactive committees were transferred to the secretariat of the Comité consultatif. Whereas Daladier's High Committee was primarily concerned with birth rates, rural and urban population, and the integration of immigrants, the Vichy incarnation dealt above all with the moral and material interests of the family and counted many leaders of family associations and Catholic movements among its members. The Comité consultatif, however, was neither prominent nor particularly effective: the captivity of its vice president, Vice Admiral de Penfentenyo, and the lack of any clearly defined objectives or plan of action contributed to its relatively low profile.

The Comité consultatif was responsible, however, for initiating one of the most significant innovations of French family policy in the twentieth century: the Gounot Law.[22] The law was named after Emmanuel Gounot, a lawyer from Lyon and professor at the Catholic Semaines sociales de France, who was the *rapporteur* of the commission deliberating the question of official representation for families. Promulgated on December 29, 1942, the Gounot Law established one official family association in each commune, department, and region that was ultimately represented in a national federation of family associations. Family associations were endowed with consultative and representational rights within the government, and they were to assist in managing all services related to the assistance and promotion of families. Open to all "legitimate" French families, they were generally led by *chefs de familles* elected through a system of family suffrage.[23] With the establishment of this new semipublic association grouping together private citizens in a representational body, the family was no longer simply assisted and protected by the State, it was recognized by the State and won a place among public institutions.[24]

Family associations in France played a singularly important role in initiating and shaping family policy in the twentieth century. The ideological and political perspectives of these groups varied, but for the most part they can be grouped into two broad categories. Pro-natalists, best represented by Fernand Boverat of the Alliance national contre la dépopulation or Paul Bureau of the Ligue pour la vie, were more likely to be republicans and were above all concerned with raising population growth rates. Familists, on the other hand, such as Achille Glorieux of La Plus grande famille, were often socially committed Catholics who sought a revival of traditional values and an enhanced place for the family in French society.[25] Michel Messu estimates there were about 500 organizations in the Fédération nationale des associations de familles nombreuses alone, representing 95,000 families, or approximately 500,000 people, not counting other familist or pro-natalist groups.[26] These groups were brought together into geographically based family associations through the Gounot Law, and all had a stake in the new partnership that was taking shape between formerly private lobbying groups and the public authorities.

In the 1930s and under the Vichy regime there were myriad opportunities to gather together with like-minded citizens to contemplate and act on behalf of the family. In May 1942, a "Maison de la famille" was even established at 28, place Saint-Georges in Paris, where the myriad family associations would join together under one roof.[27] What was lacking, however, was a common understanding of the respective roles of individuals, families, and the state, and any accord on what, exactly, the role of the state in the administration of family life should be. Inspired by different notions of the family ideal, most family associations had complex and sometimes contradictory motivations in both soliciting the support of the state and claiming an autonomous public role for themselves. Many, such as the influential Fédération nationale des associations de familles nombreuses mentioned above, held distinctly negative views about the intrusive, even exploitative nature of the state. In its inaugural issue of the journal *Familles de France,* the Federation prominently displayed the following quote:

> The weakness of the State with respect to all associations is extreme. The State can only exert force against each citizen taken alone, so it harasses [him] and overwhelms him with taxes and with humiliation. If private individuals could gather together, to associate and to federate, they would be all-powerful.[28]

Taking such statements into account, it is not surprising that conflict arose between the Vichy authorities and family activists who had for decades been agitating for social reforms in the face of what they perceived to be public indifference.

Many social reformers held powerful convictions about how the French family should be assisted and guided, and they were reluctant to cede government authorities a determining role in this process. One Parisian priest, Canon Gouget, wrote to Pétain in July 1940 enumerating his qualifications as a social commentator: he had won seven military medals of honor, he was a priest, a teacher, and also the treasurer of a family allowance fund. He expressed his worry that although the state certainly had a duty to protect the family, it should not enslave the family with excessive administration.[29] State assistance could make families lazy and dependent, and it made large families appear parasitic. Exaggerated "statism," he wrote, works against the family, for it

> gives too many people the impression that the State should bear the cost of children, because it wants to monopolize everything. In attacking the traditional notion of the family, it abolishes the taste for, the prestige associated with and the acceptance of family burdens. Large families are made fun of.

Gouget nevertheless insisted that family allowances were an important development and that they needed to be expanded and ameliorated.[30] The very support that risked demeaning the large family, therefore, also seemed essential to its survival.

Concerned individuals and leaders of family associations struggled to reconcile the need for greater redistributive justice and assistance to families with the ideal of a traditional, independent family sustained by its *chef*. One group of family activists argued that the power of public authorities should stop at the threshold of a man's home:

> As much as the captain of a ship . . . in mid-ocean, the father, head of the family, to whom the new society wishes to restore eminent dignity, is only responsible to God and to his own conscience in matters concerning his family life. Only in cases where he exhibits visibly improper use of his power as head should he be stripped of this power.[31]

The very act of requesting compensation from the government, however, belied this vision of a self-reliant ship's captain. Did the fact that many *pères de familles* demonstrated need in providing for their own suggest that the tentacles of state intervention would have to reach beyond the entrance to the home?

While some family activists argued that a father was sufficient unto himself in dealing with domestic matters, others stressed the relative weakness of a father who did not join with others in the protection of his rights and the advancement of the family cause. Some members of family associations reasoned, in fact, that the solitary *chef de famille* was incapable of representing his family effectively:

> An isolated head of a family has only his personal experience: he must join an association to add to his own experience the experience of numerous other families in order to acquire the *competence* required as well as the *authority* to represent them.[32]

A tension existed between the portrayal of fathers of families as autonomous and in full control of their families, and the depiction of their inadequacy and need as a spur to greater public assistance. Social reformers attempted to fashion a role for fathers that would make them both beneficiaries of greater state compensation and active and competent protagonists in the construction of a new familial order.

This ambiguity about soliciting the assistance of the state while fearing its negative effects was characteristic not only of family activists affiliated with private associations, but also of those within governmental circles. William Garcin, who headed the legislative office of the General Commissariat on the Family, warned that excessive state management of family associations could lead to "the expropriation of families by the State and the dispossession of children." The state had to strike a delicate balance between assisting and controlling families, all the while attending to the dangers of unhealthy dependence.

> It is incumbent on the State neither to sustain families financially from a detached distance, nor to come rushing to their aid with domestic troubles. The State is the protector of families. It is neither their providential benefactor nor their dry nurse.[33]

The state risked exceeding its mandate by offering too much support for families, and Garcin thought it best that the government refrain from excessive meddling in the associative and private lives of the nation's families.

Even the prospect of additional personnel within Vichy's complicated network of family advocates could be a cause of concern. When Mr. Brassel, the President of the League of Fathers and Mothers of Large Families, suggested to Pétain that each ministry, department, and regional administration should have its own affiliated familial delegate, William Garcin was reluctant. In a letter to Renaudin, the General Commissioner of the Family, he wrote:

> The Marshal promised Mr. Brassel to make good on this suggestion. However, its application seems to me to be quite complex. Personally it worries me a bit and I think we should take great care that the institution of these delegates doesn't create a troublesome precedent for the creation of other analogous delegates, leading finally to a kind of little "soviet" of bureaucrats.[34]

Even within the administration, family advocates evinced fears of a bloated bureaucracy that would sap the movement of its vitality. In this instance, representatives of "large families," William Garcin, and even Pétain himself vied for control of the momentum and implementation of family policy and strove to assert their own definitions and ideals for the French family.

Both family activists and government administrators believed that family policy should be grounded in the action and efforts of the associations that had been working among real families for years. A tension existed, however, between harnessing the energy of these established groups and organizing new family associations under the tutelage of the state. Garcin explained the General Commissariat's need for the collaboration of the family movement:

> In the midst of general incomprehension, the Commissariat is pursuing the delicate and obscure task of propagating a consciousness of the family within the administration and the public at large. We must help it to accomplish this task. An administration is only powerful if a movement within the country supports it. To bring about a Revolution of the family, a powerful family movement must be constituted within the country.[35]

The Commissariat found itself caught between the need to acknowledge the often well-formulated and persistent demands of established family associations and the recognition that this family movement was often an inchoate and disparate assemblage of requests in need of state coordination. All parties in this process of negotiation evinced fears that the line between assistance to and obstruction of family associations would be crossed as the new bodies of the administration struggled to find the proper balance.

If the state was to check its interference in family associations, family organizations had an important role to play within the state administration. This was particularly clear in a note from the General Confederation of Families that stipulated that the family association

> should be the locus of protection and education for the French Family. . . . After the state has granted the Association its legal status, the Association will be entitled to replace the town council in administering the various allowances and benefits owed to families.[36]

If family associations feared the encroachment of the state into their own affairs, they felt a keen sense of entitlement to intervene in the management of state administration for the family. In these transactions, however, the dominant energy and control was to be generated by families themselves, rather than by agents of the state. Families, according to the associations that claimed to represent them, possessed inalienable rights that the state had to recognize if it was to be legitimate. Far from being passive targets of state policy that usurped their rights and responsibilities, family associations fought for both an enhanced role for themselves and greater communication with bodies of the government.

The General Commissioner on the Family, Philippe Renaudin, was sensitive to this ambiguous and often paradoxical relationship. He expressed the situation delicately in a speech before regional and town council representatives in Paris:

If we must resolutely avoid wanting to *administer* the family, which calls out for guidance but will not tolerate being replaced, we must, on the other hand, make every effort possible to *administrate for* the family. This is why the General Commissariat on the Family resembles . . . a liaison body, a central meeting point for family interests emanating from all the ministries and administrations. . . . It functions as their conscience, attentive to the danger of bureaucracy crushing humanity, and keeping family preoccupations in full view.[37]

Renaudin was careful to describe the Commissariat in friendly terms, emphasizing its receptive coordinating role rather than suggesting any unwanted intervention in the lives of families.

The General Commissioner on the Family went to great lengths to explain that his administration intended to help the family to enter into the public domain rather than bring public authorities into the family sphere. Writing about the Gounot Law, Renaudin noted that such legislation endowing families with a public voice made France unique, and if properly implemented would make the National Revolution truly revolutionary. With his regional delegates, however, he stressed the need to convince a wary public that they were not agents of greater state interference (*il ne s'agit pas d'étatiser*) and to let associations develop of their own accord.

In addition, you must at all times give the impression that you are *suggesting*, rather than *imposing*, until the time comes when you must step in to mediate. Let private initiatives develop and intervene later to arbitrate or to approve.[38]

Far from placing the desires of the regional delegates and the public administration at the center of new initiatives in family policy, Renaudin encouraged his personnel to offer at least the appearance of acceding to the desires of private family associations.

Although the Gounot Law came out of the deliberations of the Consultative Committee on the Family, the idea of familial representation in government had been a long-standing goal of family associations. As these associations saw their efforts crowned with success in 1942, Renaudin noted that the onus would be on private citizens, rather than the administration, to make the law meaningful:

There is no doubt that family militants and representatives of the Family are now put to the test. . . . It is the first time that the Family has been offered an invitation to take up its national responsibilities . . . only the familists and heads of families will carry the burden. The success of the law will be theirs; its failure will be blamed only on them; no explanation, no regret will erase the brutal fact that the concerned families were unable to implement the family organization that has been offered to them for the first and undoubtedly the last time. In the constitutional history of a nation, a law of this kind is striking. Let us not fail to heed the call of history.

Rather than stifling private initiatives, Renaudin wanted to convince *chefs de famille* and members of family associations that governmental policy was dependent on their energy and commitment to the cause. Ever attentive to accusations of "statism" and interference in the lives of families, the General Commissioner repeatedly underlined the idea that Vichy's policy reforms were simply the embodiment of the heretofore unmet demands of a family-oriented public. There could be no question of competition between state and private associations, he noted, just as "the limbs cannot rebel against the body."[39]

However, this carefully orchestrated pact did not always function smoothly, and determining who was best able to represent family interests and carry out the National Revolution with respect to the family was a constant struggle. Regional delegates regularly encountered well-organized and ambitious private groups who would not defer readily to the Commissariat's control, however cooperative it might have been. In the elaborate preparations around Mother's Day celebrations, for example, the Commissariat directed each regional delegate to plan festivities for the event, but warned them that local prefects and heads of local family associations also wished to establish their own committees and activities. While Mother's Day was supposed to be a spontaneous manifestation of gratitude toward all French mothers, too much spontaneity could become chaos. A letter from Renaudin encouraged regional delegates to supervise and guide such local committees, keeping ultimate control over them even if another coordinating body was formally responsible.[40]

Conflict between the authority of the state and bids for control by other competing associations was also apparent in a letter from the "National Center for the Coordination of Family Movements" concerning the protection of public morality. The Center was an administrative body established in January 1941, grouping together twenty-three leagues and family associations with the goal of unifying the family movement and encouraging the growth of family associations. Leaders at the Center wrote to Joseph Barthélemy, the Minister of Justice, requesting authorization for family associations to intervene directly in cases of public indecency. The law needed to be expanded, the Center argued, to allow groups such as their own the right of direct citation against those who affronted public morality. Family associations were, after all, able to undertake more constant and sustained surveillance of suspect individuals than the state was. Noting that this would be a mark of confidence in these associations that struggled to protect public virtue, the Center lobbied for a more active public role in criminal pursuits. The Minister of Justice, however, saw the situation differently and was not eager to cede any of the privileges of his magistrates. Although family associations were welcome to assist the justices in tracking down pornographers or other immoral individuals through denunciations or written complaints, their role, the Minister decided, should not extend to criminal investigations. "It seems to us that in this matter the initiative and the exercise of investigations should be exclusively reserved for the public prosecutors," Barthélemy wrote.[41]

Private groups, however, could be quite adamant in their bids for a part in the administration of family policy. Sometimes the feeling of battling the indifference of a large bureaucracy led them to petition Pétain himself with their requests. The "National Association of French Families with Six Children or More" won an audience with the Marshal and published a story about their encounter, describing how moved they were by the leader's intelligent and sympathetic demeanor.[42] This enthusiasm became frustration, however, when the place they had been promised on the new Consultative Committee on the Family was not forthcoming.

> The Committee was created . . . on the 5th of June and no member of the Association was asked to take part. Nevertheless our Association, which has assumed the burden of defending the interests of the largest families—with eight children, on average—is more qualified than any other group to sit on the Committee and defend the rights of these very large families . . . these stem families have very different interests than those of medium-sized families.[43]

The Association was even more dismayed by the fact that a considerable number of bachelors were said to have won seats on the Committee.

The regional delegates had a difficult time managing the requests and resolutions emanating from various levels of the system. The Marshal was apt to make commitments that could not be carried out by the administration, or that simply were ill-advised. One regional delegate wrote to his supervisor in the Commissariat asking that requests for assistance sent directly to Pétain be, at least in questionable cases, reviewed at the local level first. He had been informed that a prostitute received a gift of 250 francs from the Marshal, and in his own district a young woman who had borne nine illegitimate children, of whom four were conceived with her brother, had received 200 francs. Such mistakes, which "had a deplorable effect on the population," he wrote, could be avoided if regional delegates were consulted first.[44]

It was not only the administrative confusion surrounding family policy or certain imprudent acts of charity that could draw complaints from the population, however. Vichy authorities had been dealing with a profusion of criticism and protests about family policy emanating from citizens and members of family associations since the summer of 1940, and indeed before. In the midst of a worsening international situation and the "phony war" of 1939–40, Daladier's offices were besieged with letters complaining about either the provisions of the Code de la famille, or the lack of its full and timely implementation. Directors of family policy under the Third Republic were concerned enough about public reactions to the Code de la famille to have censors watch local papers for any "malevolent attack sowing discord amongst families or systematically underlining the so-called inequalities" of the laws of July 29, 1939.[45]

Yet inequalities there were, and concerned members of the public did not hesitate to point these out to the various arms of the administration concerned with family policy. Vichy authorities were faced with the monstrous task of implementing the provisions of the Code de la famille in the midst of war, occupation, and changing personnel and were privately quite frank about the widespread disappointment many people felt in the Code. When Vichy officials published new conditions for the application of the Code in the *Journal officiel,* they were met with virtually unanimous disapproval. One administrator wrote to the Minister of the Interior that "since the appearance of these new conditions in the *Journal officiel* of 19 November 1940, it is no longer grievances but acerbic criticism that arrives at the Marshal's Cabinet."[46] Another memorandum reported the tremendous frustration family policy had provoked in all segments of the population and noted that the same "familists" who complained in fact "constituted the healthy segment of the country."[47]

One of the most fundamental disagreements arising out of discussions of the Code and the subsequent changes enacted in family policy under Vichy concerned the very definition of a "large" family. The French Association of Families of Six Children, for example, wrote to the Marshal that the Code was an "abominable mystification, in which the only ones to benefit in even the smallest degree were medium families of three or four children, unduly qualified as large."[48] Fernand Boverat of the Alliance Nationale even took Pétain to task for referring to the family of two children as "the minimum French family" in one of his reports. He wrote to the Marshal:

> This affirmation is, from a demographic point of view, an inconceivable heresy; a family that produces only two children in each generation is condemned to disappear. . . .
>
> The minimum family is the family of three children, and there is no more indispensable truth to be imposed on the minds of Frenchmen than this, if we wish to defeat depopulation. . . .
>
> Permit me therefore to underline how important it would be, in my opinion, for you to affirm in your upcoming speeches that the family of three children is the minimum family.[49]

The secretary charged with family affairs did not appreciate these comments and dismissed them as a simple play on words, but the letter was symptomatic of the general confusion that surrounded definitions of the "normal," "large," and "minimum" family under Vichy.

Besides receiving complaints from leaders of family associations, the administration was also deluged with letters from individuals contesting the state's definitions of the number of children required to qualify one for family allowances. In an effort to promote larger families and to spare tight wartime finances, families with only one child were no longer considered eligible for allowances. Only families with at least two children under the age of seventeen would receive aid. One *ancien combattant* wrote to Pétain complaining that he had ceased to receive any subsidy, even though he had raised three children. He argued that men who had supported children for any length of time but were no longer their guardians should still be considered as fathers of several children. "Your paternal beneficence towards us," he wrote, "prompts me to disclose my personal circumstances to you."[50] William Garcin of the legal office also recognized the injustice of considering fathers of grown children as being without offspring and making them pay into family allowance schemes at rates of assessment equivalent to bachelors when they had never benefited from family allowances themselves.[51] Instead of generating national solidarity through redistributive allowance schemes, the provisions of the Family Code often fueled even more disagreements as the interested parties squabbled over terminology and compensation.

Even the Code's provision to tax bachelors at higher rates in order to subsidize family allowances was not enough for some zealots, who wanted to penalize "sterile" individuals for their unpatriotic behavior.[52] Jean Vidales from Zarbes, for example, wrote to the Marshal suggesting not only that bachelors pay higher taxes, but also that fathers who had only one or two children be made to pay others outright for raising children. A man with only one child was, after all, essentially a "parasite," living off the good will and financial sacrifice of others in order to enjoy greater pleasures himself.[53] Another leader of a family association, Colonel Faveau of the National Association of French Families of Six Children and More, won a private interview with Pétain in which he requested that a law be passed formally prohibiting any salary increases for bachelors. In the name of "strict justice," all pay raises were to be a function of increased family allowances to worthy leaders of families.[54]

Yet despite the widespread and bitter condemnation of *célibataires*, there was little agreement on who they were, exactly, and how they should be penalized. As early as July 1939, a woman wrote to Prime Minister Daladier contesting the provisions of the Code de la famille concerning taxes on single people. Although she expressed her great satisfaction with the main principles of the Code and the logic behind the tax, she asked that single women over the age of forty-five be exonerated, because they were almost always burdened with responsibility for older, impecunious family members. Furthermore, she argued that being a *célibataire* was not the fault of women such as herself who had wanted to marry and raise children but who had been thwarted by the destruction of the First World War and the selfishness of other women with generous pensions. Single women over forty-five "suffer morally as well because their fiancés disappeared during the War or its aftermath . . . war widows, all the while, were able to remarry with their pensions, to the detriment of these poor girls about whom no one ever thinks!"[55] Such women were not the same as the "voluntarily sterile" who lived off and were defended by the children of others, but how could the law discriminate between well-meaning and unworthy *célibataires*?

Another woman who wrote to Pétain in late 1940 echoed the idea that single women were victims, rather than active agents, of their "sterility." Alicia Alleaume complained that society, and the *anciens combattants* of the last war in particular, were exceptionally cruel to single women over the age of thirty, branding them as "white widows." Unmarried women, she complained, were often labeled as ugly, misshapen, or dissolute, when nothing was unappealing about them but their luck:

> Most of these women, who are also victims of the other war because many of the men who could have been their husbands were killed, are disdained and slandered by veterans and sometimes by the very leaders of the leagues that help support veterans' widows or their wives.

These women longed for conjugal happiness and motherhood, but their dreams had been cruelly dashed by the same war that killed fighting men. Mlle Alleaume asked the Marshal to intercede with the veterans' associations on behalf of "white widows," encouraging them to improve their behavior and evince more sympathy. In the fight against "sterility," single women were not to be penalized for circumstances beyond their control and were not to be taxed at the same rates as the truly deliberate male bachelors who had only disregard for the nation's future.[56]

Disputes over tax rates for single people were symbolic of the general confusion surrounding definitions of appropriate familial (and anti-familial) behavior during the Vichy regime. If the distinctions between worthy and unworthy citizens were so important to the proper implementation of family policies, how would the state and concerned individuals discriminate between different classes of people, and what criteria would be used? The issue was valid not only for punishing bachelors, but also for rewarding family members who *had* performed their patriotic duties and offered the nation more children.

If the new state was to be truly familial, then families, and fathers in particular, were due special status and recognition that would remedy the injustices wrought by years of republican "individualism." Even before the fall of the Third Republic, in fact, some vocal *pères de famille* expressed concern about safeguarding their rights as fathers and petitioned Prime Minister Daladier to offer fathers special insignia denoting their distinguished condition. "This measure," according to René Courtier, the Senator from Seine-et-Marne who took up their case, "would offer great moral advantages as it would prevent illegitimate claims, and would leave the way clear for the justifiable demands that we all have an interest in fulfilling."[57] Although this request did not lead to the formal adoption of a badge or emblem for fathers, it signaled that the identity of the *père de famille* was both uncertain and the object of solicitation. How, therefore, were fathers singled out for special treatment under the Vichy regime, and what were the distinguishing marks of a good father?

Besides the unmistakable (and dubious) distinction of being a father stripped of his paternal rights by a state-mandated decision of forfeiture (*déchéance de la puissance paternelle*), it appeared that one of the only marks separating one father from another was the sheer number of his children. This was, after all, the logic behind several of the proposals for family suffrage that had arisen in the Chamber of Deputies and the Senate from the mid-nineteenth century on. In March 1928, a law on army recruitment had come into effect that put fathers of four or more children in the last class of the second reserve for the draft; in 1939, fathers of four or more children were sent back to their homes.[58]

The leader of the Departmental Council of the Seine, Victor Constant, also made use of such criteria in evaluating himself as a *père de famille*. In a speech before town council members at the Hôtel de Ville praising the General Commissioner of the Family, Philippe Renaudin, Constant explained that his associate, M. Taittinger, in fact had more right to speak than he did:

> Mr. Taittinger would have thanked you with more authority and with more eloquence than I will be able to. Both of us are fathers of large families, but he is the father of a larger family, and therefore he enjoys a primacy that I would not want to disavow.[59]

Although there was disagreement over just how many children constituted a "large" family, it seemed as if the number of offspring, rather than any quality inherent to the man, was still the most important factor in defining a good *père de famille*.

The Vichy regime did, however, offer fathers certain special exemptions and advantages that gave some substance to the highly publicized goal of reinstating the rights of the *père de famille*.[60] One of these benefits included a directive to regional prefects granting them the power to impose quotas for employees with families in various industries. This law of October 8, 1940, stipulated that fathers of at least three children and widows with two children in their care would benefit from a hiring priority. Another law, of December 27, 1940, mandated that fathers were to be granted priority in rehiring after losing their jobs, and were to be excluded from layoffs as industries tried to make room for demobilized soldiers (law of June 30, 1941). Through a law of September 14, 1941, candidates for jobs within the state administration who were also fathers of large families were to be accorded priority over other equally qualified candidates in hiring. In addition, the number of years required for a father to qualify for a raise was reduced by one year for every child after the third, and state employees were allowed to retire one year after the usual age limit per child in their care. *Fonctionnaires* with families were given priority in choosing a period of annual vacation— perhaps fathers would take advantage of this prerogative with their discounts on rail tickets of 30 percent for three children and 75 percent for a family of at least six children.

In addition to these laws regulating the workplace, a law of February 5, 1941, stipulated that fathers of families were not to be discriminated against in rental of domestic or professional property. Landlords could not "refuse to lease a vacant locale on the pretext of the number of children of the potential renter" and could be fined one hundred to one thousand francs if found guilty of this offense.[61] Furthermore, a series of laws passed in late 1940 and 1941 granted fathers extra allowances and bonuses for obtaining and cultivating a "worker's garden." Special cards were issued qualifying fathers for seeds, tools, fencing, and piping dispensed by the Secours national. The Agence française d'information de presse was pleased to report that in the automobile industry alone, 1,500 fathers of three children had a garden of at least 200 square meters in 1941. In 1942, fathers of one and two children created 5,500 new gardens.[62] Banks offered loans for the acquisition of the *jardins ouvriers* whose repayment schedule was based on the size of the applicant's family. Families with at least six children could therefore obtain a mortgage of up to twenty-five years for their garden plot.[63] Gardening, of course, was a most appropriate pastime for a *père de famille*, keeping him from idling away hours at the bistro and helping him to provide nourishment for his family.

Although it did not refer specifically to fathers, a new addition to article 213 of the Civil Code, concerning marital powers, was perhaps one of the most striking pieces of legislation underlining the authority of the head of household. Whereas in 1938 this article of the Code had been changed to read "the husband, head of the family," on September 22, 1942, the article was again modified to proclaim "the husband *is* the head of the family" (my italics). As a primary community, the family was to play a key role in the political future of the nation, but it had to be hierarchical and under the firm control of the *chef de famille*. Vichy legislators obviously saw fit to make this position more clear with a simple declarative sentence rather than a dependent clause.[64]

In many ways, however, this simple word change actually symbolized a subtle shift in the content of the law that made this ringing proclamation more conditional than it appeared. According to Joseph Barthélemy, the Minister of Justice in 1942, the new formulation of "the husband is the head of the family" was more a translation of a duty than a right. This phrase was, after all, followed immediately by the stipulation that the husband exercised this authority in the communal interest of the household and the children. In addition, the law added a completely new phrase indicating that the wife "collaborated with the husband in assuring the moral and material direction of the family," a recognition of the important role women—particularly those whose husbands were absent—played in managing the household.

The new article 213 of the Code was above all concerned with marital rights and responsibilities, rather than with enhancing the authority of the father of the family.[65] While the new phrasing seemed to indicate an emphatic reassertion of a man's rights, in fact the law sprang from the desire to maintain the rights of the family as a whole by endowing wives with civil powers over their children when their husbands were incapacitated or absent. Under the new regulations, for example, the wife of a prisoner could now make decisions about a child's education rather than waiting for authorization from her husband. As to the rights of fatherhood, the new law in no way expanded or reasserted a man's authority over his children, for his authority was "in no way intended to indulge his whims or serve his interests, but for the good of family community."[66] A. Théry, a professor at the Catholic Institute of Paris, commented on the law of September 22:

> As to paternal authority, changing according to the times, places, traditions and temperaments, how difficult it is to translate this complex sentiment into a legal code. This is why our legislators have remained hesitant. Here again, it concerns the protection of an incompetent, and the precautions to be taken against him—the Code is satisfied with tracing general rules and preventing draconian measures.[67]

Far from bolstering the status of the *père de famille*, therefore, the law remained vague on paternal rights, and only partially reaffirmed the position of the husband. Those seeking to reconstruct the nation on the strength of the *père de famille* would find little support in this statute. Furthermore, Théry's comments as to the inconstancy of paternal authority were hardly indicative of new respect for the timeless traditions of fatherhood.

The same ambiguity was present in new legislation on supplemental allowances to households with only one income (*salaire unique*). The law of November 17, 1941, offered assistance to families with children who relied on a single salary, usually that of the father. In cases where fathers were the sole breadwinners, families with two or more children were awarded bonuses from 10 to 30 percent of the mean Departmental wage.[68] The ideological impetus behind the law on *salaire unique* was clear: the regime wished to encourage, or to force, women back to their "natural" place by offering a stipend for stay-at-home mothers.[69] Yet although the single-salary allowance strove to sanction those "traditional" families in which the father worked and the mother raised children at home, the bonus was in fact offered to either men *or* women, and in some cases offered single women with children in their care a larger allowance.[70] It was possible, therefore, that in families where the father was unemployed and only the mother worked, the single-salary bonus would be added to *her* salary. Clearly the ideological prescriptions for family life were at odds with the realities and exigencies of occupied France, as women's work outside the home remained at relatively high levels or even increased during the war years.[71]

The *allocation du salaire unique* was intended to enforce gendered norms for family life, but by offering bonuses to both fathers and mothers it did little to enhance the personal rights of the working *père de famille* or to bolster his status as a sole breadwinner. The General Commissariat on the Family recognized that even with the single-salary bonus, the standard of living of a father of numerous children would still not equal that of a bachelor, and it therefore worked to institute a family wage that would truly balance the two circumstances. Yet this family wage never became a reality under the Vichy regime, and the *allocation de salaire unique* remained an ambiguous measure of state assistance to families that did not legally single out fathers for special treatment or added privileges.[72]

Even some of the prerogatives offered by the state to fathers of large families enjoyed less unanimity than family activists would have liked. The notion that *pères de familles nombreuses* should be rewarded with special concessions in the workplace, for example, could come into conflict with the requirements of certain professional callings. Although it seemed self-evident to many familists that fathers of large families were inherently better citizens and naturally qualified for a variety of endeavors, this idea was less compelling to others. General Huntziger, for example, vigorously opposed the idea that fathers of large families would be given special preference in the army and might be promoted before others by virtue of their family size. He protested that the measures of the 1940 law favoring fathers could never be applied in the military, for in this realm only technical qualifications could be considered.

> I believe that the principle in this above-mentioned law is particularly dangerous. . . .

Professional qualities and familial burdens are two absolutely independent issues that must each be treated in the proper context and with the appropriate means, the former in professional terms, and the latter in social terms. The main bonuses foreseen—concerning promotion, age and residence requirements—emerge from technical merit and the needs of the military, and not from one's status as the father of a large family.[73]

When the tenet that fathers of large families were superior citizens was applied in a real-life situation, it was less self-evident that the number of one's offspring was, in fact, such a determining factor in a man's worth.

The needs of the military had frequently come into conflict with the projects of family advocates, especially in the spring of 1940 as administrators struggled to enact the provisions of the Code de la famille. In particular, the stipulation that fathers of four or more children be transferred to the last category of the draft caused a considerable amount of confusion as family advocates pushed for even more rights for fathers drafted into the army. Fernand Boverat of the Alliance nationale requested that fathers of three children also be exempted from military service, but Daladier responded that the privileges granted to fathers of four children had already reduced the number of troops considerably.[74] The vice president of the High Committee on Population, Georges Pernot, a Catholic lawyer and father of seven children, then suggested that fathers of large families who had forfeited their paternal rights or had been convicted of family abandonment might be drafted into the army, and could make up for the loss of those fathers of three children whom the army could let go.[75] According to Pernot, the nation needed its good *pères de familles* at home; the army could make do with a lesser quality of man.

There were, however, problems with a law whose criteria included only the number of a man's offspring as opposed to any measure of his performance of the duties of paternity. Such special exemptions were a nod in the direction of rewarding fathers with special status, but they could recompense either a worthy or an unworthy man if the only basis for this status was a familial head count. In April 1940, Pernot noted that since the general mobilization, many "suspicious legitimizations" had been recorded, releasing more and more men from the obligations of military service. It seems that a number of men were declaring themselves the fathers of children heretofore considered illegitimate, born of unknown fathers, and were thus able to benefit from the law on military exemptions. Such undeserving men were surely not the intended beneficiaries of this law, yet they could make themselves known officially as fathers of numerous children, seriously compromising the moral impact of the legislation.[76]

Pétain himself caused an uproar among Vichy administrators when he interceded on behalf of his gardener and inadvertently trifled with the very legal definition of paternity. In an episode emblematic of the confusion and contradictions inherent in the construction of family policy during the occupation, the *Loi du jardinier* illustrated the shifting nature of paternity and the plasticity of its acquisition or disavowal. The "Gardener's Law" originated from a request from Madame la Maréchale, Pétain's wife, who wished to regularize the situation of their private gardener. This man had evidently conceived children with his mistress while married to another woman and wished to legitimate them legally, a request that was favored by both La Maréchale and Pétain himself. The law, however, passed through none of the conventional channels; it was forced through by Pétain as a virtual decree in September 1941.

The uproar caused by this radical provision was documented in telegrams and letters intercepted by censors and forwarded to those responsible for family policy within the regime. One letter, from the Légion française des combattants, intercepted in October 1941, commented on the shocking consequences of this law and noted that a father could very well have both legitimate and illegitimate children of the same age born of parallel unions and rendered equal before the law by legitimization after the fact. The author questioned whether this was simply a law "intended to give satisfaction to an eminent person, which would be inadmissible."[77] Another letter, from the social-Catholic Union féminine civique et sociale (UFCS), complained that this was one of the most nefarious acts of moral and familial legislation, for under the pretext of pity for the child it sanctioned adultery and struck a death blow to marriage itself. The UFCS cautioned that not only would the new law lead to more divorces, but it would also lead more men, particularly returning prisoners, to disavow paternity if children could be legitimated by their wives' lovers. Unfaithful wives would seek to legitimate the children born of their accomplices in adultery while their husbands were away. The law could only result in a general breakdown of legitimate family structure.[78] A note from within the administration conceded that Madame La Maréchale was simply interested in the personal case of her gardener and was "without doubt little informed of current juridical principles." M. Lavagne of the Ministry of Family and Health protested, "Not even Léon Blum and the Popular Front dared to go this far!" Even though the Director of Civil Affairs was opposed to the idea, he and the Minister of Justice, Joseph Barthélemy, "fell over themselves with servility to draw up the project, and abuse the confidence of the Marshal." The Chief of Pétain's cabinet was scandalized by this provision, as were Renaudin and Huard of the Ministry of Family and Health. Nevertheless, the law was adopted on September 3, 1941, without the signatures of the leaders whose approval was technically required for any action related to the family. A law unconditionally legitimating the children of a father's adultery contradicted every principle of family ideology professed by Vichy propagandists. It served in the eyes of many to cheapen the definition of paternity by sanctioning the irresponsible behavior of unfaithful men, and it cast doubt on the principle that fatherhood was established only through the legitimate bonds of marriage. The fact that such a paradoxical piece of legislation could be pushed through by Pétain and his wife illustrates the absence of both clear streams of authority within the regime and any compelling consensus on the goals of family policy within the administrative structures established for precisely those ends. It also cast doubt on the status of paternity itself, by bringing to light the less than honorable conditions under which children were sometimes fathered in the disordered climate of occupied France.

While the *Loi du jardinier* compromised legal definitions of paternity through the admission of adultery, other social commentators cast aspersions on fatherhood by questioning the very impulse to create children. A constant tension that was played out in debates about family size and paternal status, for example, was the question of whether a man had fathered many children out of a sense of national duty or simply out of ignorance and debauch. Internal notes from within the Vichy administration underlined the dangers inherent in the idea that all people should be encouraged to have more children regardless of their qualifications or adherence to the family mystique. What was needed, according to one man who wrote to the General Commissariat, was to select a new familial elite. The laws, however, spoke only of numbers and based the regeneration of France on masses of corrupt and imperfectible people.[79] Leaders of certain family associations tried to convince government administrators that the family of five children was the only normal and healthy family and was not peopled with imbeciles or drunkards as others might have suspected.[80] One Vichy administrator admitted privately, however, that it was clear that "a certain number of large families are due simply to alcoholism."[81] This was hardly reassuring for leaders of the National Revolution attempting to make fathers of large families the heroes of the day.

Yet it is obvious that fathers were not, in fact, heroes under the Vichy regime; they appeared as targets of state censure more often than as vanguards of the new order. This became obvious in a new law on *abandon de famille,* which the administration prosecuted with increasing rigor. In a new law of July 23, 1942, the scope of the 1924 law was expanded to include crimes of moral abandonment, and the length of time that had to elapse before the offender could be brought to trial was reduced to two months.[82] Although the law ostensibly could be applied to either fathers or mothers, criminalizing family abandonment had been a long-standing objective of the Catholic women's organization, the Union féminine civique et sociale, and it was clear that wayward fathers were the primary target of the new law.[83]

Marcelle Dutheil, a legal consultant for the UFCS, wrote a book on *L'Abandon de famille,* discussing the origins of the law and outlining the conditions for its application. In the preface to the book, the jurist André Rouast declared that "of all the measures taken since the Armistice to reinstate the family . . . the most auspicious has been the law on family abandonment." Dutheil herself was especially interested in the new stipulation in the law that mothers could be granted the rights of *puissance paternelle* when their husbands were absent or declared unfit. Up until then, she noted, "authority within marriage remained the apanage of the father, whatever his deficiencies, his inadequacies and their repercussions. One wonders about the causes of this passivity."[84]

Not only could mothers now retain the rights of paternal control and prevent their children from becoming charges of the state when their fathers abandoned them, but the law could pursue the perpetrators themselves more actively. Dutheil related the example of a social worker who had been assisting a family for several years:

> Peace had always reigned until the day the father became acquainted with a female co-worker at the factory. From then on, violent scenes followed one after the other. Finally a certain Saturday he did not come home and he notified his wife that he was taking up residence with his "friend. . . ." The law had just been published. The social worker, finding out about this, wrote to the fickle husband warning him of the penalties he was incurring through his conduct, and a few days later, after having thought about it, he came back home.[85]

Fathers were clearly the principal offenders in crimes of family abandonment, and Dutheil welcomed the law as a measure of justice against such unfit parents.

The only problem with the application of the law in 1942, according to Dutheil, was that many unfit fathers had in fact left the country to work in labor camps in Germany and were therefore less accessible to prosecutors. The "Occupying Power," she reported, had regrettably outlawed any civil suits against workers in Germany, and this made tracking down family abandoners much more difficult. She did not seem to recognize the irony of the situation, in which the Germans protected *pères de familles* from prosecution by the French authorities, the same authorities who claimed to be exalting the father in social and family policy.

Other family activists such as the omnipresent Fernand Boverat also decried the inaccessibility of men mobilized for the army, for many of them were guilty of family abandonment. He complained that such men benefited from equal or greater resources in the army, yet they refused to share their wealth with wives and children and enjoyed immunity under the law. Boverat demanded that justice be served for mothers and children, emphasizing the fortunate positions of the soldiers rather than acknowledging the fact that they were headed for combat, imprisonment, or death.[86] Family activists equated fatherhood with national duty, but it was clear that the formula

MÈRES FRANÇAISES

ÉPOUSES ABANDONNÉES,

un grand scandale va cesser

L'ABANDON DE FAMILLE

devient un délit

Au bout de 2 mois d'abandon volontaire du foyer, le père de famille, peut sur la plainte de la mère, être poursuivi pour abandon de famille et être puni d'une peine d'emprisonnement de 3 mois à 1 an, ou d'une amende de 1.000 à 20.000 francs. S'il ne verse pas la pension alimentaire à laquelle il a été condamné (après divorce ou séparation de corps) il sera passible des mêmes peines.

LA FRANCE vous défend

ET DÉFEND VOTRE FOYER

Figure 5.1. "Abandoned Wives, a Great Scandal Will Cease." Commissariat général à la famille, Propagande en faveur de la famille, Bibliothèque de documentation internationale contemporaine.

worked only one way: paternity might excuse one from the obligations of war, but military service did not absolve one of paternal responsibilities.

The prosecution of wayward fathers was underlined also in an intense propaganda campaign publicizing the new law of July 1942. In a brochure addressed to mothers, the General Commissariat on the Family vowed that France would defend them and their homes (see fig. 5.1). There was no question of the gender-neutral character of the law as the pamphlet declared:

> Abandoned wives, a great scandal is about to cease. Family abandonment has become a criminal offense. After two months of voluntary abandonment of the home, the father of a family can, on the complaint of the mother, be pursued for family abandonment and be punished with a penalty of imprisonment for three months to a year, or with a fine of one thousand to twenty thousand francs. . . .

The law stipulated that fathers who were ordered to pay food allowances to their wives after separation or divorce could be punished in the same way if they failed to keep up with payments. Although the Vichy regime offered fathers rhetorical adulation, in counter-images of propaganda and in the concrete terms of the law it seemed as if fathers were more frequently the objects of criminal investigations than of praise and status. Once again, images announcing the law on family abandonment brought to mind the persistent accusation of male inadequacy as they emphasized the absence of the father. The Ministry of Justice zealously pursued complaints of family abandonment that came into the Marshal's office, even those that were found to be without merit.[87]

Ironically, men were chastised for their irresponsibility and neglect even as young women wishing to start a family eagerly sought them out. As if to underscore the idea that men were inconstant, unavailable, or loath to make a commitment to family, women wrote in to Pétain himself asking that he help them to find a suitable marriage partner. Appealing to Pétain's "paternal" nature, young women complained that they had been unable to find anyone who corresponded to their simple desires for a companion. They were ready to "work with all their strength to remake a beautiful France," but where were the men?[88] Such requests for a matrimonial introduction may have been the touching or bizarre entreaties of a few women, but they also signaled the promotion of a new alliance joining women as future or actual mothers and the state, an association that was predicated on the estrangement of men from the family unit. Just as propaganda played up the state's solicitude for mothers and children in the face of paternal abnegation, marriage requests written to Pétain paralleled the idea that due to either their scarcity or their inconstancy, men were not easily drawn into and bound by the family sphere.

This is not to say that women and mothers were in league with the state and joined with government administrators in a grand project to "stamp out the spirit of independence of the working man," as Jacques Donzelot has asserted in reference to the late nineteenth century.[89] Women were not powerful or even unwitting agents of control over husbands and fathers, for they were often manipulated as voiceless objects of state propaganda and government intervention themselves. Several important studies have documented the restrictive gender prescriptions imposed on women throughout the Third Republic and under the Vichy regime, and the way in which state assistance to mothers worked to protect the biologically ordained role of motherhood, rather than to enhance women's rights and status within the family or society at large.[90]

Yet beyond the discourse on motherhood, the untold story of this drama involving families and the state concerns the way fathers were portrayed as marginal characters in the family sphere, and were not seen by government administrators and family activists as helpful allies in the protection of mothers and children. Although ideologically the Vichy regime paid homage to the status and sovereignty of fatherhood, enumerating their sacrifices and the rights they were due, fathers were not trusted with the essential tasks of reconstructing the nation's families. Far from being at the heart of efforts to bring about a National Revolution of the family in France, fathers were more often objects of suspicion and criminal pursuit. The *père de famille* was most evident in the machinery of government when his inadequacies prompted intervention by the state.

Such mistrust of fathers came through clearly in the payment of allowances to families. Although the benefits were calculated on the basis of a man's salary, most *caisses de compensation* paid the money directly to mothers, fearing the worst if it were added to the man's salary. This was spelled out in the Code de la famille, complemented by a statute of April 24, 1940, that indicated that allowances were to be paid

1) To the mother, or, by default, to the person effectively responsible for the maintenance and education of the children when the father is stripped of paternal powers. . . .
3) To the mother or her relatives, when payment to the father or his relatives risks depriving the children of the benefits of family allowances, according to information received.[91]

The father was scarcely mentioned in this attribution of benefits, except to underline the ways in which he might have defaulted on his paternal responsibilities or might be an unfit parent likely to keep benefits from his own children. The Vichy government did not reverse the provisions of Daladier's code; rather, it reinforced and reiterated the notion that fathers might be unfit parents who were undeserving of the benefits of the Family Code.[92]

This attitude was echoed beyond government circles, as was evident in a tract published by the Alliance nationale contre la dépopulation. Under the heading "Must one pay allowances to the mother of the family?" the Alliance noted that the more generous the benefits, the more crucial it was to prevent waste.

> The best means to achieve this is, in our opinion, to pay them to the mother of the family, as more than half of the allowance funds presently do, for when allowances are subverted from their intended destination, it is, in the great majority of cases, because the head of the family spends the money at the wine merchant. It is, on the other hand, very rare for mothers raising children to follow this unfortunate example.[93]

Not only were fathers superfluous to the partnership between mothers and the solicitude of public authorities; they were potentially active agents in the destruction of familial goods. The *père de famille* had to be circumvented, neutralized by a system that would palliate the effects of his irresponsibility. The effusive propaganda of family activists under Vichy did little to counter the marginalization of fathers in social reform and law. In this respect, the regime merely built on and accelerated a process of devaluing fathers that had begun decades before, even as it loudly proclaimed official projects for the rehabilitation of paternity.

The *père de famille* was at best inconvenient and at worst injurious to the projects of a state administration fixed on the revival of families around a core of mothers and children. Had fathers become in reality what official propaganda held them to be, their strength and independence would make state assistance appear both useless and unnecessarily meddlesome. Vichy promoters had insistently forwarded an image of *pères de famille* as a new elite, a politically astute and competent citizenry that had greater rights to participation in the government of the nation. Yet if they were more entitled to recognition in civil society and in the direction of their families, how would the nation ensure the protection of children for whom such paternal domination was dangerous? The Vichy administration struggled to strike a balance between bids for power from family associations and its own determination to shape family policy; the entreaties of individual fathers only complicated this dynamic. Demands for special privileges for fathers appeared considerably less compelling when compared with the rights of children and mothers.

One father protested, for example, that he could not get a priority ration card, a privilege that would help him to feed his large family and send packages to his two sons imprisoned in Germany. Whereas mothers of many children were offered *cartes de priorité*, this official concession was not extended to fathers. "We fathers . . . thus have only one right, to sacrifice our flesh when it's time to defend the well-being and sinecure of the voluntarily sterile, who can only offer the nation bedroom maneuvers."[94] As this father of a large family complained, there were few tangible benefits to being a father despite the effusive rhetoric about their special place in the public realm. Even requests for symbolic recognition, such as government-sponsored telegrams to men mobilized in the army announcing the births of their children, met with negative responses, and even a note of sarcasm.[95]

What were, finally, the rights and privileges offered *pères de famille* in the new France? Family suffrage was in fact instituted in elections of the regional family associations, but no father can be said to have cast an important vote in any political election, as plans for a new constitution under Vichy dissolved into an increasingly repressive and powerless regime. The authority of husbands was accentuated with one verb, "is," in article 213 of the Civil Code, but the impact of this linguistic change was hardly overwhelming. Fathers gained certain privileges in employment opportunities and protection against layoffs, but it is unclear whether such provisions had an impact on the status of the *père de famille*. Much of the debate around labor legislation under Vichy seemed to focus on preventing women from "stealing" jobs from men rather than on any real effort to promote fathers of large families over bachelors.[96] Fathers were favored in tax schedules and with reductions in railroad fares—both provisions we might consider just today, but hardly the rallying cry of a new brand of Revolutionaries. If fathers wished to embody the elite of the National Revolution, they would have to manage it on their own.

Advocates of the rights of fathers were caught in a bind. On the one hand, the government offered few rewards for the duty many fathers felt they performed by raising children for the nation. On the other hand, if they attempted to capitalize on their sacrifices and pushed for official recognition and compensation, they appeared as "eternal solicitors," whose very requests subverted the traditional prescriptions of their gender and of paternity. Vichy's ideology—that fathers should be strong, independent, and filled with initiative—contradicted its legal codes, which predicted that fathers would be untrustworthy, dishonest, and irresponsible with resources. If the Civil Code of 1804 was predicated on the notion of a just and sagacious father of means, the Code as it appeared in 1945 seemed to acknowledge a poor, alcoholic, and potentially unreliable father who was no longer the focus of the state's interaction with the family sphere.

Susan Pedersen has argued that French policymakers' emphasis on the well-being and rights of children made family policy rather agnostic with respect to gender roles and "left negotiations over gender roles to individual women and men."[97] This did not preclude the possibility that policymakers may have had deeply conventional views of relations between men and women but that such attitudes were so unchallenged as to make provisions like payment of allowances to mothers unproblematic. If a "gendering" policy is defined through its reward of certain conventional gendered behaviors, such as motherhood for women or wage-earning for men, then French policy was indeed comparatively less "gendered" than was, for example, British family policy at the same time.[98] However, the reason for this apparent passivity was that gender roles for men were in fact highly problematic, for traditional visions of fatherhood were fundamentally at odds with visions of a society in which the state took an active role in the welfare of children. For French policymakers, fathers could not be trusted to care for children in an appropriate way through increases in their salaries; instead, public authorities relied on mothers and other benefits directed at children to protect the nation's families. In this sense, therefore, French family policy was not so much "laissez-faire" in its prescription of gender roles as it was essentially hampered by the struggle between two irreconcilable ideas: paternal authority and public accountability. In a clash between ideology and policy, fathers were losers in the contest between the *père de famille* as grand adventurer and the *père de famille* as impediment to greater state involvement in private life.

The creation of family policy was not a one-sided, intrusive process in which the state moved, uninvited, into the family sphere. At times almost grudgingly, at other times with clear policy objectives, public authorities negotiated with concerned citizens, family associations, and religious groups over the government and protection of families. For Vichy authorities, however, it was easier to bargain with mothers, onto whom propaganda projected nothing but the most comfortingly traditional behavior. Whereas the ideal mother was always depicted in state propaganda as selfless, prolific, and nurturing, fathers often appeared as active agents in the destruction of the family and the nation. At their most threatening, fathers could interpose themselves between the benevolence of the state and their own children, diverting essential funds from the family and squandering resources on their own selfish pleasures.

Such negative perceptions could not help but influence family legislation in a way that ultimately undermined the status and privileges associated with paternity. Under Vichy, family activists continued to push for greater rights and protection for families, but the abstract "family" moved farther and farther away from an impermeable domestic circle firmly ruled by an all-powerful father. The family was indeed coming to the fore under the Vichy regime, but this did not mean that fathers were leading the procession. As the foundation of society itself, the family required a legal status that superseded the authority of the father. The protection of children served to justify the dismantling of paternal prerogatives in the Third Republic, and the notion of the best interests of children increasingly won out against demands for greater paternal recognition under Vichy. Even though conservative family advocates made their best efforts to link the political rejuvenation of France to traditional family structure based on "natural" hierarchy, greater awareness of the rights of families did not fulfill their cherished expectations of increased political and social power for men as individuals. Despite a repeated emphasis on fatherhood, the Vichy regime was in fact as ambiguous about the status of real-life fathers as were its Third Republic predecessors.

Who could ensure that the strong, politically powerful *père de famille* foreseen by Vichy propagandists would be the right sort of man? If children were a resource of national importance, they were *too* important to be left to the vagaries of individual men; their protection had to be assured by the nation itself. In the evolution of state concern for the family, the special rights of fathers were increasingly difficult to justify and promote as the state itself took over certain paternal roles and oversaw the protection of the family. Although the *père de famille* figured prominently in rallying cries for the family under Vichy, privileges to fathers lost out to the expanding administration of the welfare state, which continued to redefine relations of authority and submission for all citizens of the nation.

Conclusion

Epilogue: The Liberation and Beyond

Paris was liberated from German occupation on August 25, 1944. The Parisian office of the General Commissariat on the Family opened its doors again on August 28, and a few days later Robert Prigent was named interim Commissioner on the Family. For the new personnel of the Commissariat appointed by General de Gaulle and the Provisional Government of the Republic, continuity rather than change was the order of the day. Prigent praised the work of former Commissioner Philippe Renaudin and encouraged the regional delegates to continue their work on behalf of the family in a newly delivered France.[1]

The Fourth Republic remained committed to pursuing population policies inaugurated by the defunct Vichy regime and the last ministers of the Third Republic. French Radicals meeting in December 1944 expressed their pride at being the first party to integrate demography and family concerns into their program, noting with satisfaction that it was a Radical Prime Minister, Edouard Daladier, who gave the nation both the High Committee on Population and the Family Code before the war. Demographic problems, the *rapporteur* stated, were questions of vital importance, for "the entire destiny of a nation is determined by the number and quality of its members."[2] In March 1945, de Gaulle himself expressed concern for the French population before the Constituent Assembly, declaring that the lack of men, both in quantity and in quality, was the underlying cause of France's misfortunes and a principal obstacle to its regeneration. De Gaulle called for "twelve million beautiful babies" to be born in France in the next ten years.[3] These new babies were to be protected by a new law of September 1945 modifying the rights of paternal correction "to better take into account the primordial interests of the child."[4] The rights and welfare of children and the family,

186

rather than political concessions to fathers, moved increasingly to center stage. From virtually every side, the family was once again acclaimed as key to France's future, and political leaders of the Fourth Republic vied with each other as the spokesmen and true representatives of the family cause.

The historian Antoine Prost has called the period from 1938 to 1958 the "golden age of family policy" in France. Not only did the Liberation validate many of the policy initiatives of the Vichy regime, but the new republican government expanded upon them and continued to place the family at the center of its concerns. Far from being a policy of expedience, generated by the threat of war or the reactionary goals of Vichy, family policy enjoyed almost universal approval and became a lasting feature of the Fourth Republic.[5] One of the key political parties of the postwar landscape, the Mouvement républicain populaire (MRP), made family policy a high priority. Many MRP supporters had been members of social-Catholic action groups, and they rallied around the activities of such groups as the National Union of Family Associations to insure the continuity of family activism in the new Republic.[6]

After the Liberation, social commentators also observed that French birth rates had begun to inch up as early as 1942, in the midst of the occupation. France was experiencing the early stages of a "baby boom" that would continue until the 1960s, and contemporaries speculated widely on the psychological, material, and political origins of this phenomenon.[7] Alfred Sauvy, the principal architect of family policy during the Daladier administration, attributed the increase in fertility rates to a "profound transformation in mentalities" accompanied by the ascendance of a new generation into political life. Despite the failure of the National Revolution and the discrediting of the Vichy regime, Sauvy notes, the ideals of *Travail, Famille, Patrie* were not in fact compromised.[8]

One dramatic rupture wrought by the Liberation was the introduction of the vote for women, decided upon by the Provisional Government in Algiers in April 1944. A committee on legislation and the reform of the state in Algiers voted 51 to 16 to give women the same electoral rights as men, an idea that found favor with General de Gaulle.[9] At the same time, however, remnants of the past lingered in the proposals submitted to the provisional government by the Conseil national de la résistance, an umbrella organization of resistance movements, which suggested that a future government of the Republic should introduce the family vote, offering *chefs de famille* extra votes for the number of their children.[10] The Alliance nationale, for its part, continued to campaign for the family vote into 1945, arguing that the electoral system was still skewed when childless couples had the same number of votes as the mother and father of a large family.[11] The family vote had, of course, been an important component of the various drafts for a new constitution drawn up under Vichy, and the idea that men should be rewarded for paternity appeared to some as far less problematic than extending the vote to women.

Paternity continued to be a hot topic for legislators and social commentators who saw the rights of fathers as intimately connected with the reinstatement of citizens' rights and the expansion of democracy. In 1947, Paris hosted a World Congress on the Family and Population, a major event that drew participants from many nations and many institutions or associations. One session that dealt specifically with paternal authority grouped together jurists and scholars for a discussion of the impact of the war on fatherhood and on democracy. A professor at the law school in Poitiers asserted that "the control of paternal powers is a vital subject because of the moral and social factors it brings into play; it is at the very center of our civilization." Professor Savatier noted, however, that the issue of paternal power "is also a sensitive subject, in which the meaning of the words themselves suffice to illustrate a paradox, almost a contradiction." At the heart of this contradiction were the conflicting definitions of paternity as a status endowed with rights and as a function entailing obligations. How could the state make up for the "social deficiency" of many fathers who ignored their moral duties without compromising their authority or even rendering them obsolete?[12]

André Rouast, another participant at the conference and a prolific commentator on family legislation during the war, bemoaned the fact that in the modern age the judicial and social apparatus of the state was called on far more often to remedy the inadequacies of paternal power than to mediate against its excesses. Fathers in France had let themselves be transformed into bureaucrats rather than leaders of the family by relying too heavily on the assistance of the administration. The key was to achieve a proper harmony between public assistance and the autonomy of the father. According to René Capitant,

> This indispensable aid should not become a dispossession. We must research the means of making the father of a family a collaborator with these institutions. . . . Let us above all ensure that these new institutions are always required to respect the rights, the power, of the father of a family; that they put themselves at his disposal to make up for his weaknesses, or even more for life's circumstances which make it impossible for him to fulfill his duties alone, but that they never substitute for him. May this problem, which is in any case a problem for all western democracies, never be solved in the manner in which it was solved in the totalitarian regimes.[13]

The war had afflicted millions of families, overturning parental roles and changing the nature of social organization. Once again, fatherhood was at the center of debates on the structure of society and a key component in the solution of its ills.

Yet inextricably linked to these discussions on the rights and obligations of fatherhood was the ambiguity reformers faced in holding up the *père de famille* as a citizen above all others and, on the other hand, the apprehension they expressed at participating in his demise. Had the *père de famille* been worthy of his special status in the past, and what would be his new position in a society whose social assistance was predicated on his repeated failures? While debates on paternity continued to engage participants in reflection on the "burning issues of the day," no one could offer unequivocal support for the rights of fathers or a resounding affirmation of the father's importance within the family sphere. After decades of deliberation on the merits and flaws of fathers in modern France, the *père de famille* continued to reflect both the highest social and political aspirations of a society hoping to reinstate order and the worst fears of an administration aiming to protect its future citizens from paternal neglect.

The Vichy regime had made of fatherhood a political symbol and a cornerstone of the social ideology of its authoritarian politics. Not only within metropolitan France but also in the colonies, Pétain had fashioned himself as the wise father who gently disciplined his children and delivered them from their lack of foresight and accountability. Interestingly, it was perhaps only in the French colonies that the regime's paternalist rhetoric came without serious internal contradictions. Eric Jennings shows that in Madagascar, Guadeloupe, and Indochina, the cult of *Maréchalisme* was particularly strong, and images of father Pétain abounded on the streets.[14] Yet perhaps a strong, paternal French state was less likely to come into conflict with the *pères de famille* of the empire, since the French state might have had less interest in promoting strong paternal images among the colonized "natives" themselves. Richard Burton has suggested, for example, that Martinique and the rest of the French Antilles were in fact cast as filial dependents of the "mother country," subordinates relying on the goodwill of their metropolitan parent as opposed to virile, self-sufficient entities.[15] More research is needed on the gendered dynamics of relations between France and its colonies, but it seems to have been only overseas that the image of Pétain, symbol of the State, as an authoritarian father, was put forth without equivocation or concern about the autonomy of individual fathers within the colonized populations.

Within the hexagon, French family activists struggled after the Liberation to reconcile this image of fathers with a new, more democratic system in which father Pétain no longer embodied the proper relationships among family members and between citizens and the state. Disassociating paternity from the brutal politics of the Vichy period became a particularly important concern for social reformers who continued to place the *père de famille* at the center of efforts to regenerate the nation. Jean Bergeaud, for example, a member of the Fédération des associations de familles nombreuses de

France and a family activist particularly concerned with fatherhood, wrote an article in the newspaper *Familles de France* in which he encouraged fathers to turn away from the "hard" mentality of the past and to incorporate a new tenderness into relations with their families. In "*Le Père, ce tendre,*" Bergeaud wrote,

> The age belongs to those who are hard. How could it be otherwise? In reaction to the easy life of yesterday, youth who move forward into the iron years that we are experiencing must constantly fly against thousands of difficulties. . . .

Fathers, Bergeaud wrote, were constantly warned of a crisis of authority, and were instructed at all times to be leaders. Sentimentality, they believed, was not part of a father's role. Yet Bergeaud cautioned that this attitude was excessively severe and would lead only to a society of Spartan toughs.

> What has always constituted the force and durability of French households is precisely this great flow of love that circulates amongst family members more freely than elsewhere. The word "paternal" has always had, in our country, and will have, we hope, a connotation of good, indulgent, a bit serious, certainly, firm at times, careful, thoughtful, and strong. But this strength is not force, at least in the odious sense in which it was imposed by daily realities in troubled times.

In Bergeaud's article, fatherhood was being pried away from its authoritarian, hardened past and integrated into a gentler and more democratic world after the war.[16]

Family activists such as Bergeaud were at pains to depict a new, more tender side to paternity that could cement the father's relations within the family sphere. Such impassioned pleas signaled a profound uneasiness with the role of fathers in modern French society and accentuated the contradictions at the heart of discourse and legislation on paternity. Fathers were instructed to be "hard," "virile," and "audacious," the "grand adventurers" of Charles Peguy, yet this disposition could only lead to a father's alienation from his family, the very foundation of his virtue. As the Vichy regime fell apart, advocates of the *père de famille* attempted to fashion a new role for fathers that could bridge the gap between the rhetoric of paternal dominion and the increasing interest in family relations and children's welfare.[17] As part of this effort to integrate fathers into the domestic sphere, a new law was passed on May 18, 1946, granting *chefs de famille* up to three days leave at the occasion of each birth in their household.[18]

Yet the incompatibility in expectations surrounding fathers in France made the chasm between the ideal of strong, distant father-leaders and the fear of neglectful, irresponsible, progenitors exceptionally wide. Throughout the Third Republic and under Vichy, the incongruous way in which state administrators and social commentators advanced the cause of the *père de famille* precluded any concrete action or reforms granting fathers special recognition. Far from instituting family suffrage and granting fathers the political ascendancy even some members of the Resistance had suggested, leaders of the new Fourth Republic granted women the vote and a new system of social security increasingly focused on social solidarity, infant mortality, and mothers' welfare.[19] Even in arguments for the family vote appearing after the Liberation, a shift was apparent in the emphasis on whose rights were at stake in the new system of universal suffrage. One family association from the Côtes-du-Nord highlighted this focus on the family and the child in a letter to the Provisional Government:

> Just as a child is living in the womb of its mother, and only joins the family after a long period of gestation, during which it is impossible to separate it from her, so is that child a citizen, as soon as he is born, and only joins the national community after a long period of education in the bosom of the family, during which time it is impossible to separate him from the family.

The association therefore recommended that minor children be granted a vote, to be exercised by their father, mother, or legal guardian.[20] No longer was the father considered the natural and exclusive representative of a child's rights. With the democratic impulses of the Liberation, the age of the *père de famille* had come to a close.

Conclusions

Although I have emphasized the many continuities linking Vichy family policy with that of the Third and Fourth Republics, examining the role of the *père de famille* over the years enables us to see the important ruptures within these policy decisions as well. Vichy family policy did indeed draw on initiatives and debates dating from the early nineteenth century on up through the Third Republic. Many of these policy suggestions emanated from a wide variety of active and vocal social-Catholics, pro-natalists, conservatives, and Communists. Similarly, politicians such as Maurice Thorez and Charles de Gaulle picked up the strains of pro-natalist and pro-family discourse after the Liberation.[21] Yet Vichy marked both the zenith and the breaking point of a particular discourse that proclaimed the *père de famille* a key national figure worthy of expanded political rights. Although proposals for the family vote continued to pour in to the Provisional Government in 1944, this was not the direction taken by the architects of the Fourth Republic. What was extraordinary about Vichy was that given the opportunity to construct a patriarchal society based on rights for fathers of families, Vichy officials were unable and even unwilling to do so.

Both Miranda Pollard and Francine Muel-Dreyfus emphasize that alongside the apparent continuity in personnel and institutions in family policy outlined by Aline Coutrot, Vichy's "antifeminism" and specific coercion of women marked a radically different and innately violent era of French history.[22] Understanding the impact of Vichy's policies on *men* enables us to see that while men were not subject to a traditional "antimasculinism," they were nonetheless coerced into labor and ultimately were the victims of a repressive, interventionist state as well. To misunderstand this double-edged gendered discourse on men, particularly concerning fatherhood, is to misunderstand the dynamics of Vichy's policies as a whole. Beneath the public adulation of the *père de famille* under Vichy was an undercurrent of serious doubt that eventually washed away the edifice of paternal authority in social legislation.

This age of paternal rhetoric and discourse proclaiming the ascendancy of fathers had from the beginning been marred by inconsistency and implausibility. In the Third Republic, pro-natalists and family advocates attempted to make paternity synonymous with good citizenship and to link the rights of political participation with the willingness to father and raise numerous children for the Republic. At the same time, however, defenders of the Republic worried that fathers were in fact to blame for various crimes against the nation's children and families, and fathers were targeted by legislation aimed at mitigating the impact of these offenses. This identification of fathers with political and social leadership reached its apex under Pétain's regime and his public avowal of paternity. Yet even in a regime enthusiastically dedicated to reinstating "traditional" family values and the privileges of fatherhood, fathers were not granted the political and social rights that many clamored for, and they came under increasing suspicion as family deserters and wayward citizens. The ideological contradictions inherent in paternal rhetoric that both idealized and demonized fathers forestalled any unanimous affirmation of the *père de famille* as model citizen and key to the future.

Not only were the prevailing conceptions of fathers as both indispensable and injurious at irreconcilable odds; prescriptions for a father's role were also so fundamentally incoherent as to render the efforts of social reformers and government officials virtually meaningless. In campaigns for family suffrage throughout the Third Republic, for example, advocates of the *chef de famille* argued that fathers represented the interests of their wives and children and were inseparable from the concerns of the domestic sphere. Yet social reformers and family theorists maintained at the same time that fathers had to preserve a certain distance and detachment from the mundane affairs of home and hearth, and that immersion in family affairs diminished the authority of a *père de famille*. This fundamental contradiction prevented fatherhood from becoming the object of simplistic acclamation that motherhood was, and it weakened reformers' claims that fathers and their needs were commensurate with those of their families.

Under Vichy, the absurdity of proclaiming the prisoners in Germany the active, vital *chefs de famille* who would lead France into a new age demonstrated the paucity of real-life heroes the regime had at its disposal to manipulate in the interest of the National Revolution. Vichy propaganda recognized the prisoners as needy, broken victims of a greater power, yet upon their shoulders was thrust the burden of embodying the stalwart *pères de famille* whose political acumen and sense of social responsibility could save the nation. Perhaps the absurdity of this call to action was one reaction to the essential conflict Vichy reformers faced in representing defeat, and acceptance of an armistice, as an honorable and even manly thing. As the essentially voiceless prisoners became ready-made spokesmen for Vichy's own designs for the family, fathers in France itself came under increasing fire for the crimes of family abandonment and alcoholic excess and represented anything but perfect citizens. Accusations of paternal absence and inadequacy haunted discussions of family policy, even as some reformers questioned whether fathers were in fact that necessary to family life. If fathers were to constitute the cornerstone of a new France under Vichy, they were certainly off to an inauspicious start.

The history of fathers in modern France has been interpreted within the context of a downward slide from the lofty heights of pre-Revolutionary despotism to our own suspicious and psychoanalytically intrusive times.[23] Certainly in the course of the early twentieth century fathers did lose specific rights and privileges associated with paternity, such as the right to incarcerate children. French law during the Third Republic and Vichy regime also circumscribed fathers with more stringent standards of behavior and of support for children.

Yet it would be wrong to focus exclusively on this fatalistic decline, for alongside this corrosion of paternal powers in the twentieth century came the very real successes of a family movement of which fathers were an active and integral part. Fathers of large families argued that they bore a disproportionate financial burden for their patriotic sacrifice of raising many children, and over the course of the Third Republic and Vichy regime such burdens were recognized as resources and rights were channeled to needy families. Fatherhood itself was not granted rewards and honors, but many of the causes for which fathers in family associations had fought, such as a new social and political voice for the family, came to fruition under both the republican and the Vichy regimes.

What did, in fact, break down over the course of the Third Republic and

Vichy regimes was a father's claim to represent his family and to be the unproblematic channel through which resources for the family should be directed. Within the ideology of the Civil Code, fathers represented the political, social, and moral interests of members of their households. As fathers came under increasing scrutiny from social reformers, family activists, and government administrators as improper guardians of future citizens of the nation in the late nineteenth and early twentieth centuries, *pères de famille* could no longer argue that their interests were commensurate with those of their families. Although this certainly did not indicate the eradication of male power within the family, paternity was no longer as compelling an argument for privilege and financial assistance. While families as a unit moved to the center of public preoccupations in the late 1930s and 1940s and even gained a political identity under the Vichy regime and the Fourth Republic, fathers ceased to be the obvious representatives of the rights of families. Fatherhood and citizenship were two distinct concepts, and the rights and obligations associated with paternity were dissociated from the requisites for political participation. With the inauguration of a new social security system in France in 1946, social reformers targeted inequalities in men's "social risk" and unemployment benefits rather than the disparities between fathers and bachelors.

As fatherhood came to represent less in political terms, so too did discussions of the *père de famille* cease to dominate debates on child and family welfare. Fathers were, in fact, inconvenient to the state's projects of reforming family life and protecting children. Far from being malleable partners in these initiatives, fathers were seen at best as distant wage earners whose needs could be met through labor and other social policies, or at worst as negligent family members whose behavior was best corrected through the criminal justice system. Despite the concerted efforts of paternal advocates in the Third Republic and the Vichy regime, men's links to their families remained obscured by public distrust and the internal contradictions of an ideology that constantly alluded to paternal distance and absence even as it hoped to bridge such gaps.

Was the separation of men from their families a cause or an effect of the state's usurpation of paternal roles as architects of the new welfare state inaugurated social policies based on the assumption of paternal inadequacy? As welfare provisions have become less and less associated with a father's income and participation, the fear of paternal alienation from family life has only increased in our contemporary world. Debates over the status of the *père de famille* have been most salient in France, because fatherhood and its power were intimately linked to the foundation of the first Republic, which attempted to create a brotherhood, a *fraternité*, rather than to uphold the status of the father-king. Each revision of the government in the nineteenth and early twentieth centuries required, therefore, a renegotiation of the role of fathers and the state.

Although discourse on paternity has historically been most active in France, today we see that such concerns have contemporary relevance in other nations as well. In the United States, for example, current debates on fathers, welfare reform, and children demonstrate that discussions on fatherhood and the state are far from passé. In the spring of 1996, *The Wilson Quarterly* published a special issue on "A World Without Fathers," in which scholars Barbara Whitehead and David Popenoe explored "fatherlessness" as a major cause of current social ills. Popenoe began by proclaiming, "The decline of fatherhood is one of the most basic, unexpected, and extraordinary events of our time."[24] Popenoe's book, *Life Without Father: Compelling Evidence that Fatherhood and Marriage Are Indispensable for the Good of Children and Society,* has generated controversy across the political spectrum.[25] Is it helpful for the state to attempt to instill a new morality promoting fatherhood? Are children better or worse off as traditional family structures, and particularly the authoritarian rights of the father, have waned? Few today can agree on *one* definition of proper fatherhood or its impact on children and families. Just as French policymakers struggled to define what fatherhood actually meant in the early twentieth century, we face new questions of defining paternity in a world in which frozen embryos are fought over in courts. These spectacular historical trends have only begun to be explored, but the roots of such a transformation must surely be researched at the beginning of this century, at a time when social reformers and state administrators began to decry the "fatherlessness" of their own time and to set about remedying the "inadequacies" of fathers who were less than ideal.

Notes

INTRODUCTION

1.   Program Notes, Metropolitan Opera *Playbill*, March 2002, Lincoln Center, New York City.
2.   Drama critic Palamède II, quoted in Carl B. Schmidt, *Entrancing Muse: A Documented Biography of Francis Poulenc* (Hillsdale, N.Y.: Pendragon Press, 2001), 329.
3.   Ned Rorem, "Parisian Thoroughfare," Metropolitan Opera *Playbill*, March 2002, 27.
4.   To name only a few recent works exploring gender in modern France, see James F. McMillan, *France and Women, 1789–1914: Gender, Society, and Politics* (New York: Routledge, 2000); Joan Wallach Scott, *Only Paradoxes to Offer* (Cambridge: Harvard University Press, 1996); Lynn Hunt, *The Family Romance of the French Revolution* (Berkeley: University of California Press, 1992); Georges Duby and Michelle Perrot, eds., *A History of Women*, 5 vols. (Cambridge: Harvard University Press, 1994), especially vol. 4: *Emerging Feminism from Revolution to World War,* and vol. 5: *Toward a Cultural Identity in the Twentieth Century;* Angus McLaren, *Sexuality and Social Order: The Debate over the Fertility of Women and Workers in France, 1770–1920* (New York: Holmes & Meier, 1983); Kristin Ross, *Fast Cars, Clean Bodies: Decolonization and the Reordering of French Culture* (Cambridge: MIT Press, 1995); Christine Bard, *Les Filles de Marianne* (Paris: Fayard, 1995); Robert Nye, *Masculinity and Male Codes of Honor in Modern France* (New York: Oxford University Press, 1993); Elinor A. Accampo, Rachel G. Fuchs, and Mary Lynn Stewart, eds., *Gender and the Politics of Social Reform in France, 1870–1914* (Baltimore, Md.: Johns Hopkins University Press, 1995); Rachel G. Fuchs, *Poor and Pregnant in Paris: Strategies for Survival in the Nineteenth Century* (New Brunswick, N.J.: Rutgers University Press, 1992).
5.   Examples include Mary Louise Roberts, *Civilization without Sexes: Reconstructing Gender in Postwar France, 1917–1927* (Chicago: University of Chicago Press, 1994); Siân Reynolds, *France between the Wars: Gender and Politics* (New York: Routledge, 1996); Edward Berenson, *The Trial of Madame Caillaux* (Berkeley: University of California Press, 1992); Sylvia Schafer, *Children in Moral Danger and the Problem of Government in Third Republic France* (Princeton, N.J.: Princeton University Press, 1997); Laura Frader, "From Muscles to Nerves: Gender, 'Race' and the Body at Work in

France, 1919–1939," *International Review of Social History* 44, no. 7 (1999): 123–147; Elisa Camiscioli, "Intermarriage, Independent Nationality, and the Individual Rights of French Women: The Law of 10 August 1927," *French Politics, Culture and Society* 17, no. 3–4 (1999): 52–74; Karen Offen, "Body Politics: Women, Work and the Politics of Motherhood in France, 1920–1950," in *Maternity and Gender Policies: Women and the Rise of the European Welfare States, 1880s–1950s,* ed. Gisela Bock and Pat Thane (New York: Routledge, 1991), 138–159; Cheryl A. Koos, "Gender, Anti-Individualism and Nationalism: The Alliance Nationale and the Pronatalist Backlash against the *Femme moderne,* 1933–1940," *French Historical Studies* 19, no. 3 (spring 1996): 699–723; Sarah Fishman, *We Will Wait: Wives of French Prisoners of War, 1940–1945* (New Haven, Conn.: Yale University Press, 1991); Miranda Pollard, *Reign of Virtue: Mobilizing Gender in Vichy France* (Chicago: University of Chicago Press, 1998); Francine Muel-Dreyfus, *Vichy et l'éternel féminin* (Paris: Éditions du Seuil, 1996); Paula Schwartz, "The Politics of Food and Gender in Occupied Paris," *Modern and Contemporary France* 7, no. 1 (1999): 35–45; Mary Jean Green, "Gender, Fascism and the Croix de Feu: The 'Women's Pages' of 'Le Flambeau,'" *French Cultural Studies* 8, no. 2 (June 1997): 229–240.

6.   See Alisa Klaus, "Depopulation and Race Suicide: Maternalism and Pronatalist Ideologies in France and the United States," in *Mothers of a New World: Maternalist Politics and the Origins of Welfare States,* ed. Seth Koven and Sonya Michel (New York: Routledge, 1993), 188–212; Susan Pedersen, "Catholicism, Feminism, and the Politics of the Family during the Late Third Republic," in *Mothers of a New World,* ed. Seth Koven and Sonya Michel, 246–276; Elinor A. Accampo, "The Rhetoric of Reproduction and the Reconfiguration of Womanhood in the French Birth Control Movement, 1890–1920," *Journal of Family History* 21, no. 3 (July 1996): 351–371; Karen Offen, "Depopulation, Nationalism and Feminism in Fin-de-siècle France," *American Historical Review* 89, no. 3 (June 1984): 648–676; Joshua Cole, "There Are Only Good Mothers: The Ideological Work of Women's Fertility in France before World War I," *French Historical Studies* 19, no. 3 (spring 1996): 639–673; and idem, "'A Sudden and Terrible Revelation': Motherhood and Infant Mortality in France, 1858–1874," *Journal of Family History* 21, no. 4 (October 1996): 419–446, and idem, *The Power of Large Numbers: Population, Politics, and Gender in Nineteenth-Century France* (Ithaca, N.Y.: Cornell University Press, 2000).

7.   I realize that "paternity," "father," and "fatherhood" carry different meanings and connotations. I use these terms as rough equivalents to avoid repetition as well as to emphasize the interchangeability and fluidity of roles and definitions of fatherhood in early twentieth-century France. Tests for ascertainment of biological paternity were not developed until the 1950s, and therefore paternity as a concept relied on moral, social, and political standards for its definition. Paternity as a genetic fact could not be separated from the social expression of this relationship evident in legal codes, family life, and political representation.

8.   Witness recent debates surrounding legislation on the marriage rights afforded same-sex partners in France, or the PACS.

9.   See Hunt, *Family Romance,* 17–52.

10.   Only in the context of American history has the study of paternity been researched more amply. See, for example, Ralph LaRossa, *The Modernization of Fatherhood: A Social and Political History* (Chicago: University of Chicago Press, 1997); Stephen Frank, *Life with Father: Parenthood and Masculinity in the Nineteenth-Century American North* (Baltimore, Md.: Johns Hopkins University Press, 1998); Scott Coltrane, *Family Man: Fatherhood, Housework and Gender Equity* (New York: Oxford

University Press, 1996); Mark Carnes, *Secret Ritual and Manhood in Victorian America* (New Haven, Conn.: Yale University Press, 1989); Mary Frances Berry, *The Politics of Parenthood: Child Care, Women's Rights, and the Myth of the Good Mother* (New York: Viking, 1993); Robert Griswold, *Fatherhood in America: A History* (New York: Basic Books, 1993); Michael E. Lamb, ed., *The Father's Role: Cross-Cultural Perspectives* (Hillsdale, N.J.: Lawrence Erlbaum, 1987); E. Anthony Rotundo, *American Manhood: Transformations in Masculinity from the Revolution to the Modern Era* (New York: Basic Books, 1993).

11.   In the tradition of a "history of mentalities," French scholars have explored paternal images and customs from the time of the Greeks to the modern age, most notably in the monumental collection by Jean Delumeau and Daniel Roche, eds., *Histoire des pères et de la paternité* (Paris: Larousse, 1990). Others have studied the evolution of paternity through literary texts, or have made use of psychoanalytic theory to interpret the changing role of the father in the modern world. See Yvonne Kniebiehler, *Les Pères aussi ont une histoire* (Paris: Hachette, 1987); Françoise Hurstel, *La Déchirure paternelle* (Paris: Presses universitaires de France, 1996); Alain Lefèvre, *Du Père carent au père humilié, ou la tragédie du père avec Sophocle, Claudel et Lacan* (Tours: Éditions soleil carré, 1995).

12.   See the collection of articles in the *Revue française des affaires sociales*, Numéro spécial, Hors-série: *Pères et paternité* (November 1988); Françoise Hurstel, "Fonction paternelle et déracinement culturel: Qu'est-ce qui fonde la paternité?" *Bulletin de psychologie* 31, no. 10–11 (1977–78): 502–509; *Les Pères aujourd'hui*, International colloquium sponsored by the Institut national d'études démographiques (INED), Paris, 1982; Nadine Lefaucheur, "Pères absents et droit au père," *Lien social et politiques* no. 37 (1997): 11–17.

13.   See Robert Nye, *Masculinity and Male Codes of Honor in Modern France* (New York: Oxford University Press, 1993); George L. Mosse, *The Image of Man: The Creation of Modern Masculinity* (New York: Oxford University Press, 1996); Elisabeth Badinter, *XY: On Masculine Identity,* trans. Lydia Davis (New York: Columbia University Press, 1995); Angus McLaren, *The Trials of Masculinity: Policing Sexual Boundaries, 1870–1930* (Chicago: University of Chicago Press, 1997).

14.   Martha Hanna, "Natalism, Homosexuality, and the Controversy over *Corydon,*" in *Homosexuality in Modern France,* ed. Jeffrey Merrick and Bryant T. Ragan Jr. (New York: Oxford University Press, 1996), 202–224. Hanna's work has been particularly useful in describing the diatribe against bachelors in the interwar years and how homosexual men came to be identified "within this more general discourse of calumny" (Hanna, 218). On the polarization of male and female spheres during the war and in the postwar years, see Mary Louise Roberts, "This Being without Breasts, without Hips," in *Civilization without Sexes;* and Françoise Thébaud, "The Great War and the Triumph of Sexual Division," in *A History of Women,* vol. 5: *Toward a Cultural Identity in the Twentieth Century,* ed. Françoise Thébaud (Cambridge: Harvard University Press, 1994).

15.   Klaus Theweleit, *Male Fantasies,* 2 vols. (Minneapolis: University of Minnesota Press, 1987). On images of men in Nazi Germany, see Michael Burleigh and Wolfgang Wipperman, *The Racial State: Germany, 1933–1945* (Cambridge: Cambridge University Press, 1991), especially parts II and III, and George Mosse, *Nationalism and Sexuality: Respectability and Abnormal Sexuality in Modern Europe* (New York: Howard Fertig, 1985).

16.   Barbara Spackman, *Fascist Virilities: Rhetoric, Ideology and Social Fantasy in Italy* (Minneapolis: University of Minnesota Press, 1996). See also David G. Horn, *Social*

Bodies: Science, Reproduction, and Italian Modernity (Princeton, N.J.: Princeton University Press, 1994); and Victoria de Grazia, *How Fascism Ruled Women: Italy, 1922–1945* (Berkeley: University of California Press, 1992).

17.   Cheryl A. Koos, "Fascism, Fatherhood, and the Family in Interwar France: The Case of Antoine Rédier and the Légion," *Journal of Family History* 24, no. 3 (July 1999): 317–329.

18.   On Germany, see Claudia Koonz, *Mothers in the Fatherland* (New York: St. Martin's Press, 1986); and Michael Burleigh and Wolfgang Wipperman, "Men in the Third Reich," in *The Racial State: Germany 1933–1945* (Cambridge: Cambridge University Press, 1991), chap. 9. Victoria de Grazia notes that paternity was proof of masculinity in Italy, and bachelors were taxed at almost double the rate of married men in the 1930s (De Grazia, *How Fascism Ruled Women*, 69–71). Yet Barbara Spackman points out that Mussolini refused to have public references made to his role as husband and father, for the image of a family man would presumably soften his virility (Spackman, *Fascist Virilities*, 3).

19.   On the École des cadres d'Uriage, see Bernard Comte, *Une Utopie combattante: L'École des cadres d'Uriage, 1940–1942* (Paris: Fayard, 1991); John Hellman, *The Knight-Monks of Vichy France: Uriage, 1940–1945* (Montreal: McGill-Queen's University Press, 1993); Pierre Bitoun, *Les Hommes d'Uriage* (Nancy: Presses universitaires de Nancy, 1989); Antoine Delestre, *Uriage, une communauté et une école dans la tourmente, 1940–1945* (Nancy: Presses universitaires de Nancy, 1989); Limore Yagil, *"L'Homme nouveau" et la Révolution nationale de Vichy (1940–1944)* (Paris: Presses universitaires du Septentrion, 1997). On the Chantiers de la Jeunesse, see Pierre Giolitto, *Histoire de la jeunesse sous Vichy* (Paris: Perrin, 1991); W. D. Halls, *The Youth of Vichy France* (Oxford: Clarendon, 1981); Christian Faure, *Le Projet culturel de Vichy* (Lyon: Presses universitaires de Lyon, 1989); Robert Hervet, *Les Chantiers de la jeunesse* (Paris: Éditions France Empire, 1962).

20.   It is beyond the scope of this study to examine in detail the authoritarian, parafascist, or fascist character of the Vichy regime. For a concise overview of this important debate, see Sarah Fishman, "The Power of Myth: Five Recent Works on Vichy France," *Journal of Modern History* 67, no. 3 (September 1995): 666–674. My argument is that while family policy under the Vichy regime shared certain attributes with fascist policy in Germany or Italy, French concern for the *père de famille* was *not* a fascist import, and cannot be written off as symptomatic of wartime mimicry of fascist regimes. Miranda Pollard notes that gender ideology and antifeminism have unfortunately been ignored in the debate on Vichy's fascist credentials (Pollard, *Reign of Virtue*, 7). For more on fascism in interwar France, see Robert Soucy, *French Fascism: The First Wave, 1924–1933* (New Haven, Conn.: Yale University Press, 1986); and idem, *French Fascism: The Second Wave, 1933–1939* (New Haven, Conn.: Yale University Press, 1995); William Irvine, "Fascism in France and the Strange Case of the Croix de Feu," *Journal of Modern History* 63 (June 1991): 271–295; Kevin Passmore, "The French Third Republic: Stalemate Society or Cradle of Fascism?" *French History* 7, no. 4 (1993): 417–449; Roger Griffin, *The Nature of Fascism* (New York: St. Martin's Press, 1991).

21.   Scholars such as John Hellman and Limore Yagil have studied ideals of the "new man" of Vichy's National Revolution, describing how the masculine values of action and courage were held up as templates for the new state.

22.   See Susan Pedersen, *Family, Dependence, and the Origins of the Welfare State: Britain and France, 1914–1945* (Cambridge: Cambridge University Press, 1993), 368–372.

23.   Pedersen writes that the domestic ideal of the *mère au foyer* was only challenged by forces on the margins of the bourgeois polity (Pedersen, *Family, Dependence*, 422).

I would argue that domestic roles for men, however, were the subject of controversy for groups from across a wide spectrum of political and social affiliations.

24.   The rich associational life that sprang up around the defense of the family in France has been carefully documented, often by sociologists whose interests in contemporary family policy have led them to research France's unique history in this regard. In addition to Robert Talmy, *Histoire du mouvement familiale en France,* 2 vols. (Paris: CNAF, 1962), see Michel Messu, *Les Politiques familiales* (Paris: Les Éditions ouvrières, 1992); Michel Chauvière, "L'Action familiale ouvrière et la politique de Vichy: Acteurs, institutions, enjeux," and "Repères: Chronologie sommaire, les principaux acteurs 1940–1945," in *L'Action familiale ouvrière et la politique de Vichy,* Journées d'études des 28–29 novembre 1984, *Les Cahiers du GRMF* 3 (1984): 13–26; and idem, "Familialisme et régulation sociale ou aspects de la démultiplication du concept de famille," *Annales de Vaucresson* 27 (1987): 207–226. Yet one important dimension lacking in the historiography on family associations and the state is any recognition of the centrality of paternity in the formation of social policies and in the motivations of the associations themselves.

25.   See Jacques Donzelot, *The Policing of Families,* trans. Robert Hurley (New York: Pantheon Books, 1979).

26.   For a discussion of the continuity inherent in Vichy family policy, see Aline Coutrot, "La Politique familiale," in *Le Gouvernement de Vichy, 1940–1942. Institutions et politiques* (Paris: Presses de la Fondation nationale des sciences politiques, no. 18, 1972). Francine Muel-Dreyfus asserts that the widespread notion of continuity between the republican and Vichy regimes has contributed to the myth that the family was an "apolitical" concept (Muel-Dreyfus, *L'Éternel féminin,* 95). I would argue that the family remained intensely political throughout this time, but that family issues managed to rally a considerable level of consensus between different political regimes.

27.   Francine Muel-Dreyfus, *Vichy et l'éternel féminin* (Paris: Éditions du Seuil, 1996); and Miranda Pollard, *Reign of Virtue: Mobilizing Gender in Vichy France* (Chicago: University of Chicago Press, 1998).

28.   Pollard, *Reign of Virtue,* 1.

29.   A new book by Michèle Bordeaux does more to address the role of fathers, yet continues the trend of viewing women, as opposed to men, as the only "gendered" beings targeted by the Vichy regime. Michèle Bordeaux, *La Victoire de la famille dans la France défaite: Vichy 1940–1944* (Paris: Flammarion, 2002).

30.   See Muel-Dreyfus, *L'Éternel féminin,* 342, for a discussion of the opposition of masculine and feminine qualities in Vichy propaganda.

31.   This parallels Victoria de Grazia's observation that the fascist state in Italy was deeply divided "between the demands of modernity and the desire to reimpose traditional authority." This conflict was especially apparent in the regime's treatment of women, which condemned female emancipation yet "inevitably promoted some of the very changes it sought to curb" (De Grazia, *How Fascism Ruled Women,* 2).

1. PATERNITY, LAW, AND POLITICS IN THE THIRD REPUBLIC

1.   Institut national de France, *Discours qui a concouru à l'Institut national de France, sur cette question: Quelles doivent être, dans une République bien-constituée, l'étendue et les limites du pouvoir d'un Père de famille?* (Paris: Chez Étienne Charles, An IX [1801]), Avant-Propos.

2.   See Bernard Schnapper, "La Correction paternelle et le mouvement des idées

au dix-neuvième siècle," in *Voies nouvelles en histoire du droit. La Justice, la famille, la répression pénale* (Paris: Presses universitaires de France, 1991), 526; see also Lynn Hunt, *The Family Romance of the French Revolution* (Berkeley: University of California Press, 1992), 40–43; and Pierre Murat, "La Puissance paternelle et la Révolution française: Essai de régénération de l'autorité des pères," in *La Famille, la loi, l'état de la Révolution au Code civil,* ed. Irène Théry and Christian Biet (Paris: Éditions du Centre Georges Pompidou/Imprimerie nationale, 1989), 94.

3.   Schnapper, "La Correction," 523.

4.   For Françoise Hurstel, when a man became a father he "put on an overcoat filled with holes and doubts." Françoise Hurstel, "L'Affaiblissement de l'autorité paternelle: La Notion de 'carence' des pères au XXe siècle," *La Pensée* 261 (1988): 43.

5.   Institut national de France, *Discours,* 13–14.

6.   Ibid., 16.

7.   Ibid., 20.

8.   See Sylvia Schafer, *Children in Moral Danger and the Problem of Government in Third Republic France* (Princeton, N.J.: Princeton University Press, 1997), 33. On the history of *la recherche de la paternité* see also Joan Wallach Scott, "Feminist Family Politics," *French Politics, Culture, and Society* 17, no. 3–4 (summer/fall 1999): 20–30.

9.   Schnapper, "La Correction paternelle," 524.

10.   See Claudia Scheck Kselman, "The Modernization of Family Law: The Politics and Ideology of Family Reform in Third Republic France" (Ph.D dissertation, University of Michigan, 1980).

11.   Schnapper, "Autorité domestique," 565.

12.   Ibid., 568.

13.   See Schafer, *Moral Danger,* 31.

14.   See "Introduction," in Pierre Reynaud, ed., *Histoire du droit de la famille,* Encyclopédie juridique Dalloz, Tome V, 2d edition, 1992.

15.   For an analysis of workers' use of family metaphors see Joan Wallach Scott, "Work Identities for Men and Women: The Politics of Work and Family in the Parisian Garment Trades in 1848," in *Gender and the Politics of History* (New York: Columbia University Press, 1988), 93–112.

16.   Schafer, *Moral Danger,* 30.

17.   Useful scholarly works addressing the depopulation crisis include Karen Offen, "Depopulation, Nationalism and Feminism in Fin-de-siècle France," *American Historical Review* 89 (June 1984): 648–676; Alain Becchia, "Les Milieux parlementaires et la dépopulation de 1900 à 1914," *Communications* (1986): 201–243; Anne Cova, "French Feminism and Maternity: Theories and Policies, 1890–1918," in *Maternity and Gender Policies: Women and the Rise of the European Welfare States, 1880s–1950s,* ed. Gisela Bock and Pat Thane (London: Routledge, 1991), 196–212. See also the Introduction, n. 22.

18.   Alisa Klaus, "Depopulation and Race Suicide: Maternalism and Pronatalist Ideologies in France and the United States," in *Mothers of a New World: Maternalist Politics and the Origins of Welfare States,* ed. Seth Koven and Sonya Michel (New York: Routledge, 1993), 195.

19.   Martine Segalen, "Sociologies et idées de la famille," in *Sociologie de la famille,* 3d ed. (Paris: Armand Colin, 1991), 26.

20.   Ibid., 20. See also Schnapper, "Autorité domestique," 569, who reports that Le Play was particularly bitter about the fact that the proposal to give fathers total testamentary freedom received only 42 votes in favor and 199 against. For an account

of Le Play's influence on the family movement, see Robert Talmy, *Histoire du mouvement familial en France, 1896–1939,* vol. 1 (Paris: UNCAF, 1962), 41–46.

21.   Émile Durkheim, "Introduction à la sociologie de la famille," 1888, quoted in *Affaires de famille, affaires d'État: Sociologie de la famille,* ed. François de Singly and Franz Schultheis, Colloque franco-allemand, CNRS (Jarville-la-Malgrange: Éditions de l'est, 1991), 14.

22.   Segalen, *Sociologie,* 265.

23.   The law itself can be found in the *Journal officiel,* 25 July 1889, 3653–3655; see Schafer, *Moral Danger,* especially chapter 3, "The Divestiture of Paternal Authority and the Law of 1889," for much more on this law and its ramifications for the boundaries between public and private spheres.

24.   Schafer, *Moral Danger,* 121.

25.   Schnapper, "Autorité domestique," 577–581.

26.   Sylvia Schafer argues for an epistemological break in the last decades of the nineteenth century as new legislation signaled an effort to remove regulation of the family from the realm of nature and to relocate it in the realm of the social. Schafer, *Moral Danger,* 67.

27.   Schnapper, "Correction paternelle," 536. Schnapper estimates that approximately half of these children were girls, and that most demands were made in Paris and other large cities.

28.   Michelle Perrot, "Roles and Characters," in *A History of Private Life,* vol. 4, *From the Fires of Revolution to the Great War,* ed. Michelle Perrot (Cambridge: Harvard University Press, 1990), 170.

29.   Sylvia Schafer has examined dossiers of paternal correction cases in Paris from 1897 to 1908, and finds that in three sample years, single mothers accounted for between 40 and 50 percent of the cases decided by the civil tribunal. Single fathers accounted for approximately 30 percent, and decisions involving both parents made up about 20 to 30 percent of the total each year. Schafer, *Moral Danger,* 95.

30.   Georges Bonjean was a philanthropist and Chevalier of the Légion d'honneur. He also founded the Société de la protection de l'enfance abandonné.

31.   Schnapper, "Correction paternelle," 540.

32.   On Marx, see Françoise Hurstel, "L'Affaiblissement de l'autorité paternelle," 42.

33.   Schnapper, "Correction paternelle," 544.

34.   See Schafer, *Moral Danger,* 72–73.

35.   See the *Petit larousse illustré* (Paris: Larousse, 1980), as well as Schafer, *Moral Danger,* 123.

36.   Françoise Hurstel writes, "whereas historical, sociological and economic phenomena were responsible for the decline of the social image of the father, and although the elaboration of new laws ratified these phenomena and determined his status, deficiency was attributed to the man himself, as if the status of fatherhood depended on his good or ill will." Hurstel, "L'Affaiblissement de l'autorité paternelle," 46.

37.   Ibid., 43.

38.   See Schafer, *Moral Danger.*

39.   *Grande encylopédie. Assistance publique,* Tome IV (Paris: Larousse, 1900), 276, Archives nationales.

40.   See Scott, "Feminist Family Politics," 24.

41.   See Henry Lavollée, *Code manuel de la recherche de la paternité* (Paris: Librairie générale de droit et de jurisprudence, 1913), 100–139.

42. See Dalloz, *Jurisprudence générale. Supplément: paternité et filiation* (Paris: Bureau de jurisprudence générale, 1893), 492.
43. See Lavollée, *Code manuel,* 20.
44. Ibid., 136.
45. According to Yvonne Kniebiehler: "Paternity is much less obvious than maternity. It is not a fact of nature, it is a human invention. It appears as an awakening of consciousness and an investment of power at the moment when the human male wishes to decipher the biological link that unites him to his progeny." Yvonne Kniebiehler, "Le Rôle des pères à travers l'histoire," in "Pères et paternité," *Revue française des affaires sociales,* Ministère du travail, de l'emploi et de la formation professionelle, hors série (November 1988): 27.
46. Lavollée, *Code manuel,* 2.
47. AN C 5635, Projet de résolution tendant à nommer une Commission de 44 membres pour la refonte du Code civil, présenté par M. Goujat, Session extraordinaire de 1893, no. 204.
48. According to Lavollée, "natural" paternity might be established through a man's willingness to pay for a child's food, upkeep, and education; blood tests that could definitively determine that a given man was *not* the father of a child were not in fact developed until 1955.
49. AN C 5564, Arthur Groussier, Proposition de loi tendant à modifier plusieurs articles du Code civil à l'effet de donner les mêmes droits aux enfants naturels qu'aux enfants légitimes et de permettre la recherche de la paternité, Dossier 129, 1895.
50. Several years later in the Senate, Rivet offered the following statistics: in 1879 in Paris, there were 56,329 births; 14,653 of these were illegitimate, and 11,484 of these illegitimate children had not been recognized. In 1909, from January 3 to 9, there were 749 legitimate births and 263 illegitimate births, only 59 of which had been recognized. Lavollée, *Code manuel,* 2.
51. AN C 5595, Gustave Rivet, "Proposition de loi relative à la recherche de la paternité," no. 1484, Chambre des députés, Session de 1895.
52. Ann-Louise Shapiro discusses the efforts to overturn the ban on *recherche de la paternité* within the context of debates about vengeful criminal women in *Breaking the Codes: Female Criminality in Fin-de-siècle Paris* (Stanford, Calif.: Stanford University Press, 1996).
53. Lavollée, *Code manuel,* 68.
54. This would contradict Jacques Donzelot's notion of a conspiracy against working-class fathers orchestrated by wives and bourgeois reformers. See Jacques Donzelot, *The Policing of Families,* trans. Robert Hurley (New York: Pantheon Books, 1979), especially chapter 4, "The Tutelary Complex."
55. Jean Carbonnier has suggested that here Third Republican legislators were unfaithful to the desires of their "great ancestors," who affirmed that one could only become a father through one's own will and affection. Carbonnier, *Le Statut de l'enfant,* 304. Other scholars have emphasized the law's continued bias in favor of men, for the pregnancy had to be a result of "rape, kidnapping, flagrant cohabitation, misrepresentation or obvious abuse of authority, and it had to be followed by either unambiguous written acknowledgement of paternity or clear evidence of support of the child"—Nicole Arnaud-Duc, "The Law's Contradictions," in *A History of Women,* vol. 4, *Emerging Feminism from Revolution to World War,* ed. Geneviève Fraisse and Michelle Perrot (Cambridge: Harvard University Press, 1993), 105.

56.   Émile de Saint-Auban, in Lavollée, *Code manuel,* page II.

57.   Madeleine Vernet, *La Paternité,* Études sociales (Poligny: Imprimerie Alfred Jacquin, 1906), 2. Madeleine Vernet was a militant feminist and advocate of "free love" before the Great War. Her feminist activism centered on concern for mothers' rights. She was an ardent pacifist and founded the Ligue des femmes contre la guerre in 1921. See Christine Bard, *Les Filles de Marianne: Histoires des féminismes, 1914–1940* (Paris: Fayard, 1995), 139.

58.   Vernet, *Paternité,* 9.

59.   Ibid., 12.

60.   Lydie Martial established the Union de pensée féminine, a feminist discussion group, in 1902. As a speaker and writer she often dealt with topics of education. Bard, *Filles de Marianne,* 37.

61.   Lydie Martial, "Un Voeu important: L'Enseignement de la paternité à la caserne et dans les écoles de l'État," *Action du féminisme rationnel,* Union de pensée féminine, 2 March 1905, 2.

62.   Hurstel, "L'Affaiblissement," 43–44.

63.   Colin Dyer, *Population and Society in Twentieth Century France* (New York: Holmes and Meier, 1978), 40. Mary Louise Roberts also refers to these figures in her *Civilization without Sexes: Reconstructing Gender in Post-War France, 1917–1927* (Chicago: University of Chicago Press, 1994), 94.

64.   Michel Huber, *La Population de la France pendant la guerre* (New Haven, Conn.: Yale University Press, 1931), 422, quoted in Eugen Weber, *The Hollow Years: France in the 1930s,* (New York: W. W. Norton, 1996), 13.

65.   Roberts, *Civilization without Sexes,* 95. See Maurice Garden and Hervé Le Bras, "La Population française entre les deux guerres," in *Histoire de la population française,* ed. Jacques Dupâquier, vol.4, *De 1914 à nos jours* (Paris: Presses universitaires de France, 1988), 90–91.

66.   Weber, *Hollow Years,* 12.

67.   Historical demographers Maurice Garden and Hervé Le Bras estimated that in 1921 there were 120 women for every 100 men. Garden and Le Bras, "La Population française," 97; see also Weber, *Hollow Years,* 14.

68.   Mary Louise Roberts details many of these debates in her *Civilization without Sexes,* particularly in part 3, "La Femme Seule."

69.   Ibid., 89–147.

70.   AN BB[18] 2616, Dossier 1094 A 1919.

71.   Françoise Thébaud, "Femmes et guerres en France au 20ème siècle," paper presented at the European Social Science History Association, Nordwijkerhout, The Netherlands, May 1996.

72.   AN C 7643, Chambre des députés, 11ème législature, Session de 1915, séance du 19 mars 1915.

73.   AN C 7643, Sénat, Année 1916, Proposition de loi adoptée par la Chambre des députés, adoptée par le Sénat, Déterminant les conditions dans lesquelles pourront être légitimés les enfants dont les parents se sont trouvés, par la mobilisation du père et le décès de ce dernier, dans l'impossibilité de contracter mariage.

74.   Weber, *Hollow Years,* 13.

75.   AN C 7643, Chambre des députés, Session de 12 septembre, 1916, no. 2472.

76.   MM Fleurot et al., "Comment relever dans les pays envahis les foyers détruits par la guerre," *La Revue philanthropique,* 15 January 1920, 7.

77.   Anne-Marie Sohn, "Between the Wars in France and England," in *A History of*

Women, vol. 5, *Toward a Cultural Identity in the Twentieth Century,* ed. Françoise Thébaud (Cambridge: Harvard University Press, 1994), 105.

78.   Gisela Bock, "Poverty and Mothers' Rights in the Emerging Welfare States," in *A History of Women,* vol. 5, *Toward a Cultural Identity in the Twentieth Century,* ed. Françoise Thébaud (Cambridge: Harvard University Press, 1994), 416.

79.   Ibid., 419; and Seth Koven and Sonya Michel, "Introduction: 'Mother Worlds,'" in *Mothers of a New World,* 1–42.

80.   For more on Mother's Day celebrations, see Karen Offen, "Body Politics: Women, Work and the Politics of Motherhood in France, 1920–1950," in *Maternity and Gender Policies,* 138.

81.   Maria Vérone was a well-known feminist lawyer who campaigned for women's voting rights in the interwar years. Bard, *Filles de Marianne,* 30.

82.   Comité national d'études sociales & politiques, "La Natalité," Exposé de MM Vieuille, Roulleaux-Dugage, de Mmes Chevally, Maria Vérone, Bouvier, Séance du lundi 26 janvier 1925, 38.

83.   E. Lancelot, *Pour l'ordre familial: Un Plan, une organisation à réaliser* (Paris: Éditions mariage et famille, 1934), 38.

84.   Rapport de Mlle Chaptal, *Enquête sur l'enfance en danger moral,* Société des nations, Comité de la protection de l'enfance, 1920, 8.

85.   See Hurstel, "L'Affaiblissement de l'autorité paternelle," 45.

·86.   Cours de M. J. Terrel, "Les Responsabilités du père de famille," *Semaines sociales de France,* Versailles, 1913, 255.

87.   *La Famille française* was the monthly publication of the Ligue des Droits de la Famille in Paris.

88.   Jean Guirand, "La Décadence paternelle," *La Famille française,* Bulletin Périodique de la Ligue des Droits de la Famille, no. 5 (April 1930).

89.   The adjective *dénaturé* (perverted, debased) was frequently used to describe fathers in such articles. *L'Humanité,* 4 November 1936, 2.

90.   *L'Humanité,* 11 February 1937, 2.

91.   *Le Populaire de Paris,* 4 August 1939, 6.

92.   D. Parodi, "Parents et Enfants," in *Les Problèmes de la famille et le féminisme,* Conférences faites à la Ligue française d'éducation morale, n.d., Bibliothèque historique de la ville de Paris, 74–75.

93.   G. Guy-Grand, "Famille et société," in *Les Problèmes de la famille et le féminisme,* 92.

94.   Proposals for a family suffrage system came forward repeatedly in late nineteenth- and early twentieth-century France. With a system of *suffrage familial,* fathers were to be rewarded with extra votes according to the number of their children. Deputies of the Right and center championed family suffrage. Richard Tomlinson points out that 46 deputies out of 372 specifically mentioned supporting the family vote in their *barodet,* or statement of intent. Richard Tomlinson, "The Politics of Dénatalité during the French Third Republic, 1890–1940" (Ph.D. thesis, Cambridge, 1981), 344. See chapter 2 of the present volume for a more complete analysis of the family suffrage debate.

95.   For more on Fernand Boverat, see Koos, "Engendering Reaction."

96.   Robert Talmy, *Histoire du mouvement familial, 1896–1939,* vol. 2 (Paris: Union national des caisses d'allocations familiales, 1962), 245. Although the family movement was made up of many different leagues and organizations, most pressed for greater state resources and public prestige for families, particularly large families (see chapters 2 and 5).

97.   Talmy, *Histoire du mouvement familial,* vol. 2, 5.

98.   Ibid., 96.

99.   Tomlinson, "Politics of Dénatalité," 232–233.

100.   Susan Pedersen, *Family, Dependence, and the Origins of the Welfare State: Britain and France, 1914–1945* (Cambridge: Cambridge University Press, 1993), 131.

101.   On the strength of the pro-natalist lobby and its integration of a wide variety of politicians from the communist to the conservative parties, see Pedersen, *Family, Dependence,* 368–372.

102.   Ibid., 402.

103.   M. Marcel Cachin, *Annales du Chambre des députés,* 2e séance du 11 décembre, 1923, 4018.

104.   Gérard Vincent, "Communism as a Way of Life," in *A History of Private Life,* vol. 5, *Riddles of Identity in Modern Times,* ed. Antoine Prost and Gérard Vincent (Cambridge: Harvard University Press, 1991), 330–333; and Bard, *Filles de Marianne,* 374.

105.   For more on Marin as a politician and social scientist, see Herman Lebovics, who includes a chapter on his importance to conservative thought, as well as to French anthropology and ethnography, in the interwar years. Herman Lebovics, *True France: The Wars over Cultural Identity in France, 1900–1945* (Ithaca, N.Y.: Cornell University Press, 1992). For more on the law of 1924, see Michèle Bordeaux, *La Victoire de la famille dans la France défaite: Vichy, 1940–1944* (Paris: Flammarion, 2002).

106.   Louis Marin, Vice-Président de la Chambre des Députés, *L'Abandon de famille,* Proposition déposée à la Chambre des Députés, le 20 février 1923, Bibliothèque historique de la ville de Paris.

107.   Gérard Cornu, *Vocabulaire juridique* (Paris: Presses universitaires de France, 1992).

108.   One example of this is a case brought before the Court of Appeals in Paris in 1927 against a man who was being charged with family abandonment. AN BB[18] 6375, "Problèmes d'application de la loi du 17 février 1924 sur l'abandon de famille," Paris, le 4 Août 1927, Direction criminelle.

109.   AN BB[18] 3205, Dossier 1610 A 1939, A. Butillard, Union féminine civique et sociale, "La Femme sert le pays en servant la famille," Note sur l'abandon de famille, Paris, 19 juin 1939.

110.   AN BB[18] 3243, Dossier 104 A 40 and Dossier 111 A.

111.   Laura L. Frader, "Engendering Work and Wages: The French Labor Movement and the Family Wage," in *Gender and Class in Modern Europe,* ed. Laura L. Frader and Sonya O. Rose (Ithaca, N.Y.: Cornell University Press, 1996), 151.

112.   Ibid., 157.

113.   For much more on this process, see Pedersen, *Family, Dependence,* chapter 5, "Business Strategies and the Family: The Development of Family Allowances in France, 1920–1936," 224–288.

114.   Frader, "Engendering Work and Wages," 158–159.

115.   Talmy, *Mouvement familial,* 2:141.

116.   Ibid., 132–133. Laura Frader argues that the state became a powerful new partner in the discussions of family allowances following World War I. See Frader, "Engendering Work and Wages," 156.

117.   Pedersen, *Family, Dependence,* 402.

118.   See Bock, "Poverty and Mothers' Rights," 427.

119.   Pedersen, *Family, Dependence,* 380.

120.   Pedersen discusses the consensus surrounding this vision of social redistribution in *Family, Dependence,* 415–416.

121.   Schnapper, "La Correction paternelle," 552.

122.   AN F^{60} 608, Ministère de la Santé Publique, Direction de l'hygiène et de l'assistance, "Projet de décret-loi sur le renforcement de la protection de l'enfance," Paris, le 1 décembre 1937.

123.   AN F^{60} 608, *Ce que sont, Ce que veulent,* Les Comités de vigilance et d'action pour la protection de l'enfance malheureuse, 2 juin 1939, 11–15.

124.   Pedersen, *Family, Dependence,* 386.

125.   4 June 1939, quoted in Talmy, *Mouvement familial,* vol. 2, 234.

126.   The full text of the Code de la famille appears in the *Journal officiel, Lois et décrets,* 30 July 1939.

127.   Quoted in Hurstel, "L'Affaiblissement de l'autorité paternelle," 40.

2.   ICONS OF THE *PÈRE DE FAMILLE*

1.   Fernand Boverat, *Patriotisme et paternité* (Paris: Bernard Grasset, 1913), 10.

2.   AN F^{12} 12137, Georges Pernot, "Les Droits de la famille," *Le Journal des familles nombreuses* 12 (December 1929): 1.

3.   Robert Talmy suggests that in the nineteenth century the main defenders of family rights tended to belong to one of three groups. Conservatives were concerned with upholding the family, religion, and property. Social-Catholics strove for a new political economy of the family and established associations to further the rights of families. Finally, economists and statisticians with links to the government were anxious about declining birth rates and the political implications of a smaller population. Robert Talmy, *Histoire du mouvement familial en France, 1896–1939,* vol. 1 (Paris: UNCAF, 1962), 27. These three groups were often the most active participants in debates on the family, but many other political and social groups, including feminists, Communists, and Radical Republicans, also took part in discourse on the family and used the *père de famille* in the articulation of their interests.

4.   Elizabeth Thompson makes an argument that the politics of the interwar years in the French mandate of Syria and Lebanon can best be understand as a "crisis of paternity" at every level of society following World War I. Elizabeth Thompson, *Colonial Citizens: Republican Rights, Paternal Privilege, and Gender in French Syria and Lebanon* (New York: Columbia University Press, 2000).

5.   For more on Antoine Rédier and the Légion française des combattants, see Cheryl Koos, "Fascism, Fatherhood, and the Family in Interwar France: The Case of Antoine Rédier and the Légion," *Journal of Family History* 24, no. 3 (July 1999): 317–329. See also Georges Valois, *Le Père: Philosophie de la famille* (Paris: Nouvelle Librairie nationale, 1926).

6.   Many works have dealt with the depopulation crisis in France in the late nineteenth and early twentieth centuries. See, for example John R. Gillis, Louise A. Tilly, and David Levine, eds., *The European Experience of Declining Fertility* (Cambridge: Harvard University Press, 1992); Ansley J. Coale and Susan Cotts Watkins, *The Decline of Fertility in Europe: The Revised Proceedings of a Conference on the Princeton Fertility Project* (Princeton, N.J.: Princeton University Press, 1986); Michael S. Teitelbaum and Jay M. Winter, *The Fear of Population Decline* (Orlando, Fla.: Academic Press, 1985). On women, mothers, and the population debate in France, see Alisa Klaus, "Depopulation and Race Suicide: Maternalism and Pronatalist Ideologies in France and the United States," in *Mothers of a New World: Maternalist Politics and the Origins of Welfare States,* ed. Seth Koven and Sonya Michel (New York: Routledge, 1993), 188–212;

Karen Offen, "Depopulation, Nationalism and Feminism in Fin-de-siècle France," *The American Historical Review* 89, no. 3 (June 1984): 648–676; Anne Cova, "French Feminism and Maternity: Theories and Policies, 1890–1918," in *Maternity and Gender Policies: Women and the Rise of the European Welfare States, 1880s–1950s,* ed. Gisela Bock and Pat Thane (London: Routledge, 1991), 196–212; Françoise Thébaud, "Le Mouvement nataliste dans la France de l'entre-deux-guerres: L'Alliance nationale pour l'accroissement de la population française," *Revue d'histoire moderne et contemporaine* 32 (1985): 276–301. See also notes 3 and 22 in the Introduction to the present volume.

7.   On the genesis of some of these organizations, see Talmy, *Histoire du mouvement familial,* vol. 1, as well as Michel Messu, *Les Politiques familiales* (Paris: Les Éditions ouvrières, 1992); Michel Chauvière, "L'Action familiale ouvrière et la politique de Vichy: Acteurs, institutions, enjeux," in *L'Action familiale ouvrière et la politique de Vichy,* Journées d'étude des 28–29 novembre 1984, *Les Cahiers du GRMF* 3 (1984): 13–26; and idem, "Familialisme et régulation sociale ou aspects de la démultiplication du concept de famille," *Annales de Vaucresson* 27 (1987): 207–226. On Fernand Boverat of the Alliance nationale, see Cheryl Koos, "Engendering Reaction: The Politics of Pronatalism and the Family in France, 1919–1944" (Ph.D. dissertation, University of Southern California, December 1996).

8.   Maria Sophia Quine, "Fathers of the Nation: French Pronatalism during the Third Republic," in *Population Politics in Twentieth-Century Europe* (New York: Routledge, 1996), 77.

9.   See Mary Louise Roberts, *Civilization without Sexes: Reconstructing Gender in Postwar France, 1917–1927* (Chicago: University of Chicago Press, 1994), 91; on women and early welfare policies, see Seth Koven and Sonya Michel, eds., *Mothers of a New World: Maternalist Politics and the Origins of Welfare States* (New York: Routledge, 1993); Offen, "Depopulation," 648–676; Catherine Rollet-Echalier, *La Politique à l'égard de la petite enfance sous la III République* (Paris: INED, 1990).

10.   Paul Bureau, *L'Indiscipline des moeurs: Étude de science sociale* (Paris: Bloud et Gay, 1921), 2.

11.   Paul Bureau was a professor at the Faculté libre de droit and at the École des hautes études sociales in Paris. A respected social critic and prolific writer, Bureau founded the Ligue pour la vie at the Musée social in 1916. The Ligue was especially concerned with reminding men of their paternal responsibilities and the moral rules of proper sexual conduct. See Talmy, *Histoire,* 1:173–178.

12.   Ibid., 11–15.

13.   Ibid., 66.

14.   Louis Blachère, "Une Question nationale: Les familles nombreuses," *Alès-Journal* (1934): 6.

15.   According to Colin Dyer, a relative majority of families in France in 1911 chose to have only one child; more than half of French families had only one or two children. Dyer, *Population and Society in Twentieth-Century France* (New York: Holmes and Meier, 1978), 24.

16.   Judith Stone discusses how Radical Republicans were more successful at establishing "families" of peers than at creating traditional conjugal families, as many political leaders in the Radical Party in the late nineteenth and early twentieth century remained bachelors or lived in unconventional unions. Stone, *Sons of the Revolution: Radical Democrats in France, 1862–1914* (Baton Rouge: Louisiana State University Press, 1996), 39–40.

17.   Bureau, *L'Indiscipline,* 227.

18.   André Toulemon, *Le Suffrage familial* (Paris: n.p., 1933), 39.

19.   Ibid., 66.

20.   On concepts of decline and degeneration in France, see Robert A. Nye, *Crime, Madness and Politics in Modern France: The Medical Concept of National Decline* (Princeton, N.J.: Princeton University Press, 1984); and Daniel Pick, *Faces of Degeneration: A European Disorder, c. 1848–c.1918* (New York: Cambridge University Press, 1989).

21.   Emmanuel Harraca, *Sur le vote familial. Le Suffrage du chef de famille normale* (Paris, 1930), 11.

22.   Harraca, *Vote familial,* 52.

23.   Tomlinson, "Politics," 344.

24.   See Koos, "Fascism, Fatherhood," 324.

25.   AN F^{60} 495, Letter from E.Michel to E. Daladier, 23 mai 1939.

26.   E. and H. Biancini, *La Communauté familiale* (Paris: Plon, 1942), 156.

27.   AN F^{60} 606, Extrait du procès-Verbal, Institution du suffrage familial, 2 juillet 1936, Chambre de commerce d'Armentières-Hazebrouck.

28.   See Koos, "Fascism, Fatherhood," 324.

29.   The Fédération nationale des associations de familles nombreuses was established in 1921, in an effort to unite the many different groups championing family rights that had come into being following the war. Talmy estimates that the Federation grouped together about 96,000 families, or 500,000 people. Talmy, *Histoire,* 1:246–254.

30.   Henri Roulleaux-Dugage, "Le Vote familial," *Familles de France* 11 (November 1933): 2.

31.   Henri Roulleaux-Dugage, "La Natalité," *Comité national d'études sociales & politiques,* 26 January 1925, 15. Roulleaux-Dugage's numbers were in fact wrong, an error that was only pointed out several years later, after much campaigning (see Talmy, *Histoire,* 2:41).

32.   "Vous voulez une France neuve? Faites la familiale," *Familles de France* 11 (November 1936): 1.

33.   E. Harraca, *Sur le vote familial: Le Suffrage du chef de famille normale* (Paris: Marcel Giard, 1930), 9.

34.   Roulleaux-Dugage, "La Natalité," 15.

35.   For scholarly works on women's suffrage in the interwar years, see Siân Reynolds, "Rights and the Republic: The Interwar Years as Antechamber to Democracy?" in *France between the Wars: Gender and Politics* (New York: Routledge, 1996); Steven Hause and Anne Kenney, *Women's Suffrage and Social Politics in the French Third Republic* (Princeton, N.J.: Princeton University Press, 1984); Christine Bard, *Les Filles de Marianne* (Paris: Fayard, 1995); and Nicole du Roy and Albert du Roy, *Citoyennes! Il y a cinquante ans le vote des femmes* (Paris: Flammarion, 1994).

36.   For more on this, see the carton "Vote des femmes," in the Fonds Marie-Louise Bouglé, Bibliothèque historique de la ville de Paris. See also Mary Louise Roberts, *Civilization without Sexes,* esp. part 1, "La Femme Moderne," for a discussion of men's fears about women's political power.

37.   *Familles de France* 11 (November 1936): 1.

38.   Harraca, *Sur le vote familial,* 16.

39.   "Le Vote Familial," *Familles de France* 10 (October 1930): 1.

40.   AN F^{60} 606, Gouvernement provisoire de la République française, Haut comité de la population, "Note à l'attention de Messieurs les Membres du gouvernement," 24 juin 1945.

41.   See Kevin Passmore, "'Planting the Tricolor in the Citadels of Communism': Women's Social Action in the Croix de Feu and Parti Social Français," *Journal of Modern History* 7, no. 4 (December 1999).

42.   See Koos, "Fascism, Fatherhood," 324.

43.   Parti socialiste, *XXXIIe Congrès national,* Mulhouse, 9–12 June, 1935, 498.

44.   "Le Nouveau train de décrets-lois," *Le Populaire de Paris,* 28 July 1939, 3.

45.   See Susan Pedersen, *Family, Dependence, and the Origins of the Welfare State* (Cambridge: Cambridge University Press, 1993), *passim.*

46.   Paul Vaillant-Couturier, "Le Massacre des innocents," *L'Humanité,* 11 December 1935, 1

47.   On motherhood, see Anne Cova, *Maternité et droits des femmes (XIX–XX siècles)* (Paris: Economica, 1998); Karen Offen, "Body Politics: Women, Work, and the Politics of Motherhood in France, 1920–1950," in *Maternity and Gender Policies: Women and the Rise of the European Welfare States, 1880s–1950s,* ed. Gisela Bock and Pat Thane (London: Routledge, 1991), 138–159; Nadine Lefaucheur, "Maternity, Family, and the State," in *A History of Women,* vol. 5, *Toward a Cultural Identity in the Twentieth Century,* ed. Françoise Thébaud (Cambridge: Harvard University Press, 1994), 433–453.

48.   Henry Bordeaux, *Le Foyer* (Paris: Flammarion, 1937), 30.

49.   Pierre Méline, *Morale familiale* (Paris: Bloud & Gay, 1928), 91.

50.   Madeleine Danielou, *Visages de la famille* (Paris: Bloud & Gay, 1940), 95.

51.   Maurice Carité, *Le Père de famille et le foyer* (Paris: Les Éditions du temps présent, n.d.), 22.

52.   Mme A.-M. Couvreur, *Comment aimer pour être heureux,* quoted in Maurice Carité, *Père de famille,* 10.

53.   Danielou, *Visages,* 82.

54.   Ibid., 28.

55.   See, for example, the case of "Gonin contre Dame Gonin," Cour de Cassation, Chambre Criminelle, 12 April 1935, reported in the *Recueil Hebdomadaire Dalloz,* Annuel de l'année 1935, 333.

56.   AN BB[18] 6375, Le Procureur général près la Cour d'appel de Paris, "Problèmes d'application de la loi du 17 février 1924 sur l'abandon de famille," 4 août 1927. See also Michèle Bordeaux, *La Victoire de la famille dans la France défaite: Vichy 1940–1944* (Paris: Flammarion, 2002), 218–221.

57.   See Laura L. Frader, "Engendering Work and Wages: The French Labor Movement and the Family Wage," in *Gender and Class in Modern Europe,* ed. Laura Frader and Sonya O. Rose (Ithaca, N.Y.: Cornell University Press, 1996), 145.

58.   For much more on the gendered development of family allowances, see Pedersen, *Family, Dependence.*

59.   Cours du R. P. Desbuquois, "Les Réformes économiques qu'exige la restauration de la famille," *Semaines sociales de France,* Grenoble, 1923, 355.

60.   For a discussion of gender in the political economy of work and family life in the mid-nineteenth century, see Joan Scott, *Gender and the Politics of History* (New York: Columbia University Press, 1988), especially part 3, "Gender in History," 92–163.

61.   Danielou, *Visages,* 139–140.

62.   Paul Géraldy was the *nom de plume* of Paul Lefèvre, a Commandeur de la Légion d'Honneur and author of at least twelve major works of poetry and theater.

63.   Paul Géraldy, *L'Homme et l'amour,* illus. Raoul Serres (Paris: La Belle édition, n.d.), 64.

64.   Carité, *Père de famille,* 1.

65. Ibid., 18.
66. Danielou, *Visages*, 82.
67. Géraldy, *L'Homme et l'amour*, 63.
68. Carité, *Père de famille*, 14.
69. Danielou, *Visages*, 109.
70. For a discussion of the importance of the Salons des Arts Ménagers, see Ellen Furlough, "Selling the American Way in Interwar France: *Prix Uniques* and the *Salons des Arts Ménagers,*" *Journal of Social History* 26, no. 3 (1993): 491–519.
71. "Les Loisirs au foyer," *Action familiale* 70 (February 1937): 1.
72. AN F⁷ 12386, "Association de pères de famille, Modèle de statuts," *La Croix des Alpes,* 1908.
73. For more on the crucial question of education and religion during the Third Republic, see Deborah Reed-Danahay, *Education and Identity in Rural France: The Politics of Schooling* (New York: Cambridge University Press, 1996); Sarah A. Curtis, "Supply and Demand: Religious Schooling in Nineteenth-Century France," *History of Education Quarterly* 39, no. 1 (1999): 51–72; Robert Gildea, *Education in Provincial France, 1800–1914: A Study of Three Departments* (New York: Oxford University Press, 1983); André Lanfrey, *Les Catholiques français et l'école, 1902–1914* (Paris: Cerf, 1990); Jo Burr Margadant, *Madame le professeur: Women Educators in the Third Republic* (Princeton, N.J.: Princeton University Press, 1990); Raymond Grew, *School, State and Society: The Growth of Elementary Schooling in Nineteenth-Century France: A Qualitative Analysis* (Ann Arbor: University of Michigan Press, 1991); and Maurice Crubellier, *L'École républicaine, 1870–1940: Esquisse d'une histoire culturelle* (Paris: Éditions Christian, 1993).
74. "La Responsibilité du père de famille," Cours de M. J. Terrel, *Semaines sociales de France,* Versailles, 1913, 355.
75. AN F⁷ 12386, "M. le Doyen de Saint-Gilles-sur-Vie," 1908, TD.
76. AN F⁷ 12386, "Les Associations de pères de famille," *Rappel,* 26 September 1908.
77. See Steven J. Ross, "Living for the Weekend: The Shorter Hours Movement in International Perspective," *Labour* 2 (1991): 267–282.
78. For more on the eight-hour movement in France and the use of familial arguments, see Gary Cross, *A Quest for Time: The Reduction of Work in Britain and France, 1840–1940* (Berkeley: University of California Press, 1989), 67–68; idem., "*Les Trois Huits:* Labor Movements, International Reform, and the Origins of the Eight-Hour Day, 1919–1924," *French Historical Studies* 14 (1985): 240–268; idem., "The Quest for Leisure: Reassessing the Eight-Hour Day in France," *Journal of Social History* 18 (1984): 195–216; and Kristen Stromberg Childers, "Paternity and the Politics of Citizenship in Interwar France," *Journal of Family History* 26, no. 1 (January 2001).
79. The UFCS was founded by Andrée Butillard in 1925. With more than 10,000 members, the organization fought for women's civic education and for improvement in their social and economic condition. The UFCS supported the idea of a family vote and condemned "egalitarian feminism," which they believed threatened to destroy the Christian family. See Bard, *Filles de Marianne,* 275.
80. "La Famille dans la vie sociale: Petit guide pratique de la législation familiale," in *Union féminine civique et sociale* (Paris: Éditions SPES, 1937), 109.
81. AN F.22 .405, Maurice Guérin, "La 8 heures et la vie 'humaine' des travailleurs," *La Voix sociale,* 13 August 1922.
82. Cross, "Quest for Leisure," 208.

83. Ibid., 202.

84. Cross, "Origins of the Eight-Hour Day," 263.

85. Cross, "Quest for Leisure," 208.

86. M. Zirnheld, "La Famille et les revendications des travailleurs," *Semaine sociales de France,* Grenoble, 1923, 463.

87. The *Revue de la famille* was a newspaper published by the Comité central des allocations familiales. Supported by industrial interests such as the Comité des Forges and the Union des industries métallurgiques et minières, the Comité was an association of employers concerned with developing a family allowance system as a means of stabilizing the work force and keeping down wage costs. See Pedersen, *Family, Dependence,* 224–288.

88. J. F. Paul-Leclercq, "Loisirs intelligents," *Revue de la famille* 130 (15 August 1936): 3.

89. Quoted in Monique Eleb, *L'Apprentissage du "chez-soi"* (Paris: Éditions parenthèses, 1994), 54.

90. It is interesting in this regard that neither illustration from the *Revue de la famille* depicts fathers engaged in sports activities *with* their children. Whereas in the United States one suspects that it was precisely this sort of activity that fathers were supposed to share with their children, in France men appear as participants on teams with other men.

91. Carité, *Père de famille,* 41.

92. Danielou, *Visages,* 28.

93. Association pour la protection légale des travailleurs, "L'Utilisation des loisirs des travailleurs," Paris, 1925, 19.

94. *Solidarité: Exposition internationale des arts et techniques dans la vie moderne, Paris, 1937* (Paris: Éditions Edna Nicoll, 1937), 126.

95. Romy Golan traces the importance of the peasant theme in French art of the interwar years, describing an intense "conjunction of the peasantry and the moralizing climate of the *rappel à l'ordre*" that was played out by artists of the period and was manifest in the belief that what made France resistant to the crash on Wall Street was its reliance on agriculture. Romy Golan, *Modernity and Nostalgia: Art and Politics in France Between the Wars* (New Haven, Conn.: Yale University Press, 1995), especially 41, 45, and 51.

96. Eugen Weber, *The Hollow Years: France in the 1930s* (New York: W. W. Norton, 1996), 39.

97. Eugène Duthoit, "Illusions et réalités touchant le problème de la population," *Semaines sociales de France,* Grenoble, 1923, 75.

98. Mgr Lavallée, "Le Célibat écclésiastique et le problème de la population," *Semaines sociales de France,* Grenoble, 1923, 240.

99. AN F^{60} 607, "Allocution de M. l'Abbé Viollet," *Le Congrès annuel de la Confédération générale des familles et des associations familiales de France,* December 1937.

100. See Martha Hanna, "Natalism, Homosexuality, and the Controversy over *Corydon,*" in *Homosexuality in Modern France,* ed. Jeffrey Merrick and Bryant T. Ragan Jr. (New York: Oxford University Press, 1996), 202–224.

101. Roberts, *Civilization without Sexes,* 104 and 138.

102. See Bureau, *L'Indiscipline,* 15.

103. Georges Ferré, *Chroniques des temps d'après-guerre* (Paris: Éditions Jules Tallandier, 1929), ii, 19–20.

104. Toulemon, *Suffrage familial,* 15, 230.

105.   M. G. Widmer, *Les Logements pour célibataires* (Paris: Impr. Chaix, 1918), 17.

106.   La Plus grande famille was an association of bourgeois fathers of at least five children, founded in 1916 by Auguste Isaac. The association's goal was to help fathers of families to carry out their unique social obligations. See Talmy, *Histoire*, vol. 1, 179–220.

107.   AN F^{60} 607, Letter from J. B. Autissier, 23 novembre 1938.

108.   M. Amoudrou, "La Paternité," Conférences données à l'Institut d'études familiales du Nord de la France, Lille, 1943, 72.

109.   See Bernard Schnapper, "L'Autorité domestique et partis politiques de Napoléon à de Gaulle," in *Voies nouvelles en histoire du droit: La justice, la famille, la répression pénale* (Paris: Presses universitaires de France, 1991), 584–596, for a discussion of political perspectives on domestic relations. See also Bard, *Filles de Marianne*, 358–359.

110.   Bard, *Filles de Marianne*, 374. In 1937, the Communists advocated a substantial tax break for fathers, but they suggested augmenting the tax for bachelors and married couples only at high income levels. "La Reforme fiscale," *L'Humanité*, 5 February 1937, 7.

3. BUILDING ON THE FAMILY

1.   See Christian Bachelier, "L'Armée française entre la victoire et la défaite," in *La France des années noires*, vol. 1, *De la défaite à Vichy*, ed. Jean-Pierre Azéma and François Bédarida (Paris: Éditions du Seuil, 1993), 77.

2.   Robert O. Paxton, *Vichy France: Old Guard and New Order, 1940–1944* (New York: Columbia University Press, 1972), 20.

3.   See Gérard Miller, *Les Pousse-au-jouir du Maréchal Pétain*, foreword by Roland Barthes (Paris: Éditions du Seuil, 1975), 52.

4.   Philippe Pétain, "Appel du 11 juillet 1940," in *Messages d'outre-tombe du Maréchal Pétain*, ed. Monique and Jean Paillard (Paris: Nouvelles éditions latines, 1983), 22.

5.   The term "strange defeat" comes from the title of the historian Marc Bloch's commentary. See Marc Bloch, *Strange Defeat: A Statement of Evidence Written in 1940* (New York: Norton, 1968).

6.   Some scholars have placed great emphasis on the importance of Charles Maurras to the ideology of the National Revolution. While the Vichy regime did take up many of Maurras's favorite themes, such as the fight against "anti-France," Vichy ideology was a synergetic mix of influences that cannot be reduced simply to Maurrassian ideas. See Jean-Pierre Azéma, "Le Régime de Vichy," in *France des années noires*, 1:162; and idem, *From Munich to the Liberation, 1938–1944*, trans. Janet Lloyd (New York: Cambridge University Press, 1984), 56.

7.   See Norman Ingram, *The Politics of Dissent: Pacifism in France 1919–1939* (New York: Oxford University Press, 1991); and Jean Defrasne, *Le Pacifisme en France* (Paris: Presses universitaires de France, 1994).

8.   Jean-Pierre Azéma, "La France de Daladier," in *France des années noires*, 1:11–15.

9.   François Bédarida, "Huit mois d'attente et d'illusion: La 'Drôle de guerre,'" in *France des années noires*, 1:38.

10.   See Azéma, "La France de Daladier," 31–32.

11.   Edouard Herriot's words in the Chamber of Deputies, cited by Bédarida in "Huit mois d'attente," 38.

12.   The term *drôle de guerre* was coined by Roland Dorgelès in October 1939: "Non, la guerre n'est pas drôle, mais c'est tout de même une drôle de guerre. . . ." Cited in Bédarida, "Huit mois d'attente," 41.

13.   For a detailed account of France's defeat in 1940 see Alistair Horne, *To Lose a Battle: France 1940* (Boston: Little, Brown, 1969).

14.   James F. McMillan, "The Strange Defeat," in *Twentieth-Century France: Politics and Society, 1898–1991* (London: Edward Arnold, 1992), 128.

15.   This is an oversimplified version of the fall of France; for greater details see Joel Blatt, ed., *The French Defeat of 1940: Reassessments* (Providence, R.I.: Berghahn Books, 1998); Jean-Louis Crémieux-Brilhac, *Les Français de l'an 40,* 2 vols. (Paris: Gallimard, 1990); William L. Shirer, *The Collapse of the Third Republic: An Enquiry into the Fall of France, 1940* (New York: Da Capo, 1994); Jean-Baptiste Duroselle, *La Décadence, 1932–39* (Paris: Éditions du Seuil, 1983); and idem, *L'Abîme, 1939–1945* (Paris: Éditions du Seuil, 1982); and Jean-Pierre Azéma, *1940: l'Année terrible* (Paris: Éditions du Seuil, 1990).

16.   Jean-Pierre Azéma, "Le Choc armé et les débandades," in *France des années noires,* 1:102. Ernest May turns the notion of a "strange defeat" on its head in his *Strange Victory: Hitler's Conquest of France* (New York: Hill and Wang, 2000).

17.   Azéma, "Choc armé," 100.

18.   Ibid., 116.

19.   McMillan, *Twentieth-Century France,* 130. Robert Paxton writes that Maxime Weygand told General Charles-Léon Huntziger, the French representative to the armistice meeting, that he should above all reject any German attempt at control of the French Fleet or the Empire. Robert O. Paxton, *Parades and Politics at Vichy: The French Officer Corps under Marshal Pétain* (Princeton, N.J.: Princeton University Press, 1966), 4.

20.   Paxton, *Parades and Politics,* 7–8.

21.   Ibid., 11.

22.   Ibid., 10.

23.   Cited in Christian Bachelier, "L'Armée française entre la victoire et la défaite," in *France des années noires,* 1:82.

24.   This is discussed in greater detail in chapter 4. For more on the role of the army, see Paxton, "The Officers turned Schoolmaster," chapter in *Parades and Politics,* 183–213.

25.   For more on the role of the veterans, see Antoine Prost, *In the Wake of War: Les Anciens combattants and French Society* (Providence, R.I.: Berg, 1992).

26.   Paxton, *Vichy France,* 190–191. On the efforts to mobilize veterans into the Solidarité française before the war and the uses of the "veterans' mystique," see Robert Soucy, *French Fascism: The Second Wave, 1933–1939* (New Haven, Conn.: Yale University Press, 1995), 102–103.

27.   John F. Sweets, *Choices in Vichy France: The French under German Occupation* (New York: Oxford University Press, 1994), 69.

28.   Bachelier, "L'Armée française," 83.

29.   "Equipes et cadres de la France nouvelle," *Jeunes DRAC,* Bibliothèque de documentation internationale contemporaine.

30.   Philippe Pétain, Message du 8 Octobre 1940, cited in Miller, *Pousse-au-jouir,* 52. Denis Peschanski also notes Pétain's posture as father-figure in "Un Chef, un mythe," in *Images de la France de Vichy, 1940–1944: Images asservies, images rebelles* (Paris: La Documentation Française, 1988), 9, as does Christian Faure in *Le Projet culturel de Vichy:*

Folklore et révolution nationale, 1940–1944 (Lyon: Presses Universitaires de Lyon, 1989), 15.

31.   On the infantilization of the French people, see Miller, *Pousse-au-jouir,* 52; Sweets, *Choices in Vichy France,* 49, and Michèle Cointet-Labrousse, *Vichy et le fascisme* (Paris: Éditions complexes, 1987), 190–191.

32.   Miller, *Pousse-au-jouir,* 52.

33.   Pétain had no children of his own, but he married a divorced woman who had a grown son by her previous marriage. He also was reputed to have a long-standing relationship with another much younger widow with two daughters, with whom he vacationed and shared family celebrations. See Philippe Améras, *Un Français nommé Pétain* (Paris: Robert Laffont, 1995).

34.   Pétain was called upon to quell mutinies within the French army in 1917. He imposed stricter discipline but also ameliorated material conditions for the troops.

35.   "Le Don à la Patrie, Juin 1940," in *La Vie du Maréchal, petit album à colorier pour les enfants de France* (Limoges: Éd. Imagerie du Maréchal, 1941), cited in Denis Peschanski, "Un Chef, un mythe," in *Images de Vichy,* 15.

36.   Francine Muel-Dreyfus, "Le Contrôle des corps," in *Vichy et l'éternel féminin* (Paris: Éditions du Seuil, 1996), 290. Muel-Dreyfus cites Jean-Pierre Azéma, who has described this cult of veneration as *maréchalisme,* distinct and more widespread than other forms of support for the Vichy regime. Jean-Pierre Azéma, *From Munich to the Liberation, 1938–1944* (New York: Cambridge University Press, 1984), 50–73.

37.   One Senator and twenty-six Deputies did leave France for Casablanca aboard the *Massilia,* but they were detained upon arrival by North African authorities and accused of desertion and treason by pro-armistice factions in France that wanted them out of the way. McMillan, *Twentieth-Century France,* 130.

38.   Azéma, "Le Choc armé," 128.

39.   Robert Frank, "Pétain, Laval, Darlan," in *France des années noires,* 1:304.

40.   Azéma, "Le Choc armé," 124.

41.   Pétain's views in the interwar period had been those of a traditional French conservative whose opinions were best expressed by writers such as Charles Maurras or Maurice Barrès at the turn of the century. His political ideology was influenced by his peasant origins, his respect for Catholicism, and his military training. Nicholas Atkin, *Pétain* (New York: Longman, 1998), 52.

42.   See Pétain's famous speech of October 30, 1940, where he announced from Montoire: "J'entre dans la voie de la collaboration." Atkin, *Pétain,* 129.

43.   See, for example, Paxton, *Vichy France,* 139–146; and Peschanski, "Un Chef, un mythe," in *Images de Vichy,* 9–10.

44.   Azéma, "Le Régime de Vichy," in *France des années noires,* 1:154.

45.   On Pétain's attitudes toward Germany, see Frank, "Pétain, Laval, Darlan," in *France des années noires,* 1:297–306.

46.   See Peschanski, "Encadrer ou contrôler?" in *La Propagande sous Vichy, 1940–1944,* ed. Laurent Gervereau and Denis Peschanski (Nanterre: BDIC, 1990), 10.

47.   Denis Peschanski considers the year from January 1940 to February 1941 as the "golden age" of the National Revolution. Peschanski, "Un Chef, un mythe," in *Images de Vichy,* 10.

48.   Pétain was not alone in his desires and theories for a cultural revolution, and the strong influence of the right-wing parties, which had been excluded from power during the Republic, was apparent.

49. Georges Bonvoison, "La Politique familiale du Maréchal," *L'Actualité sociale* 169 (January 1942): 1.

50. Philippe Pétain, cited in Bonvoisin, "Politique familiale du Maréchal," 2.

51. The administrative structures established to deal with family issues will be discussed in greater detail in subsequent chapters. The main official associated with leadership in family policy during the early years of the occupation was Philippe Renaudin. See Aline Coutrot, "La Politique familiale," in *La Gouvernement de Vichy, 1940–1942: Institutions et politiques* (Paris: Presses de la fondation des sciences politiques, 1972), 245–263.

52. Vérine, "C'est dans les familles que se fait la France," *Education* 71 (April–May 1942): 1; emphasis in original.

53. Philippe Pétain, Message du 20 juin 1940, cited in *Messages d'outre-tombe du Maréchal Pétain: Textes officiels, ignorés ou méconnus, consignes secrètes,* ed. Monique and Jean Paillard (Paris: Nouvelles éditions Latines, 1983), 17.

54. Commissariat général à la famille, *Le Chef et la famille,* Préface de Général Lafont, 1942, BDIC, Gr. Fol. 126/18.

55. Demographic education had in fact been made compulsory in all secondary schools in the Code de la famille of July 29, 1939; the Vichy regime modified the law to make it mandatory in primary schools as well. See Aline Coutrot, "La Politique familiale," 251; also AN AJ[16] 7122, Dossier de la propagande en faveur de la famille, Le Ministre Secrétaire d'Etat à l'Education Nationale à MM les Recteurs, 5 juin 1943, TL, and AN F[60] 428, Enseignement primaire, Journal officiel du 12 mars 1942.

56. Nazi officials also used such familial problems and images in textbooks and other school materials as part of their effort to inculcate children with the proper family values. See Lisa Pine, "Education and Socialisation: Imbuing German Society with Nazi Family Ideals," in *Nazi Family Policy, 1933–1945* (New York: Berg, 1997).

57. Commissariat général à la famille, *L'Ecole et la famille,* preface by Paul Haury (Paris: Office de publicité générale, 1942).

58. Commissariat général à la famille, *L'Université devant la famille,* preface by Gilbert Gidel (Paris: Office de publicité générale, 1942).

59. Ibid.

60. Commissariat général à la famille, *Le Chef et la famille.*

61. Paul Vincent, "Quand on pouvait se marier à l'âge de trois ans," *Familles de France* 11 (1 September 1943): 1.

62. Victor Dancette, "Il était une fois un pays heureux," illustrated by P. Baudoin, Office de publicité générale, n.d., Bibliothèque historique de la ville de Paris, Fonds Actualités, Guerre, 39–45.

63. Note the crude portrayal of the black musicians and the heavily Semitic features of the audience in this illustration. Vichy racial attitudes were complicated by the fact that the French empire and its people, especially in Indochina and North Africa, were seen as a crucial bargaining card and possible means of renewal by both Vichy authorities and the Free French. See Jacques Marseille, "L'Empire," in *France des années noires,* 1:271–293. French anti-Semitism was more straightforward and ultimately more violent. See Michael Marrus and Robert Paxton, *Vichy France and the Jews* (New York: Basic Books, 1981); François and Renée Bédarida, "La Persécution des juifs," in *France des années noires,* 2:129–158.

64. The British were very concerned that the French fleet might fall into German hands and threaten the Royal Navy. On July 3, British forces launched "Operation

Catapult" and bombarded French ships docked in the North African port of Mers-el-Kébir, killing close to 1,200 French soldiers and seriously compromising Anglo-French relations.

65.   Philippe Pétain, Message du 11 Juillet 1940, "Le massacre de Mers-el-Kébir," in *Messages du Maréchal Pétain,* 22.

66.   AN 2 AG 497, Rapport de M. Paul Leclerq, "L'Intégration de la famille dans la constitution du nouvel État Français," TD.

67.   See Coutrot, "La Politique familiale," 255.

68.   *L'Actualité sociale,* founded in 1928, was a monthly periodical that addressed questions of family allowances. During the war it carried many articles on French demography, and it frequently referred to the positive examples of Italy and Germany. Muel-Dreyfus, *L'Éternel féminin,* 99.

69.   G.-M. Bonvoisin, "Bâtir sur la famille," *L'Actualité sociale* 178 (February 1943): 48.

70.   AN 2 AG 497, Philippe Renaudin, "Directives de M. le Commissaire général à la famille pour la mise en oeuvre de la loi sur les associations familiales, Loi Gounot," TD.

71.   See André Rouast, "La Famille, personne morale," *L'Actualité sociale* 169 (January 1942): 4–5.

72.   AN 2 AG 605, Rapport sur l'avant-projet de statut des associations familiales, TD.

73.   AN 2 AG 605, Discours de M. le Secrétaire d'État à la Santé et à la Famille, Conseil supérieur de la Famille, Séance plénière du 7 décembre 1943, TD.

74.   Commissariat général à la famille, *La Commune: Rempart de la famille,* preface by Charles Trochu, Office de publicité générale, 1942. The idea of a direct relationship between the state and its families was reiterated at a lecture given by Philippe Renaudin at the Sorbonne in June 1943; see Philippe Renaudin, *La Famille dans la nation,* Commissariat général à la famille, June 1943.

75.   Commissariat général, *Commune,* 25.

76.   Vice-Amiral de Penfentenyo, *Le Manuel du père de famille* (Paris: Flammarion, 1941), ii.

77.   Ibid., 150.

78.   Philippe Renaudin, *La Famille dans la nation,* Conférence du 16 juin 1943 à la Sorbonne, BDIC.

79.   Allocution de M. Pierre Taittinger, Président du Conseil municipal de Paris, Conférences d'information de l'Hôtel-de-Ville, Paris, 1943–1944, Bibliothèque administrative de la ville de Paris.

80.   "Conférence de M. Philippe Renaudin," Conférences d'information de l'Hôtel-de-Ville, 1943–1944, Bibliothèque administrative de la ville de Paris.

81.   Ibid., 4.

82.   Ibid., 5.

83.   Ibid., 5.

84.   Mme Juliette Droz, "Esprit de famille et politique familiale," in *La Politique familiale de l'État français. Textes et commentaires par Pierre Sauvage,* Collection France vivante (Paris: Editions Spes, 1941).

85.   *France 41: La Révolution nationale constructive: Un Bilan et un programme,* foreword by Raymond Postal (Paris: Éditions Alsatia, 1941), 28. *France 41* was in a sense a manifesto of the Vichy regime and gathered together essays on a variety of issues seen as crucial to the regeneration of France.

86. Commissariat général à la famille, *La Commune, Rempart de la famille.*

87. AN F⁶⁰ 607, "La Propagande pour la Journée des mères, le 30 Mai 1943," TD.

88. Eric Jennings provides an interesting perspective on the staging of such Vichy festivals in the colonial context in his *Vichy in the Tropics: Pétain's National Revolution in Madagascar, Guadeloupe and Indochina, 1940–1944* (Stanford, Calif.: Stanford University Press, 2001), especially chapter 8, "The Pétainist Festival: Staging Travail, Famille, Patrie in the Tropics," pp. 199–223. Jennings's research shows that May 1st celebrations took on more significance in the colonies during festivals in which "allegiance was sworn to Pétain, 'Father of the workers and savior of France'" (208).

89. See Frank, "Guerre des images, guerre des symboles," in *Images de Vichy,* 211–216.

90. AN F⁶⁰ 607, "Le Chef du Gouvernement Ministre Secrétaire d'État et de l'Intérieur à Messieurs les Préfets," Vichy, 16 February 1943, TL.

91. On the rhetorical power of the prisoner-of-war motif, see Miller, *Pousse-au-jouir,* 151.

92. Sarah Fishman, "Grand Delusions: The Unintended Consequences of Vichy France's Prisoner of War Propaganda," *Journal of Contemporary History* 26 (1991): 229–254.

93. Commissariat général à la famille, *Les Prisonniers et la famille* (Paris: Office de propagande générale, 1943), 72.

94. Ibid., 73.

95. AN F⁶⁰ 606, Jean Guibal, *La Famille dans la Révolution nationale,* 24 octobre 1940, TD.

96. AN F⁶⁰ 606, "Importance de la Politique familiale," 17 janvier 1941, TD.

97. The Vichy regime espoused corporatist ideas of labor and promulgated a "Charte du travail," which was to fix relationships between different social and professional groups through "social committees." The Charte du travail was to make occupational groups a sort of family for workers. See Henry Rousso, "L'Économie: Pénurie et modernisation," in *France des années noires,* 1:443–445.

98. For a comparison of policies in fascist Spain, see Mary Nash, "Pronatalism and Motherhood in Franco's Spain," in *Maternity and Gender Policies: Women and the Rise of the European Welfare States, 1880–1950s,* ed. Gisela Bock and Pat Thane (New York: Routledge, 1991), 160–177.

99. Victoria de Grazia, "How Mussolini Ruled Italian Women," in *A History of Women,* vol. 5, *Toward a Cultural Identity in the Twentieth Century,* ed. Françoise Thébaud (Cambridge: Harvard University Press, 1994), 132–133.

100. Chiara Saraceno, "Redefining Maternity and Paternity: Gender, Pronatalism and Social Policies in Fascist Italy," in *Maternity and Gender Policies,* 203–204.

101. Sophia Maria Quine, "From Malthus to Mussolini: Fascist Italy's 'Battle for Births,'" in *Population Policies in Twentieth-Century Europe* (New York: Routledge, 1996), 35–42.

102. See Claudia Koonz, *Mothers in the Fatherland: Women, the Family and Nazi Politics* (New York: St. Martin's Press, 1987), 107.

103. Gisela Bock, "Antinatalism, Maternity, and Paternity in National Socialist Racism," in *Maternity and Gender Policies,* 243.

104. For a discussion of women's special "battlefield" on the homefront, see Lisa Pine, *Nazi Family Policy, 1933–1945* (New York: Berg, 1997), 9.

105. For more on such Nazi policies, see Bock, "Antinatalism," and Pine, *Nazi Family Policy,* especially chapters 4 and 5 on "Asocial" and Jewish families.

106.   Koonz, *Mothers in the Fatherland,* 392.
107.   AN 72 AJ 1854, N.T. 9.XII.43, "Le Conseil supérieur de la famille a tenu hier sa première réunion," TD.
108.   Michèle Bordeaux, however, points to a stronger concentration of eugenicists within the Commissariat on Jewish Questions, epecially regarding the question of divorce. Bordeaux, *La Victoire de la famille,* 238–249.
109.   Pine, *Nazi Family Policy,* chapter 3.

4. MODELING THE NEW MAN

1.   Henri Vibert, "Êtes-vous des hommes?" *Réveil du peuple,* 27 December 1940, 1.
2.   See Maurizia Boscaglia, *Eye on the Flesh: Fashions of Masculinity in the Early Twentieth Century* (Boulder, Colo.: Westview Press, 1996); George Mosse, *Nationalism and Sexuality: Respectability and Abnormal Sexuality in Modern Europe* (New York: H. Fertig, 1985).
3.   For Germany, see Mosse, *Nationalism and Sexuality;* David Schoenbaum, *Hitler's Social Revolution: Class and Status in Nazi Germany, 1933–1939* (New York: W. W. Norton, 1980); Detlev Peukert, *Inside Nazi Germany: Conformity, Opposition and Racism in Everyday Life* (New Haven, Conn.: Yale University Press, 1987); Jill Stephenson, *Women in Nazi Society* (London: Croom Helm, 1975). For Italy, see Victoria de Grazia, *How Fascism Ruled Women: Italy, 1922–1945* (Berkeley: University of California Press, 1992); Barbara Spackman, *Fascist Virilities: Rhetoric, Ideology and Social Fantasy in Italy* (Minneapolis: University of Minnesota Press, 1996); and Carl Ipsen, *Dictating Demography: The Problem of Population in Fascist Italy* (New York: Cambridge University Press, 1996).
4.   Claire Andrieu, "Démographie, famille, jeunesse," in *La France des années noires,* vol. 1, *De la défaite à Vichy* (Paris: Éditions du Seuil, 1993), 474.
5.   AN 72 AJ 254, Comité d'histoire de la Deuxième guerre mondiale, "Paul de la Porte du Theil (1884–1976)," TD.
6.   Despite his position of responsibility in the Vichy government, General de la Porte du Theil was relieved of guilt by the French High Court of Justice in 1947. After instigation of the Service du travail obligatoire, the Chantiers became a prime target for German authorities to draft young men into compulsory labor service. De la Porte du Theil resisted this, and he was arrested and imprisoned in Germany in January 1944 for inciting resistance. The Chantiers were eventually closed in June 1944. De la Porte du Theil's account and other documents pertaining to the Chantiers are found at the Archives nationales, series 72 AJ 254.
7.   Andrieu, "Démographie, famille, jeunesse," 474.
8.   For more on Baden-Powell and on the German Wandervogel movement in the early twentieth century, see Boscaglia, *Eye on the Flesh,* 82–89.
9.   AN 72 AJ 254, M. Charles-Louis Foulon, "Paul de la Porte du Theil," TD.
10.   M. Georges Bertier, "Une Mystique pour les jeunes français," *Éducation* 62 and 63 (May–June 1942): 3.
11.   See Jacques Marseille, "L'Empire," in *France des années noires,* 1:271–293.
12.   AN 72 AJ 254, Propagande des Jeunes, "A Propos de la quinzaine impériale: Enseignement de l'empire," TD.
13.   Paul Cadier, "Pour ton camp de troupe: L'aventure coloniale," *Le Lien* (January 1942): 172.

14.   See Eric Jennings, *Vichy in the Tropics: Pétain's National Revolution in Madagascar, Guadeloupe and Indochina, 1940–1944* (Stanford, Calif.: Stanford University Press, 2001), 149.

15.   Such "frank gestures" would surely be in contrast to the effeminate gestures of less virile or homosexual men (see chapter 2 for images of the feminized bachelor).

16.   Jean-Jacques Chevallier, *L'Ordre viril: L'Éfficacité dans l'action,* Collection Chef et ses jeunes 7, 16–19.

17.   This indifference and lack of candor was perhaps best personified in Jean Renoir's masterpiece of 1939, *La Règle du jeu.* Several of the male characters in the film seem to lack the "frank" gestures and integrity required to fight a war—so much so that the film was deemed "demoralizing" and banned by both the Third Republic and the Vichy regime.

18.   Commissariat général à la famille, *Le Chef et la famille* (Paris: Office de la publicité générale, 1942).

19.   Commissariat général à la famille, *L'Université devant la famille* (Paris: Office de la publicité générale, 1942).

20.   AN 72 AJ 254, Chef Cassou, "La Famille dans la Révolution nationale," mardi 29 janvier, 1942, TD.

21.   AN 72 AJ 254, Association des anciens des Chantiers de la jeunesse, Province Alpes-Jura, 23–27 mars, Lyon, TD.

22.   Commissariat général à la famille, *Chef et la famille.*

23.   The Compagnons de France were another youth organization established under the Vichy regime. Fonds actualités, Guerre, 1939–1945, Bibliothèque historique de la ville de Paris. According to Claire Andrieu, approximately 30,000 youth participated in the Compagnons de France. Andrieu, "Démographie, famille, jeunesse," 473.

24.   *Éducation* was a journal founded in 1935 as a fusion of three other scholarly and family-oriented reviews. Its editors included such important figures as l'Abbé Viollet of the Confédération générale de familles; Georges Bertier, the director of the leadership school at Les Roches and a member of the advisory board at the Fondation Carrel; and Vérine, the pseudonym for Marguerite Lebrun, an outspoken supporter of traditional roles for women and the founder of the École des parents. Francine Muel-Dreyfus, *Vichy et L'éternel féminin* (Paris: Seuil, 1996), 183, 269.

25.   A. Brandt-Mieg, "La Famille, centre d'intérêt," *Éducation* 78 (March 1943): 36–37. I am grateful to Francine Muel-Dreyfus for bringing this publication to my attention.

26.   Commissariat général à la famille, *Chef et la famille.*

27.   The school at Uriage was set up in a castle near Grenoble requisitioned by the Vichy government. Its first recruits were selected by Segonzac from among demobilized officers and leaders of youth groups. See John Hellman, *The Knight-Monks of Vichy France: Uriage, 1940–1945* (Montreal: McGill-Queen's University Press, 1993), 3–44.

28.   Hellman, *Knight-Monks,* 9. See also Muel-Dreyfus, *L'Éternel féminin,* 287–288.

29.   Bernard Comte asserts that for the young men of Uriage, "the themes of virility and efficiency, so constantly repeated, were not a concession to the prestige of fascism," but rather a form of individual humanism committed to the dignity and equality of all. Comte, "L'Esprit d'Uriage: Pédagogie civique et humanisme révolutionnaire," *Les Politiques et pratiques culturelles dans la France de Vichy, Les Cahiers de l'IHTP* 8 (June 1988): 121.

30. See Mosse, *Nationalism and Sexuality,* 154.

31. See Spackman, *Fascist Virilities,* 13, and Mosse, *Nationalism and Sexuality,* 154.

32. Mosse, *Nationalism and Sexuality,* 161.

33. Ibid., 20.

34. Ibid., 154.

35. Hellman, *Knight-Monks,* 158.

36. Beuve-Méry was the first editor of *Le Monde,* established in 1945, and Mounier was the director of the journal *Esprit,* influential in setting the tone on discussion of Vichy after the Liberation, and also closely connected to the progress of the Éditions du Seuil, established by Paul Flamand in the Latin Quarter in 1945. John Hellman takes a more critical view of Uriage's goals and ideology. Bernard Comte, the French authority on the Uriage school, has written a Doctorat d'histoire on the Uriage school, abridged in his book, *Une Utopie combattante: L'École des cadres d'Uriage, 1940–1942* (Paris: Fayard, 1991). He is straightforward in his sympathy for the men and experience of Uriage, and he has defended the reputations of the school and men such as Mounier as bastions of the Resistance.

37. Andrieu, "Démographie, Famille, Jeunesse," 475.

38. Comte, "L'Esprit d'Uriage," 117. Comte suggests that approximately 3,000 interns went through the École des cadres at Uriage (126).

39. Pierre Dunoyer de Segonzac, *Réflexions pour de jeunes chefs,* Le Chef et ses jeunes, no. 5, École nationale de cadres, Uriage, n.d., 21.

40. P. Reuter, "Uriage," *Jeunesse . . . France!* 29 (March 1942): 1. *Cadres,* as the interns at Uriage and other schools were called, can be roughly translated as meaning administrators, directors, or top-level leaders, although used in this context, with associations to an elite, there is no direct English equivalent.

41. Dunoyer de Segonzac, "Réflexions pour de jeunes chefs," 21.

42. Chevallier, *L'Ordre viril,* 39.

43. R. Vuillemin, "Le Sens de la force," *Jeunesse . . . France!* 30 (April 1942): 2.

44. Mme Brunet, "La Communauté conjugale," *Jeunesse . . . France!* 31 (May 1942): 3.

45. Équipes et cadres de la France nouvelle, "Les Conditions du renouveau français," *Jeunes DRAC,* Tract 4-A-1, BDIC, Q 5072. The Équipes et cadres de la France nouvelle was another youth group founded in August 1942.

46. "Mes droits, mes devoirs," Tract 38-A-1, Équipes et cadres de la France nouvelle, *Jeunes DRAC,* BDIC Q 5072.

47. Alexis Carrel, *L'Homme, cet inconnu* (Paris: Plon, 1935).

48. Alain Drouard, *Une Inconnue des sciences sociales: La Fondation Alexis Carrel, 1941–1945* (Paris: Éditions de la Maison des sciences de l'homme, 1992), xiv–xv and 271–273.

49. Much of the work of the Foundation was devoted to research, opinion polls, and "synthesis" of existing research on a variety of human issues such as demography, work, insurance, and maternity. See Drouard, *Inconnue,* 207–269.

50. See Jacques Doriot, "Crise de l'élite," in *Je suis un homme du Maréchal* (Paris: Grasset, 1941), 61.

51. Commissariat général à la famille, *Les Prisonniers et la famille* (Paris: Office de propagande générale, 1943), 5.

52. *Femmes d'absents,* Série "Fêtes et saisons" (Paris: Les Éditions du Cerf, 1943), back cover.

53. *Femmes d'absents,* 17.

54. According to Henry Rousso, 1.5 million men, or close to 90 percent of the cap-

tives in Germany, were put to work in agriculture, transportation, and other industries. Henry Rousso, "L'Économie: Pénurie et modernisation," in *France des années noires,* 1:441.

55.   Commissariat général à la famille, *Prisonniers et la famille,* 59.

56.   Ibid., 71.

57.   Rousso, "L'Économie," 441, 448.

58.   Denis Peschanski, "Encadrer ou contrôler?" in *La Propagande sous Vichy* (Nanterre: BDIC, 1990), 26–28.

59.   In January 1943, Fritz Sauckel, the German officer responsible for requisitioning French labor, demanded that Laval turn over another 250,000 men to be sent to Germany in mid-March. The law promulgated on February 16 drafted every young man born from 1920 to 1922 into forced labor in Germany. There were subsequently protests organized at the train stations where young men were given their papers and clothes to work in Germany, and many young men responded by escaping to the hills to join the Maquis. See H. Roderick Kedward, "STO et Maquis," in *La France des années noires,* vol. 2, 273–274.

60.   See Pierre Laborie, *L'Opinion française sous Vichy* (Paris: Éditions du Seuil, 1990), 286.

61.   See Peschanski, "Encadrer ou contrôler?" 28.

62.   AN AJ 16 7122, Concours de la plus belle lettre, Première catégorie, lettres de Claude Poitrenaud, 7 ans, et Gérald Meiss, 6 ans, TD.

63.   AN AJ 16 7122, 2ème Technique, A.P.S., Composition française, TD.

64.   This is perhaps not exceptional; most wartime letters are decidedly upbeat, as most governments at war have placed restrictions on negative information passed on in letters that could affect morale. In the French case, however, there seemed to be no limit to descriptions in public discourse of the hardships endured by mothers and by prisoners because these were politically useful. It is the conspicuous reiteration of paternal absence, rather than the optimistic tone, that makes these letters noteworthy.

65.   "Jour de l'An," *Almanach de la famille française,* 1941, Bibliothèque historique de la ville de Paris.

66.   *Femmes d'absents,* 29.

67.   Ibid., 28. Sarah Fishman uses this series of booklets in her book on prisoners' wives during the occupation: see Fishman, *We Will Wait: Wives of French Prisoners of War, 1940–1945* (New Haven, Conn.: Yale University Press, 1991), 142–149. Fishman notes that there was frequently quite a disparity between the cheerful advice offered to wives and the reality of their situations; women often had a very difficult time in fulfilling the proper female gender prescriptions for a faithful wife and mother and meeting the rigorous demands of raising children and supporting a family without the "chef de famille." My argument here is that in both the projected images and the lived realities of prisoners' wives, the absence of the father is a preoccupying concern because it carried with it the potential for subversion of the "natural" order, where the father's authority and presence were obvious and unquestioned.

68.   "La Flamme du foyer," *"Ils sont là!"* Special issue of *Revue de la famille* (May 1945): 22.

69.   "Ton Papa est rentré . . . " *"Ils sont là!"* 24.

70.   Ibid., 26.

71.   Ibid., 25.

72.   "Faites revivre la maison," *Almanach de la famille française,* 1941, Bibliothèque historique de la ville de Paris.

73. One author advised prisoners' wives to treat the returnee in a "sweet and gentle way, almost maternally," but warned against treating him "like a child, for he is the head of the family." "Simples conseils," *Femmes d'absents*, 28.

74. Miranda Pollard, *Reign of Virtue: Mobilizing Gender in Vichy France* (Chicago: University of Chicago Press, 1998), 45.

75. Playing on the title of Alexis Carrel's best-selling book, *L'Homme, cet inconnu*, Francine Muel-Dreyfus writes: "si l'homme est un inconnu, la femme, elle, reste sans surprise." *L'Éternel féminin*, 92.

76. Pollard, *Reign of Virtue*, 52.

77. Francine Muel-Dreyfus, *L'Éternel féminin*, 123–124. Both Miranda Pollard and Francine Muel-Dreyfus lay out in much greater detail the political and social implications of this cult of motherhood and its importance to the regime. See also Michèle Bordeaux, *La Victoire de la famille dans la France défaite: Vichy 1940–1944* (Paris: Flammarion, 2002).

78. AN F^{60} 607, Scénario du film "Le Culte des héros," TD.

79. Miranda Pollard notes the eventual contradictions in this policy when the Vichy regime, under pressure from the Germans, began to encourage women to work. *Reign of Virtue*, 170–173.

80. *Sciences et voyages*, Numéro spécial consacré à la famille (1941), Bibliothèque nationale.

81. William Garcin, " . . . Et les pères?" *Familles de France* 13 (1 October 1943): 3.

82. Jean Bergeaud, "L'Exposition de la famille française," *Revue de la famille* 240 (July 1943): 4–5.

83. Brochure for the Exposition de la défense de la famille française, Fonds actualités, Guerre, 39–45, Bibliothèque historique de la ville de Paris.

84. Although there is no photograph of this particular diorama, the newspaper *Familles de France* reproduced a picture of another such scene from an exposition on the family that took place in Reims in 1939: *Familles de France* 6 (June 1939): 4; that picture is reproduced in fig. 4.13. The General Commissariat on the Family had its own illustrations on the dangers of alcoholism in another brochure. Fonds actualités, Guerre, 39–45, Bibliothèque historique de la ville de Paris.

85. "Audacity" was a term frequently used when talking of the *chef de famille* in France, and it can be found in the Futurists' manifesto of 1909, which contained many of the moral ideals of fascism (Spackman, *Fascist Virilities*, 49). "Strength" and "joy" are reminiscent of the Nazi "Kraft durch Freude" (Strength through Joy) program.

86. AN AJ^{16} 7122, Archives de l'Académie de Paris, "L'Exposition de la famille du Vème arrondissement," Dossier sur la propagande en faveur de la famille.

87. George Mosse makes a similar point about the mythology of family life in the Third Reich, in which the "ritualized mass meetings were, for the most part, free of references to the bliss of family life." Mosse, *Nationalism and Sexuality*, 159–160.

88. André Fabre, "Le Père de famille, est-il un chef?" *Familles de France* 11 (1 September 1943): 1.

89. Commissariat général à la famille, "Chefs de famille, Voici vos droits," AN 72 AJ 1238.

90. "Stabilité des cadres," *Le Lien*, Revue mensuelle des chefs éclaireurs unionistes de France (mai 1943): 120–121.

91. E. Coeurdevey, "L'Autorité du chef de famille," *Éducation* 70 (March 1942): 51.

92. Ibid., 53.

93.   Etienne Videcoq, "Quit doit diriger la famille?" *Revue de la famille* 236 (February 1943): 9. Francine Muel-Dreyfus interprets this article in a different light, emphasizing Videcoq's contention that female subordination is willed "by the laws of nature." Muel-Dreyfus, *L'Éternel féminin,* 204. There is no doubt that the ideology espoused by such Vichy theorists was markedly antifeminist and reactionary. On the other hand, however, this oppressive attitude toward women did not necessarily imply an unabashed promotion of men and fathers.
94.   There is no exact translation for the term "méconnu" here, for it carries with it both a sense of mistrust and misgiving and a sense of being unacknowledged or unrecognized.
95.   Jean Bergeaud, "Le Père, ce méconnu," *Fédération des associations de familles nombreuses de France* 5 (1 March 1944): 1.

5. BRINGING SOCIAL REFORM HOME

1.   Henri David, "Familles de France, adhérez à l'association familiale la plus proche de votre domicile," *Familles de France* 10 (October 1941): 1.
2.   For the most comprehensive discussion of family associations and the family movement in France, see Robert Talmy, *Histoire du mouvement familiale en France, 1896–1939,* 2 vols. (Paris: UNCAF, 1962). For more recent analyses, see Agnes Pitrou, *Associations familiales et jeu sociale,* Informations sociales (Paris: CNAF, 1978); Michel Messu, *Les Politiques familiales: Du natalisme à la solidarité* (Paris: Les Éditions ouvrières, 1992); Michel Chauvière, "1939–1944, Du Code de la famille à la Libération—Présentation de la période," in *Les Mouvements familiaux populaires et ruraux, naissance, développement, mutations 1939–1955, Les Cahiers du GRMF* 1 (August 1983).
3.   Robert Paxton argues that the Vichy regime was not a bloc, but rather was made up of "competing visions" that ranged from traditional Catholic ideas to conceptions of a society of experts needed to keep pace with the modern world. Despite these contradictory ideals and competing means of achieving them, the National Revolution was not paralyzed by inaction because these visions overlapped at a few key points. Robert Paxton, *Vichy France: Old Guard and New Order, 1940–1944* (New York: Columbia University Press, 1972), 139–145. Family policy suffered from the same contradictory directives, though most family advocates associated with the Vichy regime could agree on the common good of encouraging large families.
4.   Susan Pedersen even asserts that "the Vichy government completed the process of ceding official power to the pro-family lobby, with the creation of both the Commissariat Général à la Famille and the Conseil Supérieur de la Famille, whose members included many prominent pronatalists and familists, including Georges Bonvoisin, Paul Haury, and Georges Pernot." Susan Pedersen, *Family, Dependence, and the Origins of the Welfare State: Britain and France, 1914–1945* (Cambridge: Cambridge University Press, 1993), 387. In contrast to the predatory model of state intervention proposed by Jacques Donzelot in his *Policing of Families,* it seems clear that the development of state interest in family life and social reform was not a one-way process of state encroachment, but a much more complicated story of bargaining, negotiation, and compromise between the state, families, and the associations that claimed to represent them.
5.   Philippe Burrin has written extensively about public opinion in wartime France, describing the many nuances in attitudes toward the Germans. He estimates that

from one quarter to one fifth of French people in the Free Zone, and one fifth to one sixth of the country as a whole were actually favorably inclined toward collaboration. The projects of the National Revolution, on the other hand, drew "almost total indifference," but the regime stood high in public opinion in 1941 because it was better than direct German rule, because it attempted to make communication easier between the two zones, and because it was working for the repatriation of the prisoners. Burrin, *France under the Germans: Collaboration and Compromise* (New York: New Press, 1996), 177–190. Family policy was not seen as a project of the National Revolution, for after years of pressure from pro-natalists and familists, family policy had become a central concern for the nation, demonstrated in the *Code de la famille* of 1939 and again in the pro-family initiatives of the liberators in 1944.

6.   On the widespread popular consensus surrounding the need for new family policy, see Messu, *Politiques familiales*, 70.

7.   Aline Coutrot notes that the measures passed that were most characteristic of Vichy concerned the family institution as a whole rather than any particular member. Coutrot, "La Politique familiale," 251. Susan Pedersen argues that pro-natalists were not particularly interested in either men or women per se, but rather in couples and families. Pedersen, *Family, Dependence*, 364.

8.   Pedersen sees the formation of this committee as "the final step in the incorporation of pronatalists into government decision making," mainly because of the inclusion of three prominent pro-natalists—Fernand Boverat, Georges Pernot, and Adolphe Landry—on the High Committee. Pedersen, *Family, Dependence*, 386. The pro-natalists enjoyed remarkable success in influencing family policy during the interwar years, but the role of Catholic familist organizations must not be underestimated during these years and particularly under Vichy, when familists managed to bring about a semipublic role for family associations through the Gounot law.

9.   For a detailed description of the personnel shifts and various statutes regulating the offices of family services, see *La Politique familiale de l'Etat français, Textes et commentaires par Pierre Sauvage,* Collection France vivante (Paris: SPES, 1941).

10.   Aline Coutrot, "La Politique familiale," in *Le Gouvernement de Vichy, 1940–1942: Institutions et politiques* (Paris: Presses de la Fondation nationale des sciences politiques, 1972), 245–246. Another council was created on June 28, 1943, the Conseil supérieur de la famille, but this body had little direct impact on family policy.

11.   Coutrot, "Politique familiale," 246; Commissariat général à la famille, *Les Prisonniers et la famille* (Paris: Office de publicité générale, 1943), 61–62. See also Michèle Bordeaux, *La Victoire de la famille dans la France défaite: Vichy 1940–1944* (Paris: Flammarion, 2002), 26–32.

12.   As Philippe Burrin notes, "Dictatorships are always curious to discover the state of mind of the people they gag. Vichy and the occupier were constantly monitoring the pulse of the French people." *France under the Germans,* 177.

13.   AN F^{1a} 3701, Le Chef du Gouvernement Ministre Secrétaire d'État et d'Intérieur à Monsieur le Secrétaire d'État à l'Information, "Extrait du rapport mensuel du Préfet de la DROME," Vichy, 26 novembre 1942.

14.   Although he does not deal specifically with the question of propaganda, Pierre Laborie discusses prevailing sentiments among French citizens during the occupation in his *L'Opinion française sous Vichy* (Paris: Seuil, 1990). Laborie concludes that although Marshal Pétain enjoyed considerable popularity and veneration as a "grand chef" who represented tradition and certainty, the French population exhibited more "prudence than enthusiasm for the political projects" of the National Revolu-

tion (236). From the reports retained at the Archives nationales, and considering the penury of life in occupied France, one may conclude that bombastic propaganda on the family was not especially appreciated by the population at large.

15.   AN F^{1a} 3701, 28 août 1941, Préfet de l'Aveyron.

16.   See Rémy Lenoir, Rapporteur générale du groupe de travail, *La Politique familiale en France depuis 1945* (Paris: La Documentation française, 1985); and Messu, *Politiques familiales,* 70.

17.   Nicholas Atkin estimates that throughout the occupation more than two thousand people a day wrote in personally to the Marshal. Nicholas Atkin, *Pétain* (New York: Longman, 1998), 107. Obviously not all these letters concerned family matters, but many people did feel called upon to express such concerns to Pétain.

18.   AN 2 AG 497, "Note sur les questions familiales," Propagande familiale, Vichy, le 12 octobre 1941.

19.   *La Politique familiale de l'État français,* Textes et commentaires par Pierre Sauvage (Paris: SPES, Collection France vivante, 1941).

20.   Coutrot, "Politique familiale," 248; Commissariat général à la famille, *Prisonniers et la famille,* 62.

21.   Commissariat général à la famille, *Prisonniers et la famille,* 62.

22.   For greater detail on the Gounot law, see Michel Chauvière, "Jalons pour une socio-histoire de l'action publique dans le champ familial en France," paper presented at the conference "Changes of Family Patterns in the Western Countries," Bologna, Italy, October 1994; and idem, "De la sphère privée à la sphère publique: La Construction sociale de l'usager par un mouvement familial durant les années quarantes et ses contradictions," in *Les Usagers, entre marché et citoyenneté,* Michel Chauvière and Jacques Godbout (Paris: Harmattan, 1992); Messu, *Politiques familiales;* Bordeaux, *Victoire de la famille.*

23.   The directors of the local associations were elected by members—usually fathers—who had different numbers of votes according to the number of their children.

24.   Coutrot, "Politiques familiales," 255.

25.   Like Miranda Pollard and Cheryl Koos, Sarah Fishman asserts that the differences between pro-natalist and familialist groups should not be overemphasized. Sarah Fishman, *We Will Wait: Wives of French Prisoners of War, 1940–1945* (New Haven, Conn.: Yale University Press, 1991), 182 n. 53. Miranda Pollard, *Reign of Virtue: Mobilizing Gender in Vichy France* (Chicago: University of Chicago Press, 1998), 10; Cheryl A. Koos, "Gender, Anti-Individualism, and Nationalism: The Alliance Nationale and the Pronatalist Backlash against the *Femme moderne,* 1933–1940," *French Historical Studies* 19, no. 3 (spring 1996): 701.

26.   Messu, *Politiques familiales,* 53. For a finely detailed account of the history of family associations, see Talmy, *Histoire du mouvement familial.* The Fédération nationale des associations de familles nombreuses was founded by Auguste Isaac in Bordeaux, in 1921. It grouped together most of the important regional, federal, and national family leagues and associations, and it was thus able to speak on behalf of a majority of these groups. Its active members were fathers of at least three children. Talmy, *Histoire du mouvement familial,* 53–54.

27.   Bordeaux, *Victoire de la famille,* 68.

28.   Quote from *Paris-Midi, Familles de France* 1 (January 1932): 1.

29.   The Catholic Church's position on the role of the state in family life was laid out by Pope Leo XIII in his Encyclical Letter of 1891, *De Rerum Novarum,* in which

he stated, "To desire . . . that the civil power should enter arbitrarily into the privacy of homes is a great and pernicious error." State intervention was justified only in cases of grave violation of basic rights. Furthermore, he wrote, "[p]aternal authority is such that it can be neither abolished nor absorbed by the State, because it has the same origin in common with that of a man's own life." Quoted in Eugen Weber, *The Western Tradition: From the Renaissance to the Present,* vol. 2, 4th ed. (Lexington, Mass.: D. C. Heath, 1990), 671–672.

30.   AN 2 AG 654, Letter from Chanoine Gouget to Maréchal Pétain, 8 juillet 1940.

31.   AN 2 AG 605, Report submitted to Pétain's cabinet, "Travaux du Mont doré," septembre 1943, TD.

32.   2 AG 605, Note sur l'importance d'une législation familiale, "Vers un ordre social nouveau," 21 décembre 1940.

33.   AN 2 AG 459 CC34, William Garcin, *Principes d'une législation familiale,* 15 novembre 1940.

34.   2 AG 497, Note to Philippe Renaudin, 2 décembre 1941.

35.   AN 2 AG 654, William Garcin, *Révolution sociale par la famille* (Vichy, 1943).

36.   AN F^{60} 606, Note relative à l'organisation nationale de la famille, Abbé Viollet, Confédération générale des familles, 16 septembre 1940.

37.   Conférence de M. Philippe Renaudin, *Conférences d'information de l'Hôtel-de-Ville,* Paris, 1943–1944, Bibliothèque administrative de la ville de Paris.

38.   AN 2 AG 497, "Directives de M. le Commissaire général à la famille pour la mise en oeuvre de la loi sur les assocations familiales—Loi Gounot," n.d., TD.

39.   "Allocution de M. Renaudin, Commissaire générale à la famille, à la réunion du Centre de coordination des activités familiales, qui s'est tenu à Paris, le dimanche 12 mars 1944," *Familles de France* 7 (1 April 1944): 1.

40.   AN F^{60} 607, Commissaire générale à la famille aux Délégués régionaux de la Famille, 1 mai 1943.

41.   AN BB^{18} 3332, Centre national de coordination et d'action des mouvements familiaux à Monsieur Barthélemy, Garde des sceaux, 26 février 1941.

42.   AN F^{60} 607, "Un Entretien avec le Maréchal Pétain," *Défendons nos foyers,* 25 août 1941.

43.   AN F^{60} 607, Letter from the "Association nationale de familles françaises de six enfants et plus" to the Commissariat, 3 September 1941.

44.   AN 2 AG 459, Letter from Maurice Denis to Jacques Chevalier, Secrétaire d'état à la famille et à la santé, 3 May 1941.

45.   AN F^{60} 498, "Code de la famille, Rapport des préfets, Mai-Juin 1940," Réponses des préfectures à la circulaire no. 298 S.G. sur le Code de la famille.

46.   AN 2 AG 605, Memorandum to Monsieur le Ministre de l'intérieur, Secrétariat général à la famille et à la santé publique, Vichy, 26 December 1940.

47.   2 AG 605, "Note sur la politique familiale" Vichy, 13 janvier 1940.

48.   AN 2 AG 605, Cahier de revendications formulées et des réformes proposées par les familles françaises de plus de cinq enfants, Secrétariat Général Morlhom, Association de familles françaises de six enfants.

49.   AN F^{60} 606, Letter from Fernand Boverat to Maréchal Pétain, 13 October 1941.

50.   AN 2 AG 605, Letter from Avignon, 2 January 1941.

51.   AN 2 AG 497, William Garcin, "Cotisations dues par les travailleurs indépendants ou par les patrons pour eux-mêmes."

52.   Single people in France had to pay an additional 40 percent of the amount of

their general taxes as a penalty. As this was essentially a surtax on a tax, William Garcin complained that this only amounted to approximately 1 to 2 percent of their total income. He suggested that since a *célibataire* had costs equal to only a third of those of a *père de famille,* the gross income of bachelors should be taxed at a rate of 66 percent. William Garcin, *Révolution sociale par la famille* (Vichy: Fédération française des associations de famille, 1943), 30.

53.   AN 2 AG 605, Letter from Jean Vidales to Maréchal Pétain, 18 November 1940.

54.   Compte-rendu du Colonel Faveau, "Un Entretien avec le Maréchal Pétain," *Défendons nos foyers,* Organe trimestriel de l'Assocation nationale des familles françaises de six enfants et plus, 25 August 1941.

55.   AN F^{60} 495, 28 July 1939.

56.   AN 2 AG 605, Mlle Alicia Alleaume, Letter to Maréchal Pétain, "Éducation moral des Anciens combattants-veuves blanches" Antibes, 7 December 1940. This differentiation between male and female bachelors would support Françoise Thébaud's contention that the Second World War increased misunderstanding between the sexes in France and hampered the development of women's rights. She writes that World War II was an experience of men's failures; their world had contributed to the defeat and the occupation, and upon returning many wanted to find the world as it had been. Françoise Thébaud, "Femmes et guerres en France au 20ème siècle," paper presented at the European Social Science History Association, Nordwijkerhout, The Netherlands, May 1996.

57.   AN F^{60} 607, Sénateur René Courtier, Marcilly, le 30 janvier 1940, lettre à Monsieur Daladier, Président du Conseil.

58.   AN F^{60} 498, Note pour le Président du conseil relative à la politique familiale, 25 novembre 1939. During the 1930s, fathers were accorded special rights that delayed their conscription. These rights ranged from a reclassification to a category four years older for fathers of two living children to a total exemption from military service for fathers of six children. Yves Helleu, *Les Avantages réservés à la famille,* AN 72 AJ 1854. See also Sophia Maria Quine, "Fathers of the Nation: French Pronatalism during the Third Republic," in *Population Politics in Twentieth-Century Europe* (New York: Routledge, 1996).

59.   Allocution de M. Victor Constant, Président du Conseil départemental de la Seine, *Conférences d'information de L'Hôtel-de-Ville,* Paris, 1943–1944, Bibliothèque administrative de la ville de Paris.

60.   See especially the poster issued by the Commissariat général à la famille titled "Chefs de familles—Voici vos Droits." These rights included supplements to pensions, reduced taxes on salaries and legacies, and housing stipends for families (usually of at least three children). AN 72 AJ 1232. Robert Talmy details the privileges extended to large families during the Third Republic in his *Histoire du mouvement familiale,* 2:14–37.

61.   AN 72 AJ 1854, Yves Helleu, *Avantages réservés à la famille,* 1943.

62.   AN 72 AJ 1858, Agence française d'information de presse, Paris, 25 juin 1942.

63.   Commissariat général à la famille, *Les Prisonniers et la famille,* 45.

64.   AN 72 AJ 1854, Exposé de M. Joseph Barthélemy, Vichy, 2 novembre 1942.

65.   Francine Muel-Dreyfus discusses the law of September 22, 1942, from the perspective of women's rights and finds that although jurists proclaimed this a victory for married women and a step toward equality between spouses, the law in fact only gave women more rights in the privacy of the domestic sphere. The hierarchical structure of the family was not seriously compromised, although even these few

amendments were the subject of intense controversy. Muel-Dreyfus notes, however, that the issue of the father's authority was in fact a central problem of government, for he symbolized the unity of the family community and the fight against individualism. She reports that in August 1943, 40,000 people gathered at a family conference in Lourdes to discuss the "essential problem of the authority of the head of the family." Muel-Dreyfus, *L'Éternel féminin*, 203–205. This law did uphold men's powers as husbands, and therefore can be seen as part of what Muel-Dreyfus considers the "feminine subjection" and "familial imperialism" of the Vichy regime. But it did nothing to enhance paternal power, and therefore cannot be seen as a victory for fathers as such. Furthermore, while Muel-Dreyfus notes that jurists finessed the issue of the head of household's authority, this acknowledgment of a wife's role in household management was in fact a compromise of his absolute authority.

66.   A. Théry, *La Famille: Erreurs d'hier, réalisations d'aujourd'hui* (Paris, 1943), 41.

67.   A. Théry, *La Famille: Vérités de toujours* (Paris, 1943), 56.

68.   Commissariat général à la famille, *Les Prisonniers et la famille*, 41.

69.   For more on the single-salary allowance and its ideological prescriptions for women see Fishman, *We Will Wait*, 20 and 53–54; see also Pollard, *Reign of Virtue*, chapters 5 and 6. Francine Muel-Dreyfus also writes about the efforts to keep women at home in *L'Éternel féminin*, 124–125.

70.   Commissariat général à la famille, *Prisonniers et la famille*, 41.

71.   Muel-Dreyfus notes that the percentage of women in the work force was always comparatively high in France, amounting to approximately 40 percent of the working population from 1900 to 1946. During the war, women's salaries were often essential to a family's survival and remained at high levels despite legislative restrictions on married women's work. *L'Éternel féminin*, 119, 125.

72.   Susan Pedersen argues that the single-salary allowance was one of the most innovative acts of legislation under Vichy and that it operated *de facto* if not *de jure* to favor a certain kind of family structure because it probably encouraged married women with small children to give up work. In this sense, French family policy from the 1940s through the 1970s performed a "gendering" function by favoring families with a male earner and dependent wife. Pedersen, *Family, Dependence*, 408–410. Pedersen notes, however, that this "gendering" effect was most pronounced in the 1960s and 1970s, and I would assert that legislation that awarded allowances to women or to divorced or single parents as sole breadwinners did not privilege men either in fact or in law during the war. Few families could afford to give up a mother's salary, and female participation in the work force did not plummet during the occupation.

73.   AN F[60] 606, Le Général d'Armée Huntziger, Commandant en chef des Forces terrestres, Ministre secrétaire d'état à la guerre, à Monsieur le Ministre Secrétaire d'État à l'Économie nationale et aux finances, Vichy, le 1 septembre 1941.

74.   AN F[60] 498, Ministre de la Défense nationale et de la guerre, État-Major de l'armée, à Monsieur le President du conseil, Ministre des Affaires étrangères, Paris, 14 mai 1940.

75.   AN F[60] 498, M. le Président du conseil à M. le Vice-Président du Haut-comité de la population, Paris, 21 mai 1940. Georges Pernot had written to Daladier a little more than a month before protesting that fathers of four or more children who had been convicted of family abandonment or forfeiture of paternal rights should not benefit from the measures of the law, but should remain in the army to fight.

76.   AN F[60] 496, Le Vice-Président du Haut-comité de la population à Monsieur le Ministre de la Défense nationale et de la guerre et des Affaires étrangères, 11 April 1940.

77.   AN 2 AG 497, "L'expéditeur commente et critique une loi nouvelle concernant les enfants adultérins," 24.10.41, Dossier Famille.

78.   AN 2 AG 497, "Légitimation des enfants adultérins," UFCS, Lyon, 29 June 1942, Dossier Famille.

79.   AN 2 AG 605, 8 February 1943, "La Loi sur les associations familiales—Danger pour la famille et pour la France," TD.

80.   AN 2 AG 605, "Note sur les associations familiales—Politique nefaste des familles en France," n.d., TD.

81.   AN 2 AG 605, "Note sur l'importance du Secrétariat d'état à la famille," Vichy, le 10 mars 1941, TD.

82.   Muel-Dreyfus, *L'Éternel féminin,* 201. See also Bordeaux, *Victoire de la famille,* 221–224.

83.   For more on the UFCS, see Christine Bard, *Les Filles de Marianne. Histoires des féminismes, 1914–1940* (Paris: Fayard, 1995), 275.

84.   Marcelle Dutheil, *L'Abandon de famille,* preface by M. André Rouast (Paris, 1943), 23.

85.   Ibid., 29.

86.   AN BB[18] 3243, Fernand Boverat à Monsieur le Garde des sceaux, Ministre de la justice, Paris, 16 janvier 1940.

87.   AN BB[18] 3303. One mother of six children wrote that her husband had abandoned her while she was ill and six months pregnant. After a period of investigation she asked that the case be dropped as she had taken up residence with her husband again.

88.   AN 2 AG 605, "Demande mariage," Marseille, mardi 19 avril 1941. Francine Muel-Dreyfus uses these letters as evidence of the internalization of the ideals of maternity amoung young women for whom no options were open in the public sphere. Although the letters offer clear evidence of the cult of maternity, they nonetheless are indicative of male absence and a new alliance between mothers and the state that excludes, or at least exists without, men.

89.   Jacques Donzelot, *The Policing of Families* (New York: Pantheon Books, 1979), 36.

90.   See Seth Koven and Sonya Michel, eds., *Mothers of a New World: Maternalist Politics and the Origins of Welfare States* (New York: Routledge, 1993); Mary Louise Roberts, *Civilization Without Sexes: Reconstructing Gender in Postwar France, 1917–1927* (Chicago: University of Chicago Press, 1994); Siân Reynolds, *France between the Wars: Gender and Politics* (London: Routledge, 1996); Fishman, *We Will Wait;* Muel-Dreyfus, *L'Éternel féminin;* Anna Cova, "French Feminism and Maternity: Theories and Policies, 1890–1918," in *Maternity and Gender Policies: Women and the Rise of the European Welfare States, 1880s-1950s,* ed. Gisela Bock and Pat Thane (London: Routledge, 1991); Françoise Thébaud, *Quand nos grand-mères donnaient la vie: Maternité en France dans l'entre-deux-guerres* (Lyon: Presses universitaires de Lyon, 1986), and idem, "Le Mouvement nataliste dans la France de l'entre-deux-guerres: L'Alliance Nationale pour l'accroissement de la population française," *Revue d'histoire moderne et contemporaine* 32 (April-June 1985): 276–301; Cheryl A. Koos, "Gender, Anti-Individualism and Nationalism: The Alliance Nationale and the Pronatalist Backlash against the *Femme moderne,* 1933–1940," *French Historical Studies* 19, no. 3 (spring 1996): 669–723; Andrés Horacio Reggiani, "Procreating France: The Politics of Demography, 1919–1945," *French Historical Studies* 19, no. 3 (spring 1996): 726–754; Joshua Cole, "'There Are Only Good Mothers': The Ideological Work of Women's Fertility in France before World War I," *French Historical Studies* 19, no. 3 (spring 1996): 639–673; Elinor

A. Accampo, "The Rhetoric of Reproduction and the Reconfiguration of Woman-hood in the French Birth Control Movement, 1890–1920," *Journal of Family History* 21, no. 3 (July 1996): 351–371; Bordeaux, *Victoire de la famille*.

91.   Secrétariat géneral à la famille et à la santé, *Code de la famille: Textes annotés et mis à jour par William Garcin* (Paris: n.p., 1941), 4–5.

92.   See Pedersen, *Family, Dependence*, 402–407 for a discussion of feminists' views on the issue of payments to the mother.

93.   Alliance nationale contre la dépopulation, *Fécondité ou servitude* (Paris, 1942), 20.

94.   AN 2 AG 605, Letter to Marshal Pétain, Marseille, 5 October 1940.

95.   AN F^{60} 498, Le Président du conseil, Ministre de la défense nationale et de la guerre à Monsieur le Vice-Président du Haut comité de la population, Paris, 30 mai 1940.

96.   See Fishman, *We Will Wait*, 42–44 for a discussion on restrictions of women's work.

97.   Pedersen, *Family, Dependence*, 420.

98.   Pedersen argues that the British held to the idea of a male family wage, direct-ing income and benefits "disproportionately to men in the expectation that some would use it to support dependent wives and children." This was in contrast to the French system, in which "some portion of the earnings of all adults was forcibly ex-pended in the support of all children." Pedersen, *Family, Dependence*, 413–414.

CONCLUSION

1.   Aline Coutrot, "La Politique familiale," in *Le Gouvernement de Vichy, 1940–42: In-stitutions et politiques* (Paris: Presses de la Fondation nationale des sciences politiques, 1972), 247.

2.   Rapport de M. Landry, Ancien ministre, "La Politique sociale et démographique," Parti Républicain radical et Radical-socialiste, Petit congrès des 19–20 décembre 1944.

3.   "Déclaration du Général de Gaulle," Assemblée nationale constituente, 2 mars 1945, cited in "La Législation familiale du gouvernement provisoire de la République française," La Documentation française, *Notes documentaires et études* 452 (25 October 1946): 3

4.   " Législation familiale du gouvernement provisoire," 13.

5.   See Michel Messu, *Les Politiques familiales: Du Natalisme à la solidarité* (Paris: Édi-tions ouvrières, 1992), 70.

6.   Antoine Prost, "L'Évolution de la politique familiale en France de 1938 à 1981," *Le Mouvement social* 129 (October–December 1984): 10.

7.   See Jacques Dupâquier et al., *Histoire de la population française*, vol. 4, *De 1914 à nos jours* (Paris: Presses universitaires de France, 1988), 171–180.

8.   Alfred Sauvy, "La Population française pendant la seconde guerre mondiale," in *Histoire de la population française*, ed. Dupâquier et al., vol. 4, *De 1914 à nos jours*, 177.

9.   For a discussion of the deliberation of this committee, see Siân Reynolds, *France between the Wars: Gender and Politics* (New York: Routledge, 1996), 212–221.

10.   Ibid., 215.

11.   Alliance nationale contre la dépopulation, *Vitalité française* 372 (September–October 1945).

12.   Centre des archives contemporaines, Fontainebleau (CAC), Participation au Congrès mondial de la famille et de la population, Paris, juin 1947, 1947–1948, 9DPM 218.

13.   "Rapport de M. le Professeur Dabin sur le contrôle de la puissance paternelle" (n.p., 1947), Bibliothèque administrative de la ville de Paris.

14.   Eric Jennings, *Vichy in the Tropics: Pétain's National Revolution in Madagascar, Guadeloupe and Indochina, 1940–1944* (Stanford, Calif.: Stanford University Press, 2001), 45.

15.   Richard D. E. Burton, *La Famille coloniale: Martinique et la mère patrie, 1789–1992* (Paris: Édition l'Harmattan, 1994), 180.

16.   Jean Bergeaud, "Le Père, ce tendre," *Familles de France* 23 (15 November 1945): 3.

17.   Antoine Prost has written that the postwar period in France witnessed a transformation in attitudes toward the family, especially related to conjugal relations. Instead of emphasizing the duties of procreation, many Catholic groups came to see the family as a means of personal fulfillment and marital happiness. These changes took place within the context of widespread consensus on family policy and the general acceptance of state assistance for the family. Antoine Prost, "L'Évolution de la politique familiale en France de 1938 à 1981," *Le Mouvement social* 129 (October–December 1984): 11–12.

18.   La Documentation française, "Législation familiale du gouvernement provisoire," 14.

19.   See Messu, *Politiques familiales,* 69–79.

20.   Président de Vulpian, Centre de coordination et d'action des mouvements familiaux des Côtes-du-Nord, "Vote des femmes ou vote familial," Saint-Brieux, 25 novembre 1944. Haut comité de la population et de la famille, 1945–1970, CAC 860269.

21.   See Miranda Pollard, *Reign of Virtue: Mobilizing Gender in Vichy France* (Chicago: University of Chicago Press, 1998), 201.

22.   See Pollard, *Reign of Virtue,* 202; and Francine Muel-Dreyfus, *Vichy et l'éternel féminin: Contribution à une sociologie politique de l'ordre des corps* (Paris: Seuil, 1996), 95. For more on the continuity thesis, see Aline Coutrot, "La politique familiale," in *Le Gouvernement de Vichy, 1940–1942: Institutions et politiques* (Paris: Colin, 1972). For the most recent assessment of the historiography of Vichy in general, see Sarah Fishman et al., eds., *France at War: Vichy and the Historians* (New York: Berg Books, 2000).

23.   See, for example, Jacques Donzelot, *The Policing of Families* (New York: Pantheon, 1979); Françoise Hurstel, *La Déchirure paternelle* (Paris: Presses universitaires de France, 1996); and Alain Lefèvre, *Du Père carent au père humilié ou la tragédie du père avec Sophocle, Claudel et Lacan* (Tours: Soleil Carré, 1995). For a revision of this historiography, see Muriel Darmon, "Les 'entreprises' de la morale familiale," *French Politics, Culture and Society* 17, no. 3–4 (summer/fall 1999): 1–19.

24.   David Popenoe, "A World Without Fathers," *Wilson Quarterly* 20, no. 2 (spring 1996): 12.

25.   David Popenoe, *Life without Father: Compelling New Evidence that Fatherhood and Marriage Are Indispensable for the Good of Children and Society* (Chicago: University of Chicago Press, 1996). Frank Furstenberg describes the book as "at once a compendium of social science research on the paternal role, a passionate appeal for resurrecting men's authority as parents, and a list of prescriptions for rebuilding marital commitments and restoring the paternal role." *American Journal of Sociology* 103, no. 3 (November 1997): 803–807.

Selected Bibliography

ARCHIVAL AND MANUSCRIPT COLLECTIONS

Archives nationales, Paris, France

Académie de Paris.
    Propagande en faveur de la famille.
    AJ^{16} 7122.
Ministère de la justice, Correspondance générale de la division criminelle.
    Dossiers banaux.
    BB^{18}: 2616, 2825, 2866, 3205, 3243, 3252, 3303, 3332, 6375.
Ministère de l'intérieur, Administration générale.
    Exploitation des rapports préfectoraux.
    F^{1a}: 3701.
Police générale.
    F^7: 12386, 13179, 13186, 13955, 13962.
Commerce et industrie.
    Expositions.
    F^{12}: 11943, 12137, 12454.
Travail et securité sociale.
    Journée de huit heures.
    F^{22}: 404, 405, 406.
Services de l'information.
    F^{41}: 226, 291.
Secrétariat général du gouvernement et Services du Premier ministre.
    F^{60}: 359, 440, 495, 496, 498, 499, 528, 606, 607, 608.
Archives du cabinet du Chef de l'État.
    2 AG: 27, 459, 497, 498, 536, 543, 605, 654.
Seconde guerre mondiale.
    72 AJ: 51, 254, 257, 255, 1232, 1238, 1241, 1410, 1422, 1424, 1854, 1858.

Centre des archives contemporaines, Fontainebleau, France

760145 Familles nombreuses, 1938–1945.
760169 Prestations familiales, 1943–1966.

760173 Éducation familiale, contrôle du cinéma, protection des mineurs.
770123 Rétablissement de la légalité républicaine en 1944.
860269 Haut comité de la population et de la famille, 1945–1970.

Bibliothèque administrative de la ville de Paris, France

Conférences d'information de l'Hôtel-de-Ville, 1943–1944.

Bibliothèque de documentation internationale contemporaine, Nanterre, France

Cahiers de formation politique. Vichy, 1942–1943.
Coirard, Renée. *L'Apport des Catholiques sociaux à la politique familiale française.*
    1943. O40273.
Commissariat général à la famille. Gr. fol. 126$^{1-19}$.
Commissariat général d'action sociale pour les français travaillant en Allemagne.
"Travailleurs français, dans les 'Manoirs' vos enfants seront heureux et en sécurité."
    O pièce 26418.
"Droits respectifs de l'état, du père de famille et de l'enfant en matière de l'édu-
    cation."
    1933, O 44154.
"Éléments d'orientation sur notre politique familiale." September 1945. O pièce
    25170^{1}.
Équipes et cadres de la France nouvelle. Jeunes DRAC. Q 5072.
"La Famille française et l'esprit de famille actuel en France." Paris, Comité national
    d'études sociales et politiques, 1929. O 53 275/Col.
"Foyer retrouvé." 1942. S29166.
Guerdan, René. "Travailleur qui pars pour l'Allemagne." S26802
"La Législation familiale du gouvernement provisoire de la République française."
    4P4198^{452}.
"Le Maréchal protège la famille." Vichy, August 1943. Q pièce 4348.
Secrétariat général à la famille et à la santé. Paris, 1941. O pièce 21800$^{1-2}$.
Voix françaises familiales. 1942–44. GFP 3015.

Vidéothèque de Paris, Nouveau forum des Halles, Paris

France actualités
Newsreels: August-September 1943, October-November 1943, January-February
    1944, July-August 1944.
Paris, Réalisation anonyme. Documentaire, v.o. 1944, 11 min.
Caméras sous la botte. Film, 1944, 26 min.

PRIMARY SOURCES

Almanach de la famille française. Paris: Durassié et cie, 1941.
Amieux, Émile. *Bréviaire de la paix et de la guerre. Essai sur la nature de l'homme en
    général et du français en particulier.* Paris: OCIA, 1944.
Amoudrou, M. "La Paternité." Conférences données à l'Institut d'études familiales
    du Nord de la France. Lille, 1943.

André, Justin. *Le Suffrage universel dédié à la famille représentée par son chef le Père de famille*. Paris: Garnier, 1850.

Association pour la protection légale des travailleurs. "L'Utilisation des loisirs des travailleurs." Paris, 1925.

"Aux ouvriers, prisonniers de guerre libérés." Secrétariat général de l'information, n.p., 1941.

Barrès, Maurice. *Les Diverses familles spirituelles de la France*. Paris: Émile-Paul Frères, 1917.

Benôit-Levy, Georges. *La Maison heureuse*. Paris: Éditions des cités-jardins de France, 1921.

Biancini, E. and H. *La Communauté familiale*. Paris: Plon, 1942.

Bonjean, Georges. *Enfants révoltés et parents coupables*. Paris: Armand Colin, 1895.

Bordeaux, Henry. *La Crise de la famille française*. Paris: Flammarion, 1921.

——. *Le Foyer*. Paris: Flammarion, 1937.

——. *Les Pierres du foyer: Essai sur l'histoire littéraire de la famille française*. Paris: Plon, 1918.

Boverat, Fernand. *La Dénatalité mortelle*. Paris: Alliance nationale, 1939.

——. *Fécondité ou décadence*. Lyon: Alliance nationale, 1944.

——. *Fécondité ou servitude*. Lyon: Alliance nationale, 1942.

——. *Patriotisme et paternité*. Paris: Bernard Grasset, 1913.

Bureau, Paul. *L'Indiscipline des moeurs: Étude de science sociale*. Paris: Bloud & Gay, 1921.

Carité, Maurice. *Le Père de famille et le foyer*. Paris: Les Éditions du temps présent, 1941.

Cavaille, J. *La Journée de huit heures: La Loi du 23 avril 1919*. Paris: Marcel Rivière, 1919.

Chaptal, Mlle. *Enquête sur l'enfance en danger moral*. Société des nations, Comité de la protection de l'enfance. Geneva, 1920.

Chevallier, Jean-Jacques. *L'Ordre viril: L'Efficacité dans l'action*. Collection "Chef et ses jeunes" 7, École nationale des cadres d'Uriage, n.d.

Cheysson, Émile. "À l'Assemblée générale de la Ligue." *Ligue populaire pour le repos du Dimanche*. Paris, 1902.

——. *La Famille, l'association et l'état*. Paris: Guillaumin, 1904.

Comité national d'études sociales & politiques. "L'Enfance en danger moral." Paris, 1928.

——. "La Natalité." Exposé de MM. Vieuille, Roulleaux-Dugage, de Mmes Chevally, Vérone, Bouvier. Séance du Lundi 26 Janvier 1925.

"Comment reconquérir le français à l'idée familiale." Paris: Alliance nationale, 1942.

Commissariat général à la famille. *Le Chef et la famille*. Foreword by Général Lafont. 1942.

——. *Les Chefs de demain seront. . . .* Paris: Office de publicité générale, 1942.

——. *La Commune: Rempart de la famille*. Foreword by Charles Trochu. Paris: Office de publicité générale, 1942.

——. *L'École et la famille*. Foreword by Paul Haury. Paris: Office de publicité générale, 1942.

——. *L'Enfant unique est triste*. Paris: Office de publicité générale, 1942.

——. *Paysan: Si chaque épi ne te donnait qu'un grain. . . .* Paris: Office de publicité générale, 1942.

——. *Les Prisonniers et la famille*. Paris: Office de propagande générale, 1943.

——. *L'Université devant la famille.* Foreword by Gilbert Gidel. Paris: Office de publicité générale, 1942.

Compte-rendu du Xème Congrès international. Ligue internationale pour la vie et la famille. 2–3 August, 1937.

Corra, Émile. *La Paternité.* Paris, 1911.

Crétinon, M.A. "La Famille, source de vie: Ses relations avec l'autorité politique." *Semaines sociales de France.* Grenoble, 1923.

Dalloz, *Jurisprudence générale. Supplément: Paternité et filiation.* Paris: Bureau de jurisprudence générale, 1893.

Dancette, Victor. "Il était une fois un pays heureux." Images de P. Baudoin. Paris: Office de publicité générale, n.d.

Danielou, Madeleine. *Visages de la famille.* Paris: Bloud & Gay, 1940.

Dassonville, J. *Une Mystique familiale.* Paris: Éditions Spes, 1941.

Desbuquois, R. P. "Les Réformes économiques qu'exige la restauration de la famille." *Semaines sociales de France.* Grenoble, 1923.

Discours qui a concouru à l'Institut national de France, sur cette question: Quelles doivent être, dans une République bien-constituée, l'étendue et les limites du pouvoir d'un père de famille? Paris: Étienne Charles, 1801.

Doriot, Jacques. *Je suis un homme du Maréchal.* Paris: Grasset, 1941.

Dunoyer de Segonzac. *Réflexions pour de jeunes chefs.* Collection "Chef et ses jeunes" 5, École nationale des cadres d'Uriage, n.d.

Dutheil, Marcelle. *L'Abandon de famille.* Foreword by André Rouast. Paris, 1943.

Duthoit, Eugène. "Illusions et réalités touchant le problème de la population." *Semaines sociales de France.* Grenoble, 1923.

Étude critique sur la puissance paternelle et ses limites d'après le Code civil. Paris: L. Larose, 1898.

La Famille dans la vie du droit. Paris: Imprimerie nationale, 1944.

La Famille dans la vie sociale. Paris: E. Ramlot, 1937.

Femmes d'absents. Série "Fêtes et saisons." Paris: Éditions du Cerf, 1943.

Ferré, Georges. *Chroniques des temps d'après-guerre.* Paris: Éditions Jules Tallandier, 1929.

Fleurot, M. M., et al. "Comment relever dans les pays envahis les foyers détruits par la guerre." *La Revue philanthropique,* 15 January 1920.

Forestier, H. *La Famille ouvrière dans sa maison.* Paris: Éditions du temps présent, 1941.

France 41: La Révolution nationale constructive: Un Bilan et un programme. Foreword by Raymond Postal. Paris: Éditions Alsatia, 1941.

Garail, M. *Pour une croisade familiale.* Paris: Les Éditions mariage et famille, 1936.

Garcin, William. *Révolution sociale par la famille.* Vichy: Fédération française des associations de famille, 1943.

——. *La Famille.* Vichy: [n.p.], 1944.

Géraldy, Paul. *L'Homme et l'amour.* Paris: La Belle édition, n.d.

Guérin, M. "Les Ennemis intérieur de la famille." *Semaines sociales de France.* Limoges, 1912.

Guesdon, Victor. *Le Mouvement de création et d'extension des caisses d'allocations familiales.* Paris: La Vie universitaire, 1922.

Guibal, Jean. *La Famille dans la Révolution nationale.* Paris: Éditions Fernand Sorlot, 1940.

Guide pratique des lois familiales. Paris: Le Musée social, 1946.

Guillemin, Henri. *Lamartine et la question sociale.* Paris: Plon, 1946.

Guy-Grand, G. "Famille et société." *Les Problèmes de la famille et le féminisme.* Conférences faites à la Ligue française d'éducation morale. n.d.

Harraca, E. *Sur le vote familial: Le Suffrage du chef de famille normale.* Paris: Marcel Giard, 1930.

Helleu, Yves. *Avantages réservés à la famille.* Vichy, 1943.

Lagerhof, Selma. "Le Foyer et l'état." *La Revue scandinave* (June 1911).

Lancelot, E. *Pour l'ordre familial: Un Plan, une organisation à réaliser.* Paris: Éditions mariage et famille, 1934.

Landry, M. "La Politique sociale et démographique." Parti Républicain radical et Radical-socialiste, Petit congrès des 19–20 décembre 1944.

Laparcerie, Marie. *Comment trouver un mari après la guerre.* Paris, 1915.

Larouze, Georges. *Du Retrait de certaines droits de la puissance paternelle.* Paris, 1917.

Laskine, Edmond. *L'Union libre devant la loi et les tribunaux.* Paris: E. Muller, 1935.

Lavallée, Mgr. "Le Célibat écclésiastique et le problème de la population." *Semaines sociales de France.* Grenoble, 1923.

Lavollée, Henry. *Code manuel de la recherche de la paternité.* Paris: Librairie générale de droit et de jurisprudence, 1913.

Lemaire, J. *La Défense de la famille et la société.* Laon, 1936.

Lemarié, O. *Une Charte de la famille. Précis de morale familiale.* Paris: Éditions familiales de France, 1942.

Loez, A. "Le Problème de la famille." *XX Congrès national de l'U.N.C.* Arcachon, 18–21 May 1939.

"Les Loisirs des travailleurs." Rapports présentés au Congrès international des loisirs du travailleur. Brussels, 15–17 June 1935.

Loudes, J. *Ce qu'il faut savoir sur les assurances sociales, les congés payés, les allocations familiales.* Liège: Desoer, 1936.

Le Maintien et la défense de la famille par le droit. Paris: Receuil Sirey, 1930.

Marin, Louis. *L'Abandon de famille.* Proposition déposée à la Chambre des députés. 20 February 1923.

——. "Le Partage équitable des charges de la guerre." Discours prononcé par M. Louis Marin, Député, aux séances du Chambre des députés du mercredi 21 Janvier 1925.

Martial, Lydie. "Un Voeu important: L'Enseignement de la paternité à la caserne et dans les écoles de l'État." *Action du féminisme rationel.* Union de pensée féminine, 2 March 1905.

Mascarel, Arnold. *La Famille et la fiscalité.* Paris, 1922.

Méline, Pierre. *Morale familiale.* Paris: Bloud & Gay, 1940.

Parodi, D. "Parents et enfants." *Les Problèmes de la famille et le féminisme.* Conférences faites à la Ligue française d'éducation morale, n.d.

Passerat, Marcel. *L'Hôtel-appartement. Ce que doit être l'organisation moderne de la vie privée.* Paris: Éditions des cités-jardins, 1921.

Penfentenyo, Vice-Amiral de. *Le Manuel du père de famille.* Paris: Flammarion, 1941.

Pinard, A. *La Consommation, le bien-être et le luxe.* Paris: O. Doin, 1918.

La Politique familiale de l'État français. Textes et commentaires par Pierre Sauvage. Collection France vivante, 1941.

Une Politique gouvernementale de la natalité. Paris: L'Alliance nationale, 1924.

Première journée internationale des allocations familiales. Compte-rendu. Paris, 8 July 1937.

De la Protection légale des enfants contre les abus de l'autorité paternelle. Paris: Éd. Fuzier-Herman, 1878.

"Rapport de M. le Professeur Dabin sur le contrôle de la puissance paternelle." n.p., 1947. Bibliothèque administrative de la ville de Paris.

Renaudin, Philippe. *La Famille dans la nation*. Paris: Commissariat général à la famille, 1943.

Ripert, Georges. *Le Droit privé français au milieu du 20ème siècle*. Paris: R. Pichon, 1950.

Romanet, Émile. *Les Allocations familiales*. Lyon: Chronique sociale de France, 1922.

Rouast, André. *La Famille dans la nation*. Paris: Presses universitaires, 1941.

Sauvage, P. *La Politique familiale de l'État français. Restauration familiale et révolution nationale*. Paris: Action populaire, 1941.

Secrétariat général à la famille et à la santé. *Code de la famille: Textes annotés et mis à jour par William Garcin*. Paris, 1941.

Sennep, Jean. *Cartel et Cie: Caricatures inédites*. Paris: Bossard, 1926.

Solidarité: Exposition internationale des arts et techniques dans la vie moderne, Paris, 1937. Paris: Éditions Edna Nicoll, 1937.

Strauss, Paul. *Dépopulation et puériculture*. Paris: Fasquelle, 1901.

Tabuteau, Jacques. *La Famille*. Paris: Les Éditions ouvrières, 1944.

Terrel, M. J. "Les Responsabilités du père de famille." *Semaines sociales de France*. Versailles, 1913.

Théodore, M. *Le Petit code des familles nombreuses*. Paris: Éditions "La Femme et l'enfant," 1930.

Théry, A. *La Famille: Erreurs d'hier, réalisations d'aujourd'hui*. Paris, 1943.

——. *La Famille: Vérités de toujours*. Paris, 1943.

Toulemon, André. *Le Suffrage familial*. Paris: 1933.

Union féminine civique et sociale. "La Famille dans la vie sociale: Petit guide pratique de la législation familiale." Paris: Éditions Spes, 1937.

Valois, Georges. *Le Père: Philosophie de la famille*. Paris: Nouvelle librairie nationale, 1924.

Vérine (Marguerite Lebrun). *C'est dans les familles que se fait la France*. Paris: Édition sociale française, 1942.

Vernet, Madeleine. *La Paternité*. Poligny: Imprimerie Alfred Jacquin, 1906.

La Vie en fleur. Paris: Office de publicité générale, 1943.

La Vie familiale. Scènes et portraits. Exposition, Galerie Charpentier. Paris, 1944.

Weygand, Général. *Comment élever nos fils?* Paris: Flammarion, 1937.

Widmer, M. G. *Les Logements pour célibataires*. Paris: Imprimerie Chaix, 1918.

Zirnheld, M. "La Famille et les revendications des travailleurs." *Semaines sociales de France*. Grenoble, 1923.

NEWSPAPERS AND PERIODICALS

L'Action familiale
l'Actualité sociale
Le Bonheur du foyer
Bulletin de France et famille
Le Coin de terre et le foyer
Défendons nos foyers
Éducation
La Famille française

Familles de France
Fédération des associations de familles nombreuses
L'Humanité
Jeunesse . . . France!
Le Lien
Natalité
Le Populaire de Paris
Revue de la famille
Revue de la plus grande famille

SECONDARY SOURCES

Accampo, Elinor. "The Rhetoric of Reproduction and the Reconfiguration of Womanhood in the French Birth Control Movement, 1890–1920." *Journal of Family History* 21, no. 3 (July 1996): 351–71.

Accampo, Elinor, Rachel G. Fuchs, and Mary Lynn Stewart, eds. *Gender and the Politics of Social Reform in France, 1870–1914.* Baltimore, Md.: Johns Hopkins University Press, 1995.

L'Action familiale ouvrière et la politique de Vichy. Journées d'études des 28–29 novembre 1984. *Les Cahiers du GRMF* 3 (1984).

Adler, Laure. *Secrets d'alcôve: Histoire du couple de 1830 à 1930.* Paris: Hachette, 1983.

Ambler, John S., ed. *The French Welfare State: Surviving Social and Ideological Change.* New York: New York University Press, 1991.

Andrieu, Claire. "Démographie, famille, jeunesse." In *La France des années noires.* Vol. 1, *De la défaite à Vichy,* ed. Jean-Pierre Azéma and François Bédarida. Paris: Éditions du Seuil, 1993.

Appelbaum, Stanley. *French Satirical Drawings from "L'Assiette au Beurre."* New York: Dover, 1978.

Arnaud-Duc, Nicole. "The Law's Contradictions." In *A History of Women.* Vol. 4, *Emerging Feminism from Revolution to World War,* ed. Geneviève Fraisse and Michelle Perrot. Cambridge: Harvard University Press, 1993.

Atkin, Nicholas. *Pétain.* New York: Longman, 1998.

Audoin-Rouzeau, Stéphane. *L'Enfant de l'ennemi.* Paris: Aubier, 1995.

Azéma, Jean-Pierre. *1940: L'Année terrible.* Paris: Éditions du Seuil, 1990.

———. *From Munich to the Liberation, 1938–1944,* trans. Janet Lloyd. New York: Cambridge University Press, 1984.

———. "La France de Daladier." In *La France des années noires.* Vol. 1, *De la défaite à Vichy,* ed. Jean-Pierre Azéma and François Bédarida. Paris: Éditions du Seuil, 1993.

———. "Le Régime de Vichy." In *La France des années noires.* Vol. 1, *De la défaite à Vichy,* ed. Jean-Pierre Azéma and François Bédarida. Paris: Éditions du Seuil, 1993.

Bachelier, Christian. "L'Armée française entre la victoire et la défaite." In *La France des années noires.* Vol. 1, *De la défaite à Vichy,* ed. Jean-Pierre Azéma and François Bédarida. Paris: Éditions du Seuil, 1993.

Badinter, Elisabeth. *XY: On Masculine Identity,* trans. Lydia Davis. New York: Columbia University Press, 1995.

Bard, Christine. *Les Filles de Marianne: Histoire des féminismes, 1914–1940.* Paris: Fayard, 1995.

——. "Proletarians of the Proletariat: Women's Citizenship in France." *International Labor and Working-Class History* 48 (1995): 49–67.

Barker, Kristin Kay. "Federal Maternal Policy and Gender Politics: Comparative Insights." *Journal of Women's History* 9, no. 2 (1997): 183–91.

Becchia, Alain. "Les Milieux parlementaires et la dépopulation de 1900 à 1914." *Communications* (1986): 201–43.

Bédarida, François. "Huit mois d'attente et d'illusion: La 'Drôle de guerre.'" In *La France des années noires*. Vol. 1, *De la défaite à Vichy*, ed. Jean-Pierre Azéma and François Bédarida. Paris: Éditions du Seuil, 1993.

Bédarida, François, and Renée Bédarida. "La Persécution des juifs." In *La France des années noires*. Vol. 2, *De l'Occupation à la Libération*. Paris: Éditions du Seuil, 1993.

Bederman, Gail. *Manliness & Civilization: A Cultural History of Gender and Race in the United States, 1880–1917*. Chicago: University of Chicago Press, 1995.

Berenson, Edward. *The Trial of Madame Caillaux*. Berkeley: University of California Press, 1992.

Berlanstein, Lenard R. "Breeches and Breaches: Cross-Dress Theater and the Culture of Gender Ambiguity in Modern France." *Comparative Studies in Society and History* 38, no. 2 (1996): 338–69.

Bertin, Célia. *Femmes sous l'occupation*. Paris: Stock, 1993.

Bitoun, Pierre. *Les Hommes d'Uriage*. Nancy: Presses universitaires de Nancy, 1989.

Bloch, Marc. *Strange Defeat: A Statement of Evidence Written in 1940*. New York: Norton, 1968.

Bock, Gisela. "Antinatalism, Maternity and Paternity in National Socialist Racism." In *Maternity and Gender Policies: Women and the Rise of the Welfare States, 1880s–1950s*, ed. Gisela Bock and Pat Thane. London: Routledge, 1991.

——. "Poverty and Mother's Rights in the Emerging Welfare States." In *A History of Women*. Vol. 5, *Toward a Cultural Identity in the Twentieth Century*, ed. Françoise Thébaud. Cambridge: Harvard University Press, 1994.

Bordeaux, Michèle. *La Victoire de la famille dans la France défaite: Vichy 1940–1944*. Paris: Flammarion, 2002.

Boscaglia, Maurizia. *Eye on the Flesh: Fashions of Masculinity in the Early Twentieth Century*. Boulder, Colo.: Westview Press, 1996.

Bowlan, Jeanne. "Polygamists Need Not Apply: Becoming a French Citizen in Colonial Algeria, 1918–1938." *Proceedings of the Annual Meeting of the Western Society for French History* 24 (1997): 110–19.

Burleigh, Michael, and Wolfgang Wipperman. *The Racial State: Germany, 1933–1945*. Cambridge: Cambridge University Press, 1991.

Burrin, Philippe. *France under the Germans: Collaboration and Compromise*. New York: New Press, 1996.

Burton, Richard D. E. *La Famille coloniale: La Martinique et la mère patrie, 1789–1992*. Paris: L'Harmattan, 1994.

Camiscioli, Elisa. "Intermarriage, Independent Nationality, and the Individual Rights of French Women: The Law of August 10 1927." *French Politics, Culture and Society* 17, no. 3–4 (spring/fall 1999): 52–74.

Carbonnier, Jean. "Le Statut de l'enfant en droit civil pendant la Révolution." In *L'Enfant, la famille et la Révolution française*, ed. Marie-Françoise Lévy. Paris: Olivier Orban, 1990.

Carroll, David. *French Literary Fascism*. Princeton, N.J.: Princeton University Press, 1995.

Cena, Olivier. *Les Jardins de la sociale.* Paris: Éditions du May, 1992.

Chauvière, Michel. "L'Action familiale ouvrière et la politique de Vichy: Acteurs, institutions, enjeux." In *L'Action familiale ouvrière et la politique de Vichy.* Journées d'études des 28–29 novembre 1984, *Les Cahiers du GRMF 3* (1984).

——. "Familialisme et régulation sociale ou aspects de la démultiplication du concept de famille." *Annales de Vaucresson* 27 (1987): 207–26.

——. "1939–1944. Du Code de la famille à la Libération: Présentation du période." In *Les Mouvements familiaux populaire et ruraux, naissance, développement, mutations, 1939–1955. Les Cahiers du GRMF* 1 (August 1983).

Chauvière, Michel, and Jacques Godbout. *Les Usagers, entre marché et citoyenneté.* Paris: Harmattan, 1992.

Choquette, Leslie. "Degenerate or Degendered?: Images of Prostitution and Homosexuality in the French Third Republic." *Historical Reflections* 23, no. 2 (1997): 205–28.

Clerget, Joël. *Être père aujourd'hui.* Paris: Le Cerf, 1979.

Coale, Ansley J., and Susan Cotts Watkins. *The Decline of Fertility in Europe: The Revised Proceedings of a Conference on the Princeton European Fertility Project.* Princeton, N.J.: Princeton University Press, 1986.

Cohen, Miriam, and Michael Hanagan. "The Politics of Gender and the Making of the Welfare State, 1900–1940: A Comparative Perspective." *Journal of Social Policy* 24 (spring 1991): 469–84.

Cointet-Labrousse, Michèle. *Vichy et le fascisme.* Paris: Éditions complexes, 1987.

Cole, Joshua. *The Power of Large Numbers: Population, Politics and Gender in Nineteenth-Century France.* Ithaca, N.Y.: Cornell University Press, 2000.

——. "'A Sudden and Terrible Revelation': Motherhood and Infant Mortality in France, 1858–1874." *Journal of Family History* 21, no. 4 (October 1996): 419–46.

——. "There are Only Good Mothers: The Ideological Work of Women's Fertility in France before World War I." *French Historical Studies* 19, no. 3 (spring 1996): 639–73.

Commaille, Jacques. *Misères de la famille, question d'état.* Paris: Presses de la Fondation nationale des sciences politiques, 1996.

Comte, Bernard. "L'Esprit d'Uriage: Pédagogie civique et humanisme révolutionnaire." In *Les Politiques et pratiques culturelles dans la France de Vichy, Les Cahiers de l'IHTP* 8 (June 1988): 117–30.

——. *Une Utopie combattante: L'École des cadres d'Uriage, 1940–1942.* Paris: Fayard, 1991.

Cooper, Sandi E. "Pacifism, Feminism and Fascism in Inter-War France." *The International History Review* 19, no. 1 (1997): 103–15.

Cornu, Gérard. *Vocabulaire juridique.* Paris: Presses universitaires de France, 1992.

Coutrot, Aline. "La Politique familiale." In *Le Gouvernement de Vichy, 1940–1942: Institutions et politiques.* Paris: Presses de la Fondation nationale des sciences politiques, 1972.

Cova, Anne. "French Feminism and Maternity: Theories and Policies, 1890–1918." In *Maternity and Gender Policies: Women and the Rise of the Welfare States, 1880s–1950s,* ed. Gisela Bock and Pat Thane, 196–212. London: Routledge, 1991.

Crémieux-Brilhac, Jean-Louis. *Les Français de l'an 40.* 2 vols. Paris: Gallimard, 1990.

Cross, Gary. *A Quest for Time: The Reduction of Work in Britain and France, 1840–1940.* Berkeley: University of California Press, 1989.

Crubellier, Maurice. *L'École républicaine, 1870–1940: Esquisse d'une histoire culturelle.* Paris: Éditions Christian, 1993.

——. *Histoire culturelle de la France, XIXe-XXe siècle*. Paris: Armand Colin, 1974.

Curtis, Michael. *Three against the Third Republic: Sorel, Barrès and Maurras*. Princeton, N.J.: Princeton University Press, 1959.

Darrow, Margaret H. "French Volunteer Nursing and the Myth of War Experience in World War I." *American Historical Review* 101, no. 1 (1996): 80–106.

Darmon, Muriel. "Les 'entreprises' de la morale familiale." *French Politics, Culture and Society* 17, no. 3–4 (spring/fall 1999): 1–19.

Delaisi de Parseval, Geneviève, and Françoise Hurstel. "'Fatherhood' à la française." In *The Father's Role: Cross-Cultural Perspectives*, ed. Michael Lamb. Hillsdale, N.J.: Lawrence Erlbaum, 1986.

Delbourg-Delphis, Marylène. *Masculin singulier: Le Dandyisme et son histoire*. Paris: Hachette, 1985.

Delestre, Antoine. *Uriage, une communauté et une école dans la tourmente, 1940–1945*. Nancy: Presses universitaires de Nancy, 1989.

Déloye, Yves. *École et citoyenneté. L'Individualisme républicain de Jules Ferry à Vichy: Controverses*. Paris: Presses de la Fondation nationale des sciences politiques, 1994.

Delumeau, Jean, and Daniel Roche, eds. *Histoire des pères et de la paternité*. Paris: Larousse, 1990.

Donzelot, Jacques. *The Policing of Families*, trans. Robert Hurley. New York: Pantheon Books, 1979.

Downs, Laura Lee. "'Boys Will Be Men and Girls Will Be Boys': Division sexuelle et travail dans la metallurgie (France et Angleterre, 1914–1939)," trans. Frédéric Lefebvre. *Annales: Histoire, Sciences sociales* 54, no. 3 (1999): 561–86.

——. *Childhood in the Promised Land: Working-Class Movements and the* Colonies de Vacances *in France, 1880–1960*. Durham, N.C.: Duke University Press, 2002.

——. *Manufacturing Inequality: Gender Division in the French and British Metalworking Industries, 1914–1939*. Ithaca, N.Y.: Cornell University Press, 1995.

Drouard, Alain. *Une Inconnue des sciences sociales: La Fondation Alexis Carrel, 1941–1945*. Paris: Éditions de la Maison des sciences de l'homme, 1992.

Duby, Georges, and Michelle Perrot, eds. *A History of Women*. Vol. 4, *Emerging Feminism from Revolution to World War*, ed. Geneviève Fraisse and Michelle Perrot. Cambridge: Harvard University Press, 1993.

——. *A History of Women*. Vol. 5, *Toward a Cultural Identity in the Twentieth Century*, ed. Françoise Thébaud. Cambridge: Harvard University Press, 1993.

Duroselle, Jean-Baptiste. *L'Abîme, 1939–1945*. Paris: Éditions du Seuil, 1982.

——. *La Décadence, 1932–1939*. Paris: Éditions du Seuil, 1983.

Dutton, Paul V. *Origins of the French Welfare State: The Struggle for Social Reform in France, 1914–1947*. Cambridge: Cambridge University Press, 2002.

Dyer, Colin. *Population and Society in Twentieth-Century France*. New York: Holmes & Meier, 1978.

Eck, Hélène. "French Women under Vichy." In *A History of Women*. Vol. 5, *Toward a Cultural Identity in the Twentieth Century*, ed. Françoise Thébaud. Cambridge: Harvard University Press, 1994.

Eleb, Monique. *L'Apprentissage du "chez soi": Le Groupe des maisons ouvrières, Daumesnil, 1908*. Paris: Éditions parenthèses, 1994.

Ellis, Jack. *The Physician-Legislators of France: Medicine and Politics in the Early Third Republic, 1870–1914*. Cambridge: Cambridge University Press, 1990.

Elwitt, Sanford. *The Third Republic Defended: Bourgeois Reform in France, 1880–1914*. Baton Rouge: Louisiana State University Press, 1986.

Faure, Christian. *Le Projet culturel de Vichy.* Lyon: Presses universitaires de Lyon, 1989.

Fields, A. Belden. *"Liberté, égalité & surtout fraternité?:* The Struggle over Women's Liberation in the French Communist & Socialist Parties," *Polity* 18, no. 4 (1986): 553–76.

Fineman, Martha Albertson. *The Neutered Mother, the Sexual Family.* New York: Routledge, 1995.

Fishman, Sarah. "Grand Delusions. The Unintended Consequences of Vichy France's Prisoner of War Propaganda." *Journal of Contemporary History* 26 (1991): 229–54.

——. "The Power of Myth: Five Recent Works on Vichy France." *Journal of Modern History* 67, no. 3 (September 1995): 666–74.

——. *We Will Wait: Wives of French Prisoners of War, 1940–1945.* New Haven, Conn.: Yale University Press, 1991.

Fishman, Sarah, Laura Lee Downs, Ioannis Sinanoglou, Leonard V. Smith, and Robert Zaretsky, eds. *France at War: Vichy and the Historians.* New York: Berg, 2000.

Frader, Laura Levine. "Definir le droit au travail: Rapports sociaux de sexe, famille et salaire en France aux XIXe et XX siècles." *Mouvement social* 184 (1998): 5–22.

——. "Dissent over Discourse: Labor History, Gender, and the Linguistic Turn." *History and Theory* 34, no. 3 (1995): 213–30.

——. "From Muscles to Nerves: Gender, 'Race' and the Body at Work in France, 1919–1939." *International Review of Social History* 44, no. 7 (1999): 123–47.

Frader, Laura, and Sonya O. Rose, eds. *Gender and Class in Modern Europe.* Ithaca, N.Y.: Cornell University Press, 1996.

Frank, Robert. "Pétain, Laval, Darlan." In *La France des années noires.* Vol. 1, *De la défaite à Vichy,* ed. Jean-Pierre Azéma and François Bédarida. Paris: Éditions du Seuil, 1993.

Fuchs, Rachel G. *Poor and Pregnant in Paris: Strategies for Survival in the Nineteenth Century.* New Brunswick, N.J.: Rutgers University Press, 1992.

——. "Seduction, Paternity and the Law in Fin-de-Siècle France." *Journal of Modern History* 72 (December 2000): 944–89.

Furlough, Ellen. "Selling the American Way in Interwar France: *Prix Uniques* and the *Salons des Arts Ménagers.*" *Journal of Social History* 26, no. 3 (1993): 491–519.

Fussell, Paul. *The Great War and Modern Memory.* New York: Oxford University Press, 1975.

Garden, Maurice, and Hervé Le Bras. "La Population française entre les deux guerres." In *Histoire de la population française,* ed. Jacques Dupâquier. Vol. 4, *De 1914 à nos jours.* Paris: Presses universitaires de France, 1988.

Gervereau, Laurent, and Denis Peschanski, eds. *La Propagande sous Vichy, 1940–1944.* Nanterre: BDIC, 1990.

Gildea, Robert. *Education in Provincial France, 1800–1914: A Study of Three Departments.* New York: Oxford University Press, 1983.

Gillis, John R., Louise A. Tilly, and David Levine, eds. *The European Experience of Declining Fertility.* Cambridge: Harvard University Press, 1992.

Ginsborg, Paul. "Family, Civil Society and the State in Contemporary European History: Some Methodological Considerations." *Contemporary European History* 4, no. 3 (November 1995): 249–74.

Giolitto, Pierre. *Histoire de la jeunesse sous Vichy.* Paris: Perrin, 1991.

Gittings, Christopher E. *Imperialism and Gender: Constructions of Masculinity.* London: Villiers, 1996.

Golan, Romy. *Modernity and Nostalgia: Art and Politics in France between the Wars.* New Haven, Conn.: Yale University Press, 1995.

Goldstein, Jan. "The Uses of Male Hysteria: Medical and Literary Discourse in Nineteenth-Century France." *Representations* 34 (1991): 134–65.

Grayzel, Susan Rachel. "Women's Identities at War: The Cultural Politics of Gender in Britain and France, 1914–1919." Ph.D. dissertation, University of California, Berkeley, 1995.

de Grazia, Victoria. *How Fascism Ruled Women: Italy, 1922–1945.* Berkeley: University of California Press, 1992.

Green, Mary Jean. "Gender, Fascism and the Croix de Feu: The 'Women's Pages' of 'Le Flambeau.'" *French Cultural Studies* 8, no. 2 (June 1997): 229–40.

Grew, Raymond. *School, State and Society: The Growth of Elementary Schooling in Nineteenth-Century France: A Qualitative Analysis.* Ann Arbor: University of Michigan Press, 1991.

Griffin, Roger. *The Nature of Fascism.* New York: St. Martin's Press, 1991.

Guillemette, Racine. *Entre Hommes: Regards sur les femmes, 1880–1930.* Paris: Flammarion, 1994.

Halls, W. D. *Politics, Society and Christianity in Vichy France.* Providence, R.I.: Berg, 1995.

——. *The Youth of Vichy France.* Oxford: Clarendon, 1981.

Hanlon, Gregory. "The Perils of Patriarchy." *Journal of Social History* 30, no. 2 (1996): 503–20.

Hanna, Martha. "Natalism, Homosexuality, and the Controversy over *Corydon.*" In *Homosexuality in Modern France,* ed. Jeffrey Merrick and Bryant T. Ragan Jr. New York: Oxford University Press, 1996.

Hause, Steven, and Anne Kenney. *Women's Suffrage and Social Politics in the French Third Republic.* Princeton, N.J.: Princeton University Press, 1984.

Hausen, Karin. "Mother's Day in the Weimar Republic." In *When Biology Became Destiny: Women in Weimar and Nazi Germany,* ed. Renate Bridenthal, Atina Grossman, and Marion Kaplan. New York: Monthly Review Press, 1984.

Hawthorne, Melanie, and Richard J. Golsan, eds. *Gender and Fascism in Modern France.* Hanover, N.H.: Dartmouth College, 1997.

Hellman, John. *The Knight-Monks of Vichy France: Uriage, 1940–1945.* Montreal: McGill-Queen's University Press, 1993.

Hervet, Robert. *Les Chantiers de la jeunesse.* Paris: Éditions France Empire, 1962.

Heuer, Jennifer. "Adopted Daughter of the French People: Suzanne Lepeletier and Her Father, the National Assembly." *French Politics, Culture and Society* 17, no. 3–4 (summer/fall 1999): 31–51.

Higonnet, Margaret Randolph, and Jane Jenson, eds. *Behind the Lines: Gender and the Two World Wars.* New Haven, Conn.: Yale University Press, 1987.

Holt, Richard. "Women, Men and Sport in France c. 1870–1914: An Introductory Survey." *Journal of Sport History* 18, no. 1 (1991): 121–34.

Horne, Alistair. *To Lose a Battle: France, 1940.* Boston: Little, Brown and Company, 1969.

Hunt, Lynn, ed. *Eroticism and the Body Politic.* Baltimore, Md.: Johns Hopkins University Press, 1990.

——. *The Family Romance of the French Revolution.* Berkeley: University of California Press, 1992.

Hurstel, Françoise. "L'Affaiblissment de l'autorité paternelle: La Notion de 'carence' des pères au 20ème siècle." *La Pensée* 261 (1988): 35–49.

———. *La Déchirure paternelle.* Paris: Presses universitaires de France, 1996.

———. "Fonction paternelle et déracinement culturel: Qu'est-ce qui fonde la paternité?" *Bulletin de psychologie* 31, no. 10–11 (1978–79): 502–9.

Huss, Marie-Monique. "Pronatalism and Popular Ideology of the Child in Wartime France: The Evidence of the Picture Postcard." In *The Upheaval of War: Family, Work and Welfare in Europe, 1914–1918,* ed. Richard Wall and Jay Winter. Cambridge: Cambridge University Press, 1989.

———. "Pronatalism in the Interwar Period in France." *Journal of Contemporary History* 25 (1990): 39–68.

Irvine, William. "Fascism in France and the Strange Case of the Croix de Feu." *Journal of Modern History* 63 (June 1991): 271–95.

Jennings, Eric. *Vichy in the Tropics: Pétain's National Revolution in Madagascar, Guadeloupe and Indochina, 1940–1944.* Stanford, Calif.: Stanford University Press, 2001.

Kedward, Roderick, and Roger Austin, eds. *Vichy France and the Resistance: Culture & Ideology.* Totowa, N.J.: Barnes & Noble, 1985.

Klaus, Alisa. "Depopulation and Race Suicide: Maternalism and Pronatalist Ideologies in France and the United States." In *Mothers of a New World: Maternalist Politics and the Origins of Welfare States,* ed. Seth Koven and Sonya Michel. New York: Routledge, 1993.

———. *Every Child a Lion: The Origins of Maternal and Infant Health Policy in the United States and France, 1890–1920.* Ithaca, N.Y.: Cornell University Press, 1993.

Kniebiehler, Yvonne. *Les Pères aussi ont une histoire.* Paris: Hachette, 1987.

———. "Le Rôle des pères à travers l'histoire." In "Pères et paternité." *Revue française des affaires sociales.* Hors-série (November 1988).

Koonz, Claudia. *Mothers in the Fatherland.* New York: St. Martin's Press, 1986.

Koos, Cheryl A. "Engendering Reaction: The Politics of Pronatalism and the Family in France, 1919–1944." Ph.D. dissertation, University of Southern California, 1996.

———. "Fascism, Fatherhood and the Family in Interwar France: The Case of Antoine Rédier." *Journal of Family History* 24 (July 1999): 317–29.

———. "Gender, Anti-Individualism and Nationalism: The Alliance Nationale and the Pronatalist Backlash against the *Femme moderne,* 1933–1940." *French Historical Studies* 19, no. 3 (spring 1996): 639–73.

———. "'*On les aura!*': The Gendered Politics of Abortion and the Alliance Nationale Contre la Dépopulation, 1938–1944." *Modern and Contemporary France* 7, no. 1 (1999): 21–33.

Koven, Seth, and Sonya Michel. "Introduction: Mother Worlds." In *Mothers of a New World: Maternalist Politics and the Origins of Welfare States,* ed. Seth Koven and Sonya Michel. New York: Routledge, 1993.

Laborie, Pierre. *L'Opinion française sous Vichy.* Paris: Éditions du Seuil, 1990.

Lanfrey, André. *Les Catholiques français et l'école, 1902–1914.* Paris: Cerf, 1990.

Lamb, Michael E., ed. *The Father's Role: Cross-Cultural Perspectives.* Hillsdale, N.J.: Lawrence Erlbaum, 1987.

LaRossa, Ralph. *The Modernization of Fatherhood: A Social and Political History.* Chicago: University of Chicago Press, 1997.

Lebovics, Herman. *True France: The Wars over Cultural Identity, 1900–1945.* Ithaca, N.Y.: Cornell University Press, 1992.

Le Bras, Hervé. "La Famille n'est pas la family." *Politis—La Revue* 8 (November-December 1994–January 1995): 55–67.

Lees, Lynn. *The Solidarities of Strangers: The English Poor Laws and the People, 1700–1948.* New York: Cambridge University Press, 1998.

Lefaucheur, Nadine. "Maternity, Family, and the State." In *A History of Women.* Vol. 5, *Toward a Cultural Identity in the Twentieth Century,* ed. Françoise Thébaud. Cambridge: Harvard University Press, 1994.

——. "Pères absents et droit au père." *Lien social et politiques* 37 (1997): 11–17.

——. "En l'Absence du père." *Informations sociales* 49–50 (1996): 56–67.

Lefèvre, Alain. *Du Père carent au père humilié, ou la tragédie du père avec Sophocle, Claudel et Lacan.* Tours: Éditions soleil carré, 1995.

Legendre, Pierre. *Les Enfants du texte.* Paris: Fayard, 1992.

Legendre, P., and A. Papageorgiou. *Filiation.* Paris: Fayard, 1990.

Lenoir, Remi. "L'État et la construction de la famille." *Actes de recherche en sciences sociales* 91–92 (1992): 20–36.

——. "Family Policy in France since 1938." In *The French Welfare State: Surviving Social and Ideological Change,* ed. John Ambler. New York: New York University Press, 1991.

Lévy, Jean-Philippe. "Le Droit familial français." In *La Famille, la loi, l'état de la Révolution au Code civil,* ed. Irène Théry and Christian Biet. Paris: Éditions Centre Georges Pompidou/Imprimerie nationale, 1989.

Magniadas, Jean. "La Politique familiale: Genèse, développements, enjeux actuels." *La Pensée* 298 (1994): 45–69.

Margadant, Jo Burr. *Madame le Professeur: Women Educators in the Third Republic.* Princeton, N.J.: Princeton University Press, 1990.

Marseille, Jacques. "L'Empire." In *La France des années noires.* Vol. 1, *De la défaite à Vichy,* ed. Jean-Pierre Azéma and François Bédarida. Paris: Éditions du Seuil, 1993.

Maugue, Annelise. *L'Identité masculine en crise au tournant du siècle (1871–1914).* Paris: Éditions Rivages, 1987.

——. "The New Eve and the Old Adam." In *A History of Women.* Vol. 4, *Emerging Feminism from Revolution to World War,* ed. Geneviève Fraisse and Michelle Perrot. Cambridge: Cambridge University Press, 1993.

McLaren, Angus. *Sexuality and Social Order: The Debate over the Fertility of Women and Workers in France, 1770–1920.* New York: Holmes & Meier, 1983.

——. *The Trials of Masculinity: Policing Sexual Boundaries, 1870–1914.* Chicago: University of Chicago Press, 1997.

McMillan, James F. *Twentieth-Century France: Politics and Society, 1898–1991.* London: Edward Arnold, 1992.

Messu, Michel. *Les Politiques familiales.* Paris: Les Éditions ouvrières, 1992.

Micale, Mark S. "Charcot and the Idea of Hysteria in the Male: Gender, Medical Science, and Medical Diagnostics in Late Nineteenth-Century France." *Medical History* 34, no. 4 (1990): 363–411.

Miller, Gérard. *Les Pousse-au-jouir du Maréchal Pétain.* With a foreword by Roland Barthes. Paris: Éditions du Seuil, 1975.

Milza, Pierre. *Fascisme français: Passé et présent.* Paris: Flammarion, 1987.

Mosse, George L. *The Image of Man: The Creation of Modern Masculinity.* New York: Oxford University Press, 1996.

——. *Nationalism and Sexuality: Respectability and Abnormal Sexuality in Modern Europe.* New York: Howard Fertig, 1985.

Muel-Dreyfus, Francine. *Vichy et l'éternel féminin.* Paris: Éditions du Seuil, 1996.

Mulliez, Jacques. "'*Pater is est* . . . 'La Source juridique de la puissance paternelle du droit révolutionnaire au Code civil." In *La Famille, la loi, l'état de la Révolution au Code civil,* ed. Irène Théry and Christian Biet. Paris: Éditions du Centre Georges Pompidou/Imprimerie nationale, 1989.

Murat, Pierre. "La Puissance paternelle et la Révolution française: Essai de régénération de l'autorité des pères." In *La Famille, la loi, l'état de la Révolution au Code civil,* ed. Irène Théry and Christian Biet. Paris: Éditions du Centre Georges Pompidou/Imprimerie nationale, 1989.

Nash, Mary. "Pronatalism and Motherhood in Franco's Spain." In *Maternity and Gender Policies: Women and the Rise of the Welfare States, 1880s-1950s,* ed. Gisela Bock and Pat Thane. London: Routledge, 1991.

Nord, Philip. "The Welfare State in France, 1870–1914." *French Historical Studies* 18, no. 3 (spring 1994): 821–38.

Nye, Robert. *Masculinity and Male Codes of Honor in Modern France.* New York: Oxford University Press, 1993.

——. *The Medical Concept of National Decline.* Princeton, N.J.: Princeton University Press, 1984.

O'Donovan, Katherine. *Family Law Matters.* Boulder, Colo.: Pluto Press, 1993.

Offen, Karen. "Body Politics: Women, Work and the Politics of Motherhood in France, 1920–1950." In *Maternity and Gender Policies: Women and the Rise of the Welfare States, 1880s to 1950s,* ed. Gisela Bock and Pat Thane. London: Routledge, 1991.

——. "Depopulation, Nationalism and Feminism in Fin-de-siècle France." *The American Historical Review* 89, no. 3 (June 1984): 648–76.

Ohlander, Ann-Sofie. "The Invisible Child? The Struggle for Social Democratic Family Policy in Sweden, 1900–1960s." In *Maternity and Gender Policies: Women and the Rise of the Welfare States, 1880s to 1950s,* ed. Gisela Bock and Pat Thane. New York: Routledge, 1991.

Paillard, Monique, and Jean Paillard, eds. *Messages d'outre-tombe du Maréchal Pétain.* Paris: Nouvelles éditions latines, 1983.

Paret, Peter. *Persuasive Images: Posters of War and Revolution from the Hoover Institution Archives.* Princeton, N.J.: Princeton University Press, 1992.

Passmore, Kevin. "Boy Scouting for Grown-ups? Paramilitarism in the Croix de Feu and the Parti Social Français." *French Historical Studies* 19, no. 2 (fall 1992): 527–57.

——. "The French Third Republic: Stalemate Society or Cradle of Fascism." *French History* 7, no. 4 (1993): 417–49.

Paxton, Robert O. *Parades and Politics at Vichy: The French Officer Corps under Marshal Pétain.* Princeton, N.J.: Princeton University Press, 1966.

——. *Vichy France: Old Guard and New Order, 1940–1944.* New York: Columbia University Press, 1972.

Pedersen, Jean Elisabeth. "Regulating Abortion and Birth Control: Gender, Medicine and Republican Politics in France, 1870–1920." *French Historical Studies* 19, no. 3 (1996): 673–98.

Pedersen, Susan. "Catholicism, Feminism, and the Politics of the Family during the Late Third Republic." In *Mothers of a New World: Maternalist Politics and the Origins of the Welfare States,* ed. Seth Koven and Sonya Michel. New York: Routledge, 1993.

——. *Family, Dependence, and the Origins of the Welfare State: Britain and France, 1914–1945.* Cambridge: Cambridge University Press, 1993.

"Pères et paternité." *Revue française des affaires sociales,* Numéro spécial, hors-série (November 1988).

Perrot, Michelle. "Roles and Characters." In *A History of Private Life.* Vol. 4, *From the Fires of Revolution to the Great War,* ed. Michelle Perrot. Cambridge: Harvard University Press, 1990.

Peschanski, Denis. "Un Chef, un mythe." In *Images de la France de Vichy, 1940–1944: Images asservies, images rebelles.* Paris: La Documentation française, 1988.

Peukert, Detlev. *Inside Nazi Germany: Conformity, Opposition and Racism in Everyday Life.* New Haven, Conn.: Yale University Press, 1987.

Pick, Daniel. *Faces of Degeneration: A European Disorder, c. 1848–1918.* New York: Cambridge University Press, 1989.

Pine, Lisa. *Nazi Family Policy, 1933–1945.* New York: Berg, 1997.

Pitrou, Agnes. *Associations familiales et jeu sociale.* Informations sociales. Paris: CNAF, 1978.

Popenoe, David. "A World without Fathers." *Wilson Quarterly* 20, no. 2 (spring 1996): 12–29.

Popkin, Jeremy. *A History of Modern France.* Englewood Cliffs, N.J.: Prentice-Hall, 1994.

Prost, Antoine. "Catholic Conservatives, Population and the Family in Twentieth-Century France." In *Population and Resources in Western Intellectual Traditions,* ed. Michael S. Teitelbaum and Jay M. Winter. Cambridge: Cambridge University Press, 1989.

——. "L'Évolution de la politique familiale en France de 1938 à 1981." *Le Mouvement social* 129 (October–December 1984).

——. *In the Wake of War: Les Anciens combattants and French Society.* Providence: Berg, 1992.

Quine, Maria Sophia. *Population Politics in Twentieth-Century Europe.* New York: Routledge, 1996.

Reggiani, Andrés Horacio. "Procreating France: The Politics of Demography, 1919–1945." *French Historical Studies* 19, no. 3 (spring 1996): 726–54.

Rémond, René. *The Right Wing in France from 1815 to de Gaulle.* Trans. James M. Laux. 2d ed. Philadelphia: University of Pennsylvania Press, 1969.

Reynaud, Pierre, ed. *Histoire du droit de la famille.* Encyclopédie juridique Dalloz, Tome V. 2d ed. 1992.

Reynolds, Siân. *France between the Wars: Gender and Politics.* New York: Routledge, 1996.

Roberts, Mary Louise. "Acting Up: The Feminist Theatrics of Marguerite Durand." *French Historical Studies* 19, no. 4 (1996): 1103–38.

——. *Civilization without Sexes: Reconstructing Gender in Postwar France, 1917–1927.* Chicago: University of Chicago Press, 1994.

——. "Gender, Consumption and Commodity Culture." *American Historical Review* 103, no. 3 (1998): 817–44.

Rollet-Echalier, Catherine. *La Politique à l'égard de la petite enfance sous la IIIème République.* Paris: INED, 1990.

Rosanvallon, Pierre. *La Nouvelle question sociale: Repenser l'État-providence.* Paris: Seuil, 1995.

——. *Le Sacre du citoyen: Histoire du suffrage universel en France.* Paris: Gallimard, 1992.

Rosario, Vernon A. "Pointy Penises, Fashion Crimes and Hysterical Mollies: The

Pederasts' Inversions." In *Homosexuality in Modern France,* ed. Jeffrey Merrick and Bryant T. Ragan Jr. New York: Oxford University Press, 1996.

Ross, Kristin. *Fast Cars, Clean Bodies. Decolonization and the Reordering of French Culture.* Cambridge: MIT Press, 1995.

Rousso, Henry. *Les Années noires. Vivre sous l'occupation.* Découvertes Gallimard. Paris: Gallimard, 1992.

——. "L'Économie: Pénurie et modernisation." In *La France des années noires.* Vol. 1, *De la défaite à Vichy,* ed. Jean-Pierre Azéma and François Bédarida. Paris: Les Éditions du Seuil, 1993.

——. "Qu'est-ce que la Révolution nationale?" *L'Histoire* 129 (January 1990).

de Roy, Nicole, and Albert de Roy. *Citoyennes! Il y a cinquante ans le vote des femmes.* Paris: Flammarion, 1994.

Rueschemeyer, Dietrich, and Theda Skocpol, eds. *States, Social Knowledge, and the Origins of Modern Social Policies.* Princeton, N.J.: Princeton University Press, 1996.

Sabatier, Pierre. *La Déchéance de la puissance paternelle et la privation du droit de garde.* Paris: Montchrestien, 1982.

Saraceno, Chiara. "Redefining Maternity and Paternity: Gender, Pronatalism and Social Policies in Fascist Italy." In *Maternity and Gender Policies: Women and the Rise of the Welfare States, 1880s-1950s,* ed. Gisela Bock and Pat Thane. London: Routledge, 1991.

Sauvy, Alfred. "La Population française pendant la seconde guerre mondiale." In *Histoire de la population française.* Vol. 4, *De 1914 à nos jours,* ed. Jacques Dupâquier et al. Paris: Presses universitaires de France, 1988.

Schafer, Sylvia. "Between Paternal Right and the Dangerous Mother: Reading Parental Responsibility in Nineteenth-Century French Civil Justice." *Journal of Family History* 23 (April 1998): 173–90.

——. *Children in Moral Danger and the Problem of Government in Third Republic France.* Princeton, N.J.: Princeton University Press, 1997.

——. "When the Child Is the Father of the Man: Work, Sexual Difference and the Guardian-State in Third Republic France." *History and Theory* 31, no. 4 (1992): 98–115.

Schnapper, Bernard. "Autorité domestique et partis politiques de Napoleon à de Gaulle." In *Voies nouvelles en histoire du droit. La Justice, la famille, la répression pénale.* Paris: Presses universitaires de France, 1991.

——. "La Correction paternelle et le mouvement des idées au dix-neuvième siècle." *Revue historique* 263 (1980): 319–49.

Schoenbaum, David. *Hitler's Social Revolution: Class and Status in Nazi Germany, 1933-1939.* New York: Norton, 1980.

Schwartz, Paula. "Partisanes and Gender Politics in Vichy France." *French Historical Studies* 16, no. 1 (spring 1989): 126–52.

——. "The Politics of Food and Gender in Occupied Paris." *Modern and Contemporary France* 7, no. 1 (1999): 35–45.

Scott, Joan Wallach. *Gender and the Politics of History.* New York: Columbia University Press, 1988.

——. "Feminist Family Politics." *French Politics, Culture and Society* 17, no. 3–4 (summer/fall 1999): 20–30.

Scriven, Michael, and Peter Wagstaff, eds. *War and Society in Twentieth Century France.* Providence, R.I.: Berg, 1991.

La Seconde guerre mondiale. Guide des sources conservées en France, 1939–1945. Paris: Archives nationales, 1994.

Segalen, Martine. *Sociologie de la famille.* 3d ed. Paris: Armand Colin, 1991.

Sherman, Daniel J. "Monuments, Mourning and Masculinity in France after World War I." *Gender & History* 8, no. 1 (1996): 82–107.

Shirer, William L. *The Collapse of the Third Republic. An Enquiry into the Fall of France, 1940.* New York: Da Capo, 1994.

Shope, Janet Hinson. "Separate but Equal: Durkheim's Response to the Woman Question." *Sociological Inquiry* 64, no. 1 (1994): 23–36.

Siegel, Mona. " 'To the Unknown Mother of the Unknown Soldier': Pacifism, Feminism, and the Politics of Sexual Difference among French *Institutrices* between the Wars." *French Historical Studies* 22, no. 3 (1999): 421–51.

de Singly, François, and Franz Schultheis, eds. *Affaires de famille, affaires d'état: Sociologie de la famille.* Jarville-la-Malgrange: Éditions de l'est, 1991.

Skocpol, Theda. *Protecting Soldiers and Mothers: The Political Origins of Social Policy in the United States.* Cambridge: Harvard University Press, 1992.

Smart, Carol, and Selma Sevenhuijsen, eds. *Child Custody and the Politics of Gender.* London: Routledge, 1989.

Sohn, Anne-Marie. "Between the Wars in France and England." In *A History of Women.* Vol. 5, *Toward a Cultural Identity in the Twentieth Century,* ed. Françoise Thébaud. Cambridge: Harvard University Press, 1994.

Solomon-Godeau, Abigail. "Male Trouble: A Crisis in Representation." *Art History* 16, no. 2 (1993): 286–312.

Soucy, Robert. *French Fascism: The First Wave, 1924–1933.* New Haven, Conn.: Yale University Press, 1986.

———. *French Fascism: The Second Wave, 1933–1939.* New Haven, Conn.: Yale University Press, 1995.

Sowerwine, Charles. "Militantisme et identité sexuelle: La Carrière politique et l'oeuvre théorique de Madeleine Pelletier." *Mouvement social* 157 (1991): 9–32.

Spackman, Barbara. *Fascist Virilities: Rhetoric, Ideology and Social Fantasy in Italy.* Minneapolis: University of Minnesota Press, 1996.

Stephenson, Jill. *Women in Nazi Society.* London: Croom Helm, 1975.

Sternhell, Zeev. *Ni droite ni gauche: L'Idéologie fasciste en France.* Paris: Seuil, 1983.

Stone, Judith. *Sons of the Revolution: Radical Democrats in France, 1862–1914.* Baton Rouge: Louisiana State University Press, 1996.

Stuart, Robert. " 'Calm, with a Grave and Serious Temperament, Rather Male': French Marxism, Gender and Feminism, 1882–1905." *International Review of Social History* 41, no. 1 (1996): 57–82.

———. "Whores and Angels: Women and the Family in the Discourse of French Marxism, 1882–1905." *European History Quarterly* 27, no. 3 (July 1997): 339–70.

Sullerot, Evelyne. *Quel père? Quel fils?* Paris: Fayard, 1992.

Sweets, John F. *Choices in Vichy France: The French under German Occupation.* New York: Oxford University Press, 1994.

Szramkiewicz, Romuald. *Histoire du droit français de la famille.* Paris: Dalloz, 1995.

Talmy, Robert. *Histoire du mouvement familial en France, 1896–1939.* 2 vols. Paris: Union nationale des caisses d'allocations familiales, 1962.

Teitelbaum, Michael S., and Jay M. Winter. *The Fear of Population Decline.* Orlando, Fla.: Academic Press, 1985.

Thalmann, Rita, ed. *Femmes et fascismes.* Paris: Éditions Tierce, 1986.

Thébaud, Françoise. "Le Mouvement nataliste dans la France de l'entre-deux-guerres: L'Alliance nationale pour l'accroissement de la population française." *Revue d'histoire moderne et contemporaine* 32 (1985): 276–301.

——. *Quand nos grand-mères donnaient la vie: La Maternité en France dans l'entre-deux-guerres.* Lyon: Presses universitaires de Lyon, 1986.

——. "The Great War and the Triumph of Sexual Division." In *A History of Women.* Vol. 5, *Toward a Cultural Identity in the Twentieth Century,* ed. Françoise Thébaud. Cambridge: Harvard University Press, 1994.

Theweleit, Klaus. *Male Fantasies.* 2 vols. Minneapolis: University of Minnesota Press, 1987.

Thompson, Elizabeth. *Colonial Citizens: Republican Rights, Paternal Privilege, and Gender in French Syria and Lebanon.* New York: Columbia University Press, 2000.

Tumblety, Joan. "The Real and the Imaginary: Political Discourse and Gender in France during the Occupation, 1940–1944." *European Legacy* 1, no. 1 (1996): 31–35.

Vincent, Gérard. "Communism as a Way of Life." In *A History of Private Life.* Vol. 5, *Riddles of Identity in Modern Times,* ed. Antoine Prost and Gérard Vincent. Cambridge: Harvard University Press, 1991.

Watkins, Susan. *From Provinces into Nations: Demographic Integration in Western Europe, 1870–1960.* Princeton, N.J.: Princeton University Press, 1991.

Weber, Eugen. *The Hollow Years: France in the 1930s.* New York: W. W. Norton & Company, 1996.

Weeks, Jeffrey. *Sex, Politics and Society: The Regulation of Sexuality since 1800.* 2d ed. London: Longman, 1981.

Whitney, Susan B. "Embracing the Status Quo: French Communists, Young Women and the Popular Front." *Journal of Social History* 30, no. 1 (fall 1996): 29–54.

——. "History through the Lens of Gender." *Journal of Women's History* 11, no. 1 (1999): 193–202.

Whitney, Walton. "Writing the 1848 Revolution: Politics, Gender and Feminism in the Works of French Women of Letters." *French Historical Studies* 18, no. 4 (1994): 1001–24.

Winter, Jay M. "Socialism, Social Democracy and Population Questions in Western Europe, 1870–1950." In *Population and Resources in Western Intellectual Traditions,* ed. Michael S. Teitelbaum and Jay M. Winter. Cambridge: Cambridge University Press, 1989.

Wipperman, Wolfgang. *Faschismustheorien. Zum Stand der gegenwärtigen Diskussion.* Darmstadt: Wissenschaftliche Buchgesellschaft, 1972.

Yagil, Limore. *"L'Homme nouveau" et la Révolution nationale de Vichy (1940–1944).* Paris: Presses universitaires du Septentrion, 1997.

Zelizer, Viviana A. *The Social Meaning of Money.* New York: Basic Books, 1994.

Index